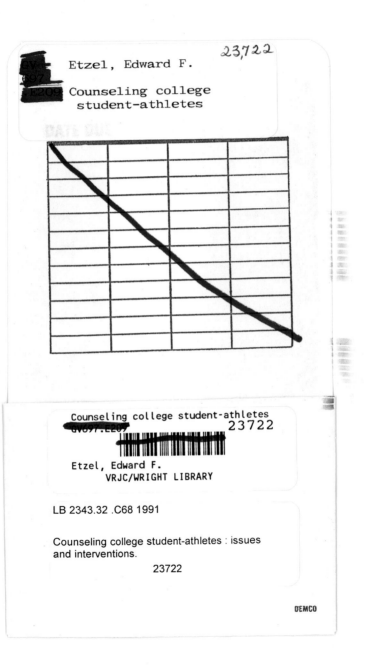

COUNSELING
COLLEGE
STUDENT-ATHLETES:
ISSUES AND INTERVENTIONS

EDITED BY

Edward F. Etzel
WEST VIRGINIA UNIVERSITY

A. P. Ferrante
THE OHIO STATE UNIVERSITY

James W. Pinkney
EAST CAROLINA UNIVERSITY

FITNESS INFORMATION TECHNOLOGY, INC.
MORGANTOWN, WV 26505

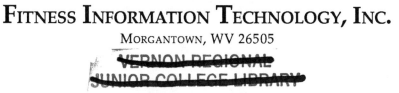

Library of Congress Catalog Card Number: 91-73215

ISBN 0-9627926-1-6

Cover Design: Brian Caudill
Copy Editor: Sandra R. Woods
Printed by: Book Crafters

Printed in the United States of America
10 9 8 7 6 5 4 3 2 1

Fitness Information Technology, Inc.
Box 4425, University Avenue
Morgantown, WV 26505 USA
(800) 477-4FIT (4348)
(304) 599-3482

To the student-athletes whom we
have had the privilege to work
with, learn from, and come to know.

Contents

Contributing Authors

Dennis Alexander is a licensed psychologist who serves as Clinical Director of the Counseling and Consultation Service at the Ohio State University.

Rod Compton is Director of the Sports Medicine Division at East Carolina University. He was the recipient of 1990 National Athletic Trainers Association Outstanding Athletic Trainer award.

Diana Damer is completing her doctorate in clinical psychology at West Virginia University. She has been associated as a therapist and as a research assistant with the Eating Disorders Program at WVU and Chestnut Ridge Hospital in Morgantown, WV.

John Damm is a licensed psychologist and certified addictions counselor working for the Federal Corrections Institute, Morgantown, WV. He has developed a drug education program for college student-athletes.

Edward Etzel is a licensed psychologist with the Counseling and Psychological Services Center at West Virginia University where he works as the outreach psychologist for the Department of Intercollegiate Athletics. He is an assistant professor with the School of Physical Education where he teaches applied sport psychology and research methods. Ed is a 1984 Olympic Gold Medalist in shooting. He also served as coach of the five time NCAA Champion WVU Rifle Team for thirteen years.

A.P."Budd" Ferrante is the Psychologist for Athletics at The Ohio State University. He is a Diplomate in Counseling Psychology of the American Board of Professional Psychology and is listed on the U.S. Olympic Committee's Registry for the Psychology of Sport. Budd served as sport psychologist with the 1988 U.S. Olympic Team in Seoul, Korea.

Laura Finch is a doctoral candidate in the Department of Exercise and Sport Science at the University of North Carolina at Greensboro.

Dan Gould is a professor in the Department of Exercise and Sport Science of the School of Health and Human Performance at the University of North Carolina-Greensboro. He is past-president of the Association for the Advancement of Applied Sport Psychology.

Contributing Authors (cont'd)

John Leard is the Athletic Training Curriculum Coordinator for graduate and NATA-approved undergraduate programs at West Virginia University. He is an assistant professor in the School of Physical Education and currently completing his doctoral studies in curriculum and instruction.

Christine Lottes is the coordinator of health education at Gettysburg College. She also works for the Counseling Service and is coordinator of drug and alcohol educational services. Christine is a consultant with various athletic teams on the GC campus.

Rebecca Parker is an Associate Director in the Office of Residence Life and Dining Halls at The Ohio State University. She is currently a doctoral candidate in higher education at The Ohio State University.

James Pinkney is a professor in the Counseling Center at East Carolina University. He currently serves on the editorial board of the Journal of College Student Development.

Le'Roy Reese is an Assistant Area Coordinator for the Office of Residence Life and Dining Halls at The Ohio State University. Le'Roy is a doctoral student in Counseling Psychology at OSU. He is also a former collegiate all-conference football and track athlete.

Kathleen Riffee is an academic counselor with the Department of Athletics at The Ohio State University.

James Scales is the Director of Career Development and Testing Services at Southern Illinois University at Carbondale.

Richard Seime is associate professor in the Department of Behavioral Medicine and Psychiatry at the West Virginia University School of Medicine. He is Chief, Section of Psychology and Director of the Eating Disorders Program at the Chestnut Ridge Hospital in Morgantown, WV, and a Diplomate in Clinical Psychology of the American Board of Professional Psychology.

Roy Tunick is a professor in the Department of Counseling Psychology and Rehabilitation at West Virginia University and the Coordinator of the Vocational Education Training Program at WVU. He is a licensed psychologist, licensed professional counselor, certified rehabilitation counselor, and certified vocational evaluator.

Foreword

Athletic coaches, administrators, and staff have always had the obligation of assisting the young men and women entrusted to them to become mature and productive people. Today, the principles remain the same, honest and dedicated interest in student-athlete development. However, in the 1990s the mechanics have become more difficult.

Today's student-athletes can run faster, jump higher, and throw harder than their bygone brethren. They are more intelligent, better coached, stronger, and just as dedicated as their earlier counterparts. Unfortunately, some of them come to us not as well prepared personally and academically, diverted by media attention and dreams of professional careers in athletics. While not discouraging such legitimate aspirations, we need to encourage a balanced outlook on college based on solid academic achievement and the earning of a valuable degree. Study halls, tutorial assistance, counseling, and career planning services are a few of the resources used to guide these young men and women toward that very important goal.

While recent NCAA philosophy and legislation aim to make student-athletes as much like the regular students as possible, in fact, they cannot be like them. There are great demands placed on student-athletes to excel both academically and athletically whereas they also have normal social expectations.

Experienced and interested coaches and administrators will emphasize the need to give academic pursuits precedence, while athletic endeavors during the season should come next if there is to be any hope of individual and team excellence. Properly managing time and responsibilities as well as setting realistic priorities are signs of maturation. The institution and its representatives must send clear signals to student-athletes that will encourage personal development. Lip service is not enough: it results only in confusion and cynicism.

The authors outline modern methods of developing the student-athlete's whole person using positive approaches to combat several negative influences in today's world. They are a collection of experienced and dedicated professionals who can assist you to identify, organize, and prioritize your efforts in this most worthwhile endeavor--helping student-athletes become successful, well-adjusted people.

John W. Kaiser, Director
Department of Athletics
St. John's University
Queens, NY

Preface

"In the tradition of meaningful education, properly conducted athletic programs are essential in sociocultural development at every level, including higher education. Beyond the lessons in self-discipline and self-motivation for student-athletes, beyond the impact of athletic programs on student bodies and loyal (contributing) alumni, the rationale for college sports reduces to the need to educate *the total person* [emphasis added] in pursuit of human excellence." (Mihalich, 1984, p.72)

Student-athletes are a diverse lot. They come in all colors, shapes and sizes, from all races and creeds. Each year tens of thousands of these young men and women participate in intercollegiate athletics from the community college ranks up to those of large universities. Although we are just beginning to understand the complexities of student-athlete life, clearly there is much more to the student-athlete experience of this diverse group than many people assume. There is much more to the student-athlete experience than attending class and playing for the alma mater—activities that the public sees and reads about.

Despite the bad press about college sports and student-athletes, we believe that intercollegiate athletics is a positive thing for young people. More student-athletes are successful and well adjusted than are not. Most of the young people who participate in intercollegiate athletics are aspiring students who are also involved in an especially demanding experience, which makes them different from their non athlete peers. In our opinion, the "student-athlete" is not an oxymoron.

Unfortunately, much of the negative press surrounding intercollegiate athletics and student-athletes is true. Intercollegiate athletics is a microcosm of society, and so we see college sports becoming a big business in our country (the only place in the world where this has occurred). Huge sums of money are made from the entertainment value of student-athlete competition, primarily in football and men's basketball. This trend will probably continue. Therefore, institutions involved in the business should become concerned not only about student-athlete academic and physical health and well-being but also about their psychosocial needs vis-a`-vis the considerable stress related to their lives.

A central purpose of this book is to increase awareness of the uniquely demanding lifestyles of college student-athletes in the 1990s. Another intent is to modify the reader's perspective on this special population, that is, to encourage those who work with, and are responsible for the welfare of student-athletes to neither think of them as athletes first (as many do) nor as students first (as some do or would like to do). We encourage readers to view student-athletes not just as the players they coach, provide medical care to, or administrate over. Rather, we want readers to see student-athletes first and foremost as developing young people. After they have perused the work of our contributors, we hope that readers will consider what they do with and how they interact with student-athletes; that readers who work with student-athletes will adopt a more holistic perspective, that reflects a sensitivity for the total person, as Mihalich has suggested above. We hope that readers will use the information in this text to stimulate innovative outreach programming for this often misunderstood population. We hope you enjoy and find useful what follows.

This work is seen as an appropriate textbook for students enrolled in upper-division undergraduate and graduate courses in counseling, psychology or sport psychology. In addition, helping professionals (counselors and psychologists), student affairs professionals (advisors and residence life personnel), and athletic department staff (coaches and trainers) who work with college student-athletes will find this a useful resource.

The text is organized in the following manner. Chapters 1-3 serve as an introduction. They provide an overview of the life-styles and concerns of student-athletes, the need to assist this special population, and describe a pair of general models for the provision of services to them.

Chapters 4 and 5 explore developmental issues and interventions appropriate for use with precollegiate and African-American student-athletes.

The next three chapters, Chapters 6-8 provide useful information about student-athlete career development and the essential skills of time management and test taking.

Chapters 9-11 discuss various clinical issues and interventions surrounding drug use, eating disorders and work with injured and disabled student-athletes.

Chapter 13 examines issues and provides suggestions helpful to athletic trainers' and residence hall professionals' efforts to assist student-athletes.

Finally, we would like to express our sincere appreciation to the many people who helped us with the production of this book. The three of us are especially grateful for the exceptional efforts of our contributing authors. We would also like to thank Dr. Robert Brown, University of Nebraska-Lincoln and Dr. Al Petitpas, Springfield College, for their reviews of our manuscript and our copy editor Sandra Woods. We also want to express our appreciation for the guidance provided by our publishers, in particular, Dr. Andrew Ostrow. We also want to recognize the efforts of Chris Godfrey, Tina Hatch, Millie Root, Jan Thompson, Lisa Quinn, and Janet Brownfield for their secretarial assistance. Finally, we want to thank our spouses Pam, Susan, and Kathy for their encouragement and support over the course of the past busy year.

Edward Etzel
A.P. Ferrante
James Pinkney, **Editors**

REFERENCES

Mihalich, J. (1984). College sports: Decisions for survival. In A. Shriberg, & F. Brodzinski (Eds.), *Rethinking services for college athletes*, (pp.71-84). San Francisco: Jossey-Bass.

CHAPTER 1

Counseling College Student-Athletes: The Problem, the Need

A.P. Ferrante and Edward Etzel

College student-athletes represent a special population on campuses across the nation. They are young people who lead stressful lives that are influenced by the unique demands placed upon them. Special services are needed to assist them to become well-adjusted, successful adults.

When students arrive at college they have much unfinished business insofar as attaining maturity is concerned. Yet this is the period which society more or less arbitrarily assumes as marking the beginning of adulthood. College administrators and teachers make the same assumption, or they should make it, yet with reservations based on the knowledge that no one can make the transition from childhood to adulthood without firm support for a while, from those who love and respect them most (Farnsworth, 1966, p.35).

College student-athletes are young people in transition, developing individuals who, like the rest of us, must confront the challenges of life in their own distinctly human ways. However, the critical difference for this group is that, unlike their nonathlete counterparts, these young men and women must function within an environment that presents a unique, complex set of demands. Furthermore, they frequently must do so under an atypical degree of public scrutiny. Their dual roles as students and entertainers also serve to complicate their experiences and have been shown often to impede their personal development (Blann, 1985; Chartrand & Lent, 1987; Nelson, 1983). It has become clear over time that the consequences of participation in intercollegiate athletics, both positive and negative, have a great impact on many aspects of their lives.

Today, more helping professionals are trying to better understand the experiences of college student-athletes and support their efforts during their busy tenure on campus (Shriberg & Brodzinski, 1984). Nevertheless, critical perceptual biases which may hamper efforts to effectively provide helping services to this special population often influence many who work with them. These biases involve the failure to recognize the fundamental importance of attending to the developmental needs of student-athletes.

This person-oriented perspective contrasts with the position publicly espoused by many colleges and universities, namely a concern for the individual student-athlete. In practice, though, many colleges and universities create systems that focus their efforts on training and retaining groups of skilled, academically eligible entertainers, for the purpose of producing highly visible and profitable winning teams (Sperber, 1990). By not fully appreciating and practicing the alternative, more humanistic view, helpers may not possess the necessary understanding of student-athlete's situation required to help them develop personal competence as young adults, the primary goal of the college experience (Chickering, 1981).

What unique challenges do student-athletes face today? First, as *students*, they are confronted with formidable academic tasks that all students must master (e.g., attending classes, doing required studying, and passing exams). These tasks are in themselves time consuming on a daily basis and in the long run can require five or more years of classroom work to earn a college diploma.

For student-athletes, however, completion of regular class work demands time that they often have little of (willingly or unwillingly) because of their extensive athletic commitments. Unfortunately, noncompletion of these tasks can have far reaching effects. For example, failure to succeed in the classroom can create great personal stress, jeopardize student-athlete's athletic eligibility, and consequently threaten their current levels of functioning and psychological well-being.

Becoming academically ineligible can also result in the end of the student's enrollment in school and thus have a major impact on those who do not survive; this is not unusual. Indeed, it is commonly assumed that many student-athletes admitted to the university, often based upon their athletic prowess alone, are not ready upon graduation from high school to meet the academic challenges of college. Recent research indicates that this is unfortunately true: student-athletes in general, and basketball and football players in particular, are not as well prepared as other college student peers to function successfully in the college classroom (American Institutes for Research, 1988; Purdy, Eitzen, & Hufnagel, 1982). Whether they recognize and/or admit it, student-athletes' ability to meet these academic challenges has personal relevance because their lives will be affected well beyond the end of their involvement in the collegiate athletic experience; that is, this ability will affect personal identity and occupational opportunities.

Second, as *athletes*, student-athletes are public performers who week after week are placed in arenas where their efforts are both praised and criticized. This occurs publicly through the media, where they are provided with an artificial, yet influential measure of their worth and privately where the relative value of their efforts is scrutinized by those they have never even met. Depending on their particular sport and the competitiveness level of their school's program, student-athletes often are required to invest nearly as much time during the academic year in structured sport-related activities as one would in performing a full-time job (i.e., in excess of 30 hours per week) if not much more (American Institutes for Research, 1988). It is not difficult then to appreciate how such activity can leave these young people in a state of mental and physical exhaustion, frequently nursing injuries and possessing limited energy to devote to other areas of interest, responsibility and long-term benefit.

As *people*, student-athletes are faced with mastering the developmental tasks associated with the college years--tasks that are formidable in their own right for all young adults (Chickering, 1969; Farnsworth, 1966). Initially, the developing individual faces the task of developing personal competence while evolving from a position of relative dependence upon parents and other significant adults to a position of relative independence. Also, during these years students are challenged to make major life decisions relating to a sense of purpose and a chosen career, developing lasting and meaningful relationships, and identifying and modifying personal values regarding love, sexuality, friendship, and trust. Learning to accept and meet responsibilities, as well as to deal effectively and cooperatively with authority are other tasks that must be mastered by the young person who is a student-athlete.

Clearly, each of us has been faced with the press to master academic challenges and to resolve the developmental tasks of young adulthood in our own ways. However, most of us have not had to do so in addition to performing in the pressure cooker that intercollegiate athletics has become in the 1990s. Today's student-athletes are presented with complex personal challenges in three major areas (i.e., personal, academic, and athletic), challenges that many often lack the ability to meet. Accordingly, their holistic development as people can become a very difficult, stressful process. Ironically, student-athletes, who are offered what seems to be an exceptional opportunity of becoming part of the intercollegiate athletic experience, may in fact be handed a long-term set of demands they are not prepared to meet. This mismatch between individual abilities and environmental demands can result in failure to meet daily responsibilities and work through the developmental tasks in a timely way. It may also lead to maladjustments, personal dissatisfaction, increased stress, and psychological disorders (Huebner & Lawson, 1990). In view of all of the demands placed upon these young people, it is a wonder that so many manage to perform successfully and ultimately graduate.

THE PROBLEM

Recent research suggests that involvement in intercollegiate athletics does not facilitate the accomplishment of developmental tasks that student-athletes must deal with. Blann (1985) found that student-athletes at a high level of competition were less able to formulate mature educational and career plans than were college students in general. Sowa and Gressard (1983) reported significant differences between student-athletes and nonathletes on three subscales of the Student Developmental Task Inventory (Winston, Miller, & Prince, 1979) (i.e., educational plans, career plans, and mature relationships with peers).

Several other factors seem to contribute to a different or slower rate of development. In addition to attending to and mastering academic responsibilities and developmental tasks, student-athletes must cope with other demands that are unique to their experience (Ferrante, 1989).

The time required to train, to practice, to attend film sessions and meetings, and to learn sport-specific material can be substantial. The physical effort devoted to a sport is often exhausting and painful. The physical and psychological effects of sport-related injury, or the specter of injury, are often disruptive. Indeed, rehabilitation can be more time consuming than the sport itself and may alienate the injured (Ermler & Thomas, 1990). The stress of competition and the obligation to perform are great and distracting. Relationships with coaches and teammates must be maintained, often in public and distressing circumstances.

The student-athlete also has enhanced visibility on campus and in the community. Worse, the student-athlete (sometimes referred to as the university's most visible ambassador) has a public image, which implies that his or her behavior is being scrutinized both on and off the playing field. Misconduct, arrest, fumbles, missed shots, academic problems, and technical fouls are examples of behavior that can haunt the student-athlete for months and even years through gossip and the follow-up of the media. Although such issues are not collectively shared by all student-athletes vis-a`-vis the sport they participate in (typically non-revenue sports will attract less media attention), the level of competition (NCAA Division I institutions attract more national media coverage than

Division III), and other factors, it is apparent that student-athletes live, study, play, and develop under conditions that make a normal college experience difficult, if not impossible.

LIFE STRESS AND THE STUDENT-ATHLETE

Reported stress among student-athletes also appears to create an atypical collegiate experience and represents another critical factor that can negatively influence the course of personal development among this student subgroup. Because the effects of stress upon psychological development and functioning are so far reaching, there are a number of issues that directly relate to stress and the lives of student-athletes.

Based upon our experience and the limited amount of literature that exists, we maintain that student-athletes experience complex internal and external stressors that seem to make them more vulnerable than most college students to encounter greater frequencies and higher levels of personal and social forms of distress. Pinkerton, Hinz, and Barrow (1987) support this view and suggest that student-athletes form an "at-risk" group who are more susceptible than other students to experiencing psychological distress due to the unique trials and tribulations of the athletic experience.

In a large-scale descriptive study of student-athletes at a medium-size land-grant (NCAA Division I-A) institution, Etzel (1989) investigated the patterns of life stress sources, stress reactions, and perceptions of personal control over life situations of 263 male and female student-athletes. Participants reported that they perceived experiencing significantly greater amounts of overall life stress, and cognitive stress symptoms (e.g., anxiety, worry, irritability), and reported possessing a chance-oriented, external locus of control.

Lanning (1982) observed that student-athletes who receive athletic scholarships have additional stresses that qualify them to receive much more attention from helping professionals. He maintained that student-athletes could benefit from direct counseling aimed at self-concept, peer relationships, injury, career choice, study skills, and time management.

Ferrante (1989) has noted that the advent of mandatory drug testing in intercollegiate athletics, has provided student-athletes with one more stress source (i.e., constant surveillance of private behavior and serious sanctions for positive tests) that possesses the potential to negatively affect their collegiate experience and beyond. To empower the individual more fully, he proposed that student-athletes could benefit from drug education programs that incorporate specific training/teaching components and proactive, direct counseling services into existing and future program curricula (e.g., assertiveness training, values clarification, communication skills, self-exploration, and one-to-one counseling).

Yet another risk associated with experiencing multiple sources of stress is athletic injury. Indeed, stressful life events may predispose athletes to suffer sport-related injuries (Rotella & Heyman, 1986). Given their demanding lifestyles, college student-athletes are at risk to experience abnormally high frequencies of physical impairment (ironically by the very system that wants to keep them healthy). They are vulnerable to losses in physical functioning that not only remove them from athletic activities but also prompt their having to cope with those losses, something they are often ill-prepared or unwilling to do. Frequently, the injured experience some form of grief reaction, the nature of which varies with each person and the severity of the injury (May & Sieb, 1987). This is an area the counselor or psychologist can be extremely helpful.

BARRIERS TO THE USE OF CAMPUS SERVICES

Most colleges and universities offer a wide range of helping services typically available to all fee paying students through their respective divisions of student life (e.g., counseling, health, and career services). These services and their respective personnel offer considerable potential benefit to the student-athlete. Although the literature offers limited evidence about the use of helping services today by student-athletes, overall it is apparent that they have typically underutilized such services as a group (Carmen, Zerman, & Blaine 1968; Pierce, 1969; Pinkerton, Hinz, & Barrow, 1987; Reinhold, 1973; Segal, Weiss, & Sokol, 1965). Unfortunately, numerous barriers make it difficult or impossible for many student-athletes to use or be inclined to use those services. Such barriers include 1) the student-athlete's high visibility on campus; 2) little available time, sport related pressure; 3) myths about the student-athlete persona; 4) the closed nature of many athletic situations; and often 5) the personal attributes of the student-athletes themselves.

Visibility. Student-athletes may be reluctant to visit or schedule an appointment with a counseling center or psychological services agency because of their high on-campus visibility. Many do not want to be seen at such an agency for fear of jeopardizing their status as campus "heroes" by revealing a perceived need for help. Furthermore, there are concerns over the possible assumptions that other students, coaches, teammates, or faculty might make about the student-athlete, for example, his or her ability to perform or to handle pressure. Seeking help and guidance for most students is a largely anonymous act. This is not so, however, for the often easily recognizable student-athlete. In fact, seeking help can quickly become a very public act for student-athletes, a public act that may generate considerable gossip and impinge upon their lives and privacy.

Time Limitations. As noted, practice and competition can drastically reduce the amount of free time the student-athlete has available for accessing needed services. Indeed, research indicates that student-athletes in general spend more time on the average involved in athletic activities than they devote to preparing for and attending class (American Institutes for Research, 1988). To compound the problem, student affairs services and programs are frequently offered in the afternoon when most practices occur. For the student-athlete, mornings are typically crowded with classes that are squeezed into time slots that will not conflict with practices or other athletically related activities. Evening programs may be accessible to some student-athletes, but they are offered at a time when student-athletes are least likely to be able to benefit from the content (i.e., when they are fatigued) or when their schedule is still tied into required athletically related activity (e.g., study hall). The availability of direct-service contact (e.g., one-to-one counseling) is also limited because most service center staff members end their working day at 5 p.m. and are no longer on campus except in emergency situations.

The effects of the high visibility of student-athletes and the factors that relate to time compression may in many ways combine to present the student-athlete with numerous social and recreational opportunities that may be perceived as far more attractive than academic or personal development/growth-oriented programming. Involvement in such activities may be regarded by the student-athlete as both stress reducing and far more personally enjoyable.

Myths. Several myths about student-athletes, if believed, would argue against student affairs agencies providing outreach services to the student-athlete. For example, if one were to assume that an athletic department's own counselors are meeting the needs of the student-athlete, outreach and/or cooperative outreach efforts from student affairs agencies are unlikely. Interestingly, this seems to be an assumption held by many personnel inside and outside athletic departments (i.e., faculty, administration and other students).

An important yet overlooked issue relative to the type and quality of internal services provided by athletic department staff involves the identity and qualifications of service providers. In an attempt to examine the roles, responsibilities, and professional preparation of athletic counselors, Brooks, Etzel and Ostrow (1987) found that athletic advisors and counselors surveyed at the NCAA Division I level reportedly are predominantly male ex-athletes with a master's degree in education whose major charge and time commitment is spent almost exclusively on academic advising. If these findings are generalizable, then little time, energy, and professional expertise are being made available to assist student-athletes "in house" with their personal, social and developmental concerns. This may be because maintenance of academic eligibility commands a high priority, or because internal staff are not generally trained to provide personal counseling services, or perhaps because untrained staff are informally providing counseling services on their own, unknown to others. It appears, however, that such staffing patterns may be gradually changing as more trained counselors are hired to provide special assistance in areas such as substance abuse and career counseling.

Student-athletes are commonly portrayed as a pampered minority with extraordinary personal privileges that include special admissions criteria, separate living and dining facilities, and preferential class scheduling. If professionals focus on such "perks" and assume that all must be well because of such care or perhaps feel resentful, outreach programming by student-affairs agencies and personnel to student-athletes may not be offered by on-campus agencies. Remer, Tongate, and Watson (1978) observed, however, that student-athletes are in reality a group truly in need of help that is often unaware of that need. Thus, others may make the same false assumptions as well. This finding may hold particular relevance to athletic department administrators, coaches, and trainers, who may also be unaware of student-athlete personal needs or be more concerned with other pressing problems.

Another myth is that coaches, athletic department staff members (e.g., trainers), family, friends, and teammates are somehow meeting all of the student-athlete's needs. Over time, the student-athlete may begin to assume this is true and not be inclined to trust or seek assistance outside of the athletic department "family." Student-athletes may be openly or indirectly discouraged to seek campus services by coaches and athletic department personnel who suggest that the student-athlete's situation may not be understood or cared about by outsiders. The attitude of "We can take care of our own problems" (except when emergencies arise) is frequently sensed. The astute professional should remember that this reluctance to refer a student-athlete to extradepartmental helpers by many athletic department personnel may be very difficult to overcome, athletic staff may fear that referral may be perceived by outsiders as a failure on their part to serve the student-athlete; therefore athletic department staff may be quite protective of their student-athletes.

Closed Environments. Whether it is fact or fiction, many athletic departments see themselves and are perceived by some members of the campus community as independent entities, uniquely separate from the rest of the university and quite closed to outsiders (except on game days). Some maintain that athletic departments, especially "big time" departments, are in fact independent on-campus businesses that have very little, if any, connection to the other functional activities of their school (Sperber, 1990). Such an independent view can easily be internalized by student-athletes and may inadvertently lead them to ignore available campus services, and to look instead to athletic staff and teammates for needed support.

Remer et al. (1978) have described collegiate athletics as a self-perpetuating system that is difficult for outsiders to enter. They concluded that though many student-athletes are protected and supported by that system, they may not necessarily be helped by that system as much as they could be, except in areas of athletic performance and academic eligibility. Ironically, Bergandi and Wittig (1984) reported that 75% of the athletic directors they surveyed claimed to hold positive attitudes about the benefits of support service outreach programs for their student-athletes. However, relatively few institutions have since moved to implement such potentially useful programs.

Relatedly, efforts are often made by many institutions to enhance the leadership abilities of student-athletes by capitalizing on their notoriety for the purpose of institutional public relations (e.g., requiring public speaking engagements and providing other community services). These efforts stand in opposition to offering more useful alternative opportunities for personal development. For example, given the time to participate, student-athletes may benefit more from education, training, or service involvements within the team and institution (e.g., leadership skills training, peer assistance activities, participation in alcohol/drug education programming). Opportunities for public speaking and community service hold potential benefit for some student-athletes. Nevertheless, it seems that opportunities should be offered first that will help develop student-athlete life skills. Otherwise, such efforts ultimately run the risk of being regarded by others and by the public as exploitative. At the very least, the student-athlete is faced with yet one more demand to be added to an often already overtaxed daily schedule.

Taken together, efforts to protect or control student-athletes are seen as detrimental to their well-being. At the very least, protectionism fails to provide the opportunity that other nonathlete peers have to learn about assuming personal responsibility through experience. However well meaning, such efforts shelter the student-athlete from facing the logical consequences of his or her behavior, a shelter that for many may significantly inhibit personal growth and sense of "how the world works."

This sheltering of student-athletes may extend differential treatment patterns by significant others that begin early in life. As children, athletically talented young people (identified early as "players") may be cared for by people who directly or indirectly support the athletic system (e.g., youth coaches, teachers, parents). Such care may foster a sense of personal specialness as well as a dependency on or a need to please powerful others. Encouragement to spend large amounts of time in sport-related activities may discourage these children from participating in a wider range of life experiences. In a sense, young student-athletes-to-be may be shaped to acquire an external locus of control that is associated with various life skill deficits, as well as immature, unrealistic values, goals and expectations that are carried with them to the college campus.

Personal Attributes. Student-athletes themselves can form a barrier to services routinely available to them and used by the general student population. Athletes may ignore services by relying on powerful others (e.g., coaches) or by having a false sense of self-reliance. Some student-athletes may own an unrealistic faith in the ameliorative powers of athletic performance. That is to say, they believe that as long as they put forth a high degree of effort and play reasonably well, they will somehow maintain control over their destiny, and subsequently everything else will work out fine.

Many student-athletes also cling to an acquired "macho" attitude characterized by the assumption that athletes are supposed to be tough and that tough people just "suck it up" or "tough it out." Accordingly, both male and female student-athletes may be reluctant to seek help for personal concerns because they believe that only weak people admit that they could benefit from someone else's help.

Furthermore, some student-athletes (like many nonathlete students) may attempt to cope with their difficulties and stress by using alcohol and drugs. Clearly, this ineffective strategy can in fact further exacerbate problems. Also, for the student-athlete who is required to participate in mandatory drug testing, substance use may contribute to a denial of problems and a reluctance to seek help from service providers because of fears surrounding the trusting of professionals with personal information about their private habits. Substance use by student-athletes can make the professional's job of helping to resolve their problems a difficult, and frustrating one.

The stereotypic misperception of counselors and psychologists as "shrinks" who analyze sick or crazy people, represents another barrier to service that may further contribute to the student-athlete's reluctance to seek assistance or for others to refer them for assistance for personal concerns. If the student-athlete, coaches, athletic trainers, or others closely involved with the student-athlete hold this inaccurate view, the chances of a timely referral or self-referral become quite remote.

Finally, yet another roadblock to helping the student-athlete that the helping professional may encounter is the expectation of obtaining a "quick fix." This refers to the unrealistic assumption that personal concerns can be resolved in a brief period (and often with little effort expended on the part of the person referred or the people who made the referral). Although personal difficulties can sometimes be overcome in a brief period of time, it seems that many student-athletes and athletic staff are not sensitive to the complexity of presenting problems or the nature of the process of counseling or psychotherapy, and thereby often expect the helping professional to fix the student-athlete's difficulties with an injection of simple advice. Those who work with this population should be sensitive to this false assumption and be actively engaged in efforts to educate clients and referral sources about the nature and limitations of the help that can be provided.

Overall, many student-athletes appear to possess a wide range of unmet needs. Unfortunately, they are directly or indirectly prevented by such factors as time compression, scheduling conflicts, fears of social or institutional repercussions, myths about counseling and psychology, and societal conditioning from accessing many of the services that our colleges and universities have established to meet those needs. Certainly, it is to the benefit of the student-athlete and the institutions they so visibly represent to have the capacity and willingness to promote more effectively the growth and development of the student-athlete as a whole person, a whole person who will master the developmental tasks of young adulthood, actively pursue a course of study that possesses relevance to his or her life, and hopefully graduate in a timely fashion.

THE NEED

We believe that student-athletes represent a special population on our campuses much like women, minorities, and people with disabilities. They are a group of students who possess unique problems and pressures that serve to negatively influence their holistic development as people. Unfortunately, many of those who are in a position to positively influence action on behalf of student-athletes (e.g., university and athletic department administrators, faculty, student development professionals, sports medicine practitioners) may possess little awareness or sensitivity to the critical factors that contribute to the unmet developmental needs of these young people. Based upon what we now know about student-athletes, their unique needs, and the obstacles that can serve to inhibit their development as young adults, it is clear that we are challenged by a problem that invites action.

Given the intercollegiate athletics system as it exists, it is arguable that student-athletes can be seen, in a sense, as employees of their institutions and therefore should be considered and treated as highly valuable "human assets." As a group, they often help generate significant amounts of publicity and revenue for their schools. In light of what we now know about student-athletes, if institutions choose to support the business of intercollegiate athletics in the 1990s (and it is highly probable that many will, given the huge sums of money available to many of those who choose to), it seems reasonable that they should strive to assume increased responsibility to provide expanded care for their student-athletes. These services, however, should extend beyond financial aid, coaching, training, rehabilitation, and academic advising and take the form of expanded professional helping services, much like the services that businesses provide for their workers through employee assistance programs.

As a necessary precondition for such action, there must be both an interest and a willingness on the part of educational institutions and their respective athletic departments, faculty, and student affairs agencies to recognize the need to provide expanded outreach services with the intent of assisting this special student subgroup. To meet the problem head on, programming that links existing campus and community services seems to be the most reasonable starting point (see Chapter 2).

Hopefully, institutions will begin to recognize and meet the needs of this special group as the business of intercollegiate athletics continues to grow at an amazing rate. We hope that institutions that sponsor intercollegiate athletics, especially highly competitive programs, recognize the value of meeting the personal developmental needs of their student-athletes and offer expanded human services to these young people. It is important that this be done because, we see the potential for student-athletes (especially those involved in highly competitive programs) to become progressively devalued and used by intercollegiate athletic systems--by those very people who are entrusted with the promotion of student-athlete welfare. One observer, Reverend Theodore Hesburgh, President Emeritus of Notre Dame and a leading member of the Knight Commission, recently described the treatment of many student-athletes, in particular those who participate in highly competitive, big-time programs. College student-athletes, he stated, "are brought in, used up and then discarded like ... rubbish on the trash heap of humanity" (Commission, 1991, p. 10).

We do not believe that this is the case everywhere. Many athletic programs do value the welfare of their student-athletes. These programs work toward making their student-athletes' academic and athletic experiences positive and growth oriented. Nevertheless, we sincerely hope that helping professionals who work with student-athletes will actively seek and create opportunities to increase awareness and sensitivity to the student-athlete's plight. More is asked of college student-athletes today than most people imagine. We encourage athletic department and university administrators, faculty and helping professionals to work together on behalf of student-athletes in an effort to develop and implement programs to insure that they have a greater opportunity to succeed as people in college and in life once the game is over. The transition from childhood to adulthood is tough enough.

REFERENCES

American Institutes for Research (1988). *Summary results from the 1987-88 national study of intercollegiate athletics.* (Report No.1). Palo Alto, CA: Center for the Study of Athletics.

Bergandi, T, & Wittig, A. (1984). Availability of and attitudes toward counseling services for the collegiate athlete. *Journal of College Student Personnell, 25,* 557-558.

Blann, W. (1985). Intercollegiate athletic competition and students' educational and career plans. *Journal of College Student*

Personnel, 26, 115-118.

Brooks, D., Etzel, E., & Ostrow, A. (1987). Job responsibilities and backgrounds of NCAA Division I athletic academic advisors and counselors. *The Sport Psychologist, 1*, 200-207.

Carmen, L., Zerman, J., & Blaine, G. (1968). Use of Harvard psychiatric service by athletes and non-athletes. *Mental Hygiene, 52*, 134-137.

Chartrand, J., & Lent, R. (1987). Sports counseling: Enhancing the development of the student-athlete. *Journal of Counseling and Development, 66*, 164-167.

Chickering, A. (1969). *Education and identity*. San Francisco: Jossey-Bass.

Chickering, A. (1981). *The modern American college*. San Francisco: Jossey-Bass.

Commission calls for athletic reform. (1991, March 20). *Daily Athenaeum*, p.10.

Ermler, K., & Thomas, C. (1990). Interventions for the alienating effect of injury. *Athletic Training, 25*, 269-271.

Etzel, E. (1989). *Life stress, locus of control, and competition anxiety patterns of college student-athletes*. Unpublished doctoral dissertation, West Virginia University, Morgantown.

Farnsworth, D. (1966). *Psychiatry, education, and the young adult*. Springfield, IL: Charles C. Thomas.

Ferrante, A. (1989). Glory or personal growth: The plight of the student-athlete. *ECU Report, 20* (2), 6.

Heubner, L., & Lawson, J. (1990). In D. Creamer & associates (Eds.), *College student development: Theory and practice for the 1990s* (pp.127-151). Alexandria, VA: American College Personnel Association.

Lanning, W. (1982). The privileged few: Special counseling needs of athletes. *Journal of Sport Psychology, 4*, 19-23.

May, J., & Sieb, G. (1987). Athletic injuries: Psychological factors in the onset, sequelae, rehabilitation, and prevention. In J. May & M. Asken (Eds.). *Sport psychology: The psychological health of the athlete* (pp.157-185). Great Neck, NY: PMA Publishing.

Nelson, E. (1983). How the myth of the dumb jock becomes a fact:

A developmental view for counselors. *Counseling & Values,27*(3), 176-185.

Pierce, R. (1969). Athletes in psychiatry: How many, how come? *Journal of American College Health, 12,* 244-249.

Pinkerton, R., Hinz, L., & Barrow, J. (1987). The college student athlete: Psychological consideration and interventions. *Journal of American College Health, 37,* 218-226.

Purdy, D., Eitzen, D., & Hufnagel, R. (1982). Are athletes also students? *Social Problems, 29,* 439-448.

Reinhold, J. (1973). Users and nonusers of college counseling and psychiatric services. *Journal of American College Health, 21,* 201-208.

Remer, R., Tongate, F., & Watson, J. (1978). Athletes: Counseling the overprivileged minority. *Personnel and Guidance Journal, 56,* 626-629.

Rotella, R., & Heyman, S. (1986). Stress, injury, and the psychological rehabilitation of athletes. In J. Williams (Ed.). *Applied sport psychology: Personal growth to peak performance.* (pp. 343-362). Palo Alto, CA: Mayfield.

Segal, B., Weiss, R., & Sokol, R. (1965). Emotional adjustment, social organization, and psychiatric treatment rates. *American Sociological Review, 30,* 545-556.

Shriberg, A., & Brodzinski, F. (Eds.) (1984). *Rethinking services for student-athletes.* San Francisco: Jossey-Bass.

Sowa, C., & Gressard, C. (1983). Athletic participation: Its relationship to student development. *Journal of College Personnel, 24,* 236-239.

Sperber, M. (1990). *College sports inc.: The athletic department versus the university.* New York: Henry Holt.

Winston, R., Miller, T., & Prince, J. (1979). *Student developmental task inventory.* (Rev. 2nd ed.). Athens, GA: Student Development Associates.

CHAPTER 2

A Model for Accessing Student-Athletes with Student-Affairs Resources

A.P. Ferrante, Edward Etzel and James Pinkney

The authors provide a conceptual framework within which comprehensive helping services may be provided by existing on-campus service units.

Barron's (1984) classifies the University of Miami as a "competitive" Category I institution with a 17:1 student to faculty ratio. Entering freshmen at Miami have an average SAT combined score of 1,104, and President Foote has insisted on higher standards that will rival the Ivy League. It sounds like an excellent place to go to college, and a parent reading Barron's description might very well be impressed.

Unfortunately, far more parents are likely to read *Sports Illustrated* and other news reports where Miami has also been recently described. Sullivan (1987) highlights the football team and its behavior over the last two years. A parent would be less impressed to read of alleged cheating, steroid abuse, various criminal charges, assault, and brawling. Given that the circulation rate of *Sports Illustrated* is almost 3 million, the public at large is likely to form an opinion about the University of Miami from its well publicized championship football team. It may not be fair to characterize an institution based on only one percent of the student body, but that one percent is highly visible with national exposure.

Student service providers have a vested interest in promoting the development of all students, in particular those who have special needs. Yet it appears that the counseling services that most student-athletes can access are typically limited to academic advising, psychological sport performance enhancement skills, and counseling for the person in trouble (Brooks, Etzel, & Ostrow, 1987; Chartrand & Lent, 1987). Clearly, programming directed toward the goal of enhancing the holistic development of student-athletes as people would be helpful to this group and their universities (Danish & Hale, 1981).

Although many authors have suggested that more comprehensive services should be provided to student-athletes (Chartrand & Lent, 1987; Lanning, 1982; Nelson, 1983; Pinkerton, Hinz, & Barrow, 1987; Sowa & Gressard, 1983), little has been written about specific models for providing helping services to student-athletes (Danish, D'Augelli, & Ginsberg, 1984; Jordan & Denson, 1990). Therefore, we provide a model that describes the authors' thinking about how existing on-campus helping services may be organized and offered to student-athletes in need.

A SERVICE PROVISION MODEL FOR STUDENT-ATHLETES

The model we propose for reaching student-athletes with student-affairs programming has two prerequisite elements: 1) the support of the chief student affairs officer (CSAO) and athletic director (AD) and 2) the presence of a highly trained student affairs professional (e.g., counselor or psychologist) assigned specifically to work with student-athletes.

The active support of the chief student affairs officer and the athletic director is crucial to the success of such a service provision system. Student-athletes and athletic department staff must know that these two influential people not only are concerned with the athletic and financial successes of their programs but also more importantly, demonstrate a greater concern for the welfare and personal development of student-athletes. Without their support, effective networking with on-campus service providers will probably not become well developed. Consequently, staff will not become aware of how such service providers can help student-athletes. Staff will often be quite reluctant to consult with helping professionals, to invite them to meet with their teams, and to refer needy team members for assistance with their difficulties.

The support of the CSAO is particularly important to the success of expanded service provision to student-athletes. He or she is generally charged with the considerable responsibility of attending to the personal development and welfare of all students. Since participation in athletics can be ideally seen as a developmental experience for student-athletes, some believe that athletic departments should be under the administrative control of the CSAO (Golden, 1984). More often than not, because intercollegiate athletics has unfortunately become such a big business, this will probably not be the case on the majority of campuses. Nevertheless, college and university presidents and chancellors should actively involve the CSAO in overseeing the provision of services to student-athletes.

The AD is perhaps the most important person behind the success of any efforts to assist student-athletes. Unless the AD solidly supports expanded programming for student-athletes, attempts to assist student-athletes will probably fail. Especially when programming efforts are in their early stages, the AD must be involved in "selling" the benefits of student-athletes seeking assistance and in encouraging staff to refer their charges to on-campus service providers-- something that many will resist. The AD regularly needs to communicate a commitment to such activities to staff (e.g., coaches, trainers, advisors) and to student-athletes.

For example, the AD must support outreach efforts on the part of helping professionals such as meeting staff and attending team practices. Many athletic practices occur during or after normal working hours, and some facilities and practice sessions are closed to the public. An unfamiliar counseling staff member who attends practices or visits training rooms at such times may be perceived as an outsider or perhaps as an individual unwelcome fan, not as a professional resource for the student-athlete and coach. Only the CSAO and AD, through their assistants, can clarify for coaches and athletes that a professional consultant is being made available to help teams and why. Only a careful handling at a high administrative level of the intent and potential benefits of the helping professional's involvement with student-athletes will help avoid the potential political confusion and mistrust often associated with the delicate, time-consuming process of establishing relationships between student service-providers and coaches and student-athletes. Establishing a clear, trusting relationship with student-athletes and staff is crucial to the success of such novel outreach efforts.

The second essential element is the presence of a well-trained readily identifiable student-affairs staff member (e.g., a professional counselor or psychologist). This person must be genuinely interested in working with student-athletes, truly aware of the uniqueness of the student-athletes' experience, and willing to learn about applied sport psychology (if one is not already knowledgeable). These qualities cannot be shortchanged or faked. Indeed, many student-athletes have been asked to do things for others most of their young lives. They quickly recognize insincerity, the hot and cold nature of a fan's approval or interest, and the fact that people often want to take from them rather than the other way around. Many student-athletes frequently are reluctant to make contact with a new person, especially someone who may represent a threat to them, as psychologists and counselors often are perceived.

As mentioned earlier, coaches too will often be sensitive to perceived insincerity as well as to efforts that may affect their people and programs. Understandably, many are individuals who resist change except when initiated by familiar insiders. Establishing positive, trusting relationships with some coaches can be a very challenging and frequently frustrating experience for the new helping professional.

Developing trust and credibility with student-athletes, athletic staff, and others who work with student-athletes does not happen overnight and is often not an easy job given the barriers associated with student-athletes using services (see Chapter 1.) Regular effort must be expended by the helping professional to meet regularly with these people to help them understand and use the services available to assist student-athletes. Meeting with individual staff members, attending team meetings and practices (with the permission of coaches), and regularly dropping by training rooms are some ways that the helping professional can work toward becoming an accepted resource.

As noted, it is extremely important that the helping professional be knowledgeable about all the on-campus resources of student affairs and be clearly identified as the contact point for student-athletes and coaches. The very issues that make student-athletes a unique population (e.g., high visibility, time pressures, role conflicts) dictate that student-athletes be able to identify and access a person available to them for help with concerns unlikely to be discussed with coaches, teammates, or friends.

ADMINISTRATIVE ASPECTS OF THE MODEL

Two options exist relative to the administrative location of the student-athlete helping professional. First, he or she could be a staff member of an organization outside the athletic department (e.g., a counseling service staff member). Jordan and Denson (1990) indicate that such a unique arrangement can be quite advantageous, because it provides an opportunity for student-athletes to access a broad-based set of on-campus services outside the sphere of influence of coaches and athletic staff. An external base of operations is also seen as a way to avoid potential conflicts of interest and unethical dual relationships with the population the professional has been hired to help. This approach (described in greater detail later) is seen as a realistic option for most institutions that wish to initiate special programming for student-athletes. However, there unfortunately still remain many barriers to student-athletes' accessing services that may undermine this arrangement. (See Chapter 1 for a discussion of barriers to the use of services.)

An alternative to having a helping professional from an organization external to the athletic department is the hiring of an "in-house" professional who is also a member of the university counseling service staff--something a small number of universities have done (e.g., Ohio State University and West Virginia University). On most campuses financial considerations will probably make this arrangement will probably be the exception and not the rule. Nevertheless, the athletic-department-based helping professional associated with another helping service unit can function as effectively as an external helper. However, the person in this position must keep in mind who he or she is serving (i.e., the student-athlete) so as to avoid potential ethical difficulties as noted above. In the end, the administrative location of the helping professional depends on the particular situation and needs of each institution.

Another recommended aspect of this service provision model is the establishment of a network of contacts between the primary student-athlete student affairs staff member and representatives of other key on-campus service units. More specifically, it will be useful for this person to make contact with at least one person from the offices of those who will potentially make or receive student-athlete referrals (e.g., the academic advising center, the student health service, the counseling service, and the residence life office).

Creating a good working relationship with a member of the athletic department administration is also seen as indispensable to the efficient functioning of the network. This person should probably be someone other than the athletic director (e.g., an assistant athletic director or associate athletic director) who would likely be more readily available and capable of focusing more of his or her energies on student-athlete service related issues.

Traditionally, the mission of university counseling and psychological services centers has been the provision of developmental programming that incorporates individual and group counseling/psychotherapy for students who present with personal, social, career, and academic concerns. As part of their overall programs, many centers have additionally offered both in-house seminars and workshops as well as out-reach programs covering preventive, developmental, and educational topics for students. Because these centers are typically staffed by credentialed human service professionals who are in the business of meeting the developmental needs of students and are familiar with existing campus and community resources, the proposed student-athlete service provision model is seen as a natural, yet specialized extension of this student affairs agency.

Though the specific administrative structure may differ for each institution, a diagram depicting the general organization of the proposed model is provided in Figure 1.

As can be seen in Figure 1, the proposed model can be graphically

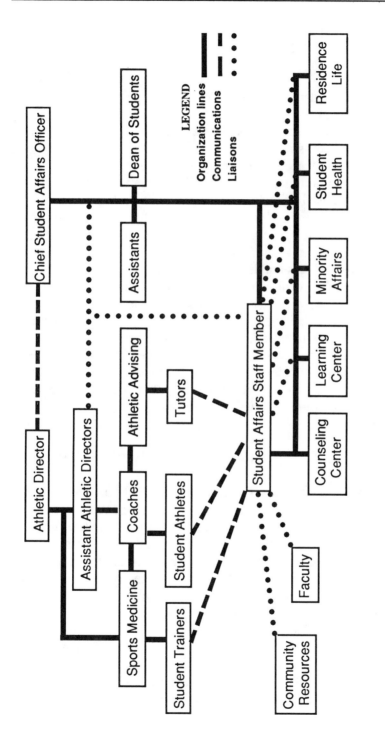

Figure 1. Organizational communications of the service provision model for student-athletes.

displayed as a two-way network of liaison between the designated helping professional and those service agencies likely to be needed by student-athletes. Especially at first, this may be most efficient and responsive to student-athletes' needs if a single person in each service agency were designated to work with student-athletes. This would insure a consistent resource person in each agency who could function as either a referral source (for the student affairs staff member) or a referral target (for specialized service from each agency).

Regular communication among all network members is a key to the successful establishment and maintenance of this network. Furthermore, the identified student-athlete helping professional (or program coordinator) should initially arrange for outreach seminars for all network representatives, coaches, and administrators as well for all team members and incoming student-athletes (i.e., freshmen and transfers). The central purpose of these seminars is to identify the program coordinator, describe the role and function of the program proper, educate participants on the unique problems and pressures experienced by student-athletes, and to identify the concerns and stresses that may be presented and experienced by student-athletes. Although these seminars are viewed as particularly important in the initial stages of program development, they should nonetheless continue to be conducted periodically throughout the course of the academic year.

PROGRAM COMPONENTS AND INTERVENTIONS

The proposed service provision model for student-athletes is comprehensive in nature and is based upon a developmental, educational, preventive, and cooperative approach. Though the unique needs of each institution and student-athlete population may suggest the need for some modification, five major program functions/services are suggested as providing the basis for an effective and successful program. They are: 1) education, 2) clinical/counseling services, 3) assessment, 4) consultation, and 5) referral.

Education. The most commonly used education/intervention approach has incorporated a group format that allows for the dissemination of information and encourages the discussion and processing of this material. This format can be effectively implemented to present virtually any topics that are viewed as relevant and useful to student-athletes and network personnel. Such topics might include: a) career choice and planning, b) choosing an academic major, c) orientation to the university, d) alcohol and substance abuse issues, e) stress management, f) assertiveness training, g) multicultural issues, h) men's/women's issues, i) dating and relationships, j) communication skills, k) adjustment issues, and l) sport performance enhancement techniques.

As the education component can clearly incorporate so many relevant topics, the program coordinator can draw upon any number of professionals from both the campus and the community to assist with presentations.

Clinical/Counseling Services. This program component offers individual and/or group counseling/psychotherapy covering the full range of potential concern areas for student-athletes. Such services are provided in a professional and confidential fashion. It is critical to note, however, that "reaching out" to student-athletes is a major focus of the current program. Therefore, the program's coordinator also must be willing to be accessible, for example, outside the confines of the counseling center and after 5 p.m. Provisions should be made for office space in areas where convenience for the student-athletes and coaches raises the potential of taking responsibility for seeking these services.

The reasons for student-athletes seeking individual counseling or psychotherapy are also endless. Generally, however, individual counseling/psychotherapy interventions will be focused upon: a) personal concerns, b) social concerns, c) career/vocational concerns, d) academic concerns, e) team-related concerns, f) athletic performance issues/enhancement, and g) crisis intervention.

Assessment Services. Whereas these services may often be incorporated into both the educational and clinical/counseling components of the program, assessment may also be a practical beginning point that could prove useful to student-athletes in a number of areas. Some of these areas include but are not limited to: a) alcohol and substance abuse, b) aptitude and career assessment, c) recruitment, d) athletic performance related issues, and e) program evaluation.

Consultation. In this service area, the program coordinator is seen as a resource for each student-athlete and coach as well as for each department and agency directly involved with them. Consultation helpful to student-athletes and their respective institutions might include efforts directed toward the following individuals and agencies: a) coaches, b) sports medicine staff, c) faculty, d) academic advising/tutoring personnel, e) student health services, f) admissions, g) parents, h) athletic department staff, i) legal and student affairs officers, and j) sports information departments.

Referral. In those instances when the student-athlete can be better served outside the domain of the existing program, or when they present issues that are beyond the expertise of the program coordinator, referral will be most appropriate. It is at these times that the full impact of an effectively developed and maintained referral network will be most important.

SUMMARY

Student affairs agencies have a wide range of services and resources that are highly relevant to the developmental needs of student-athletes. Unfortunately, there are a number of barriers that work against these students being able to access such services and resources. This article outlines a service delivery model that covers the nature and extent of the services and communications needed to effectively reach student-athletes with appropriate services. Ultimately this program intends to stimulate interest, awareness, and use of a broad spectrum of existing campus programs. The support and cooperation of the chief student affairs officer, the athletic director, and a designated professional staff member with a background in applied sport psychology are considered to be the critical elements needed for the model to effectively student-athletes.

The resources to meet the needs of a unique segment of the student body, student-athletes, are already available within our student affairs divisions. There are a number of compelling reasons why taking the time and effort needed to reach student-athletes can be beneficial not only to them but also to the institution that they so visibly represent.

REFERENCES

Barron's College Division (1984). *Barron's Guide to the Best, Most Popular, & Most Exciting Colleges* (4th Ed.). New York, NY: Barron's Educational Series.

Brooks, D., Etzel, E., & Ostrow, A. (1987). Job responsibilities and backgrounds of NCAA Division I athletic academic advisors and counselors. *The Sport Psychologist, 1*(3), 200-207.

Chartrand, J., & Lent, J. (1987). Sports counseling: Enhancing the development of the student-athlete. *Journal of Counseling & Development, 66,* 164-167.

Danish, S., D'Augelli, A., & Ginsberg. M. (1984). Life development intervention: Promotions of mental health through the development of competence. In. S. Brown, & R, Lent (Eds.), *Handbook of Counseling Psychology* (pp.520-544). New York: Wiley.

Danish, S. & Hale, B. (1981). Toward an understanding of the practice of sports psychology. *Journal of Sports Psychology,* 3, 90-99.

Golden, D. (1984). Supervising college athletics: The role of the chief student affairs officer. In A. Shriberg, & F. Brodzinski (Eds.). *Rethinking services for college athletes* (pp.59-70). San Francisco: Jossey-Bass.

Jordan, J., & Denson, E. (1990). Student services for athletes: A model for enhancing the student-athlete experience. *Journal of Counseling & Development. 69,* 95-97.

Lanning, W. (1982). The privileged few: Special counseling needs of athletes. *Journal of Sport Psychology, 4,* 19-23.

Nelson, E. (1983). How the myth of the dumb jock becomes a fact: A developmental view for counselors. *Counseling and Values, 27*(3), 176-185.

Pearson, R., & Petitpas, A. (1990). Transitions of athletes: Developmental and preventive perspectives. *Journal of College Student Development, 29*(5), 454-460.

Pinkerton, R., Hinz, L., & Barrow, J. (1987). The college student-athlete: Psychological considerations and intervention strategies. *Journal of American College Health, 37,* 218-226.

Pinkney, J. (1989). But what does a sport psychologist do? *The ECU Report, 20*(2), p.7.

Pinkney, J., Ferrante, A., & Etzel, E. (March, 1989). *A learning center dilemma: Enhancing the student in student-athletes.*Paper presented at the meeting of the American College Personnel Association, Washington, D.C.

Pinkney, J., Ferrante, A., & Etzel, E. (1990). *Isolation and ethics:*

Shared issues for minorities and student-athletes. Paper presented at the annual meeting of the Association of College Student
Personnel, St. Louis, MO.

Remer, R., Tongate, F., & Watson, J., (1978). Athletes: Counseling
the over-privileged minority. *Personnel and Guidance Journal,
56,* 626-629.

Sowa, C., & Gressard, C. (1983). Athletic participation: Its relationship to student development. *Journal of College Student Personnel, 24,* 236-239.

Sullivan, R. (1987). Time to play Foote ball? *Sports Illustrated, 67*
(27), 58-60, 63.

CHAPTER 3

A "Whole-istic" Model of Counseling Student-Athletes on Academic, Athletic, and Personal-Social Issues

Christine Lottes

The author provides the results of a Delphi panel survey of several expert student service professionals that describes a model of comprehensive service provision to college student-athletes.

For over twenty years there have been informal support service programs for college student-athletes. However, their success in dealing with today's student-athlete is being called into question. Recently student-athletes have reported a variety of academic, athletic, and personal/social concerns, such as social isolation, alcohol and drug abuse, stress and burnout, poor academic performance, difficult academic and career/vocational choices, fear of success, and identity conflicts (American Institutes for Research [AIR], 1988; AIR, 1989a; AIR, 1989b; AIR, 1989c; Bruno, 1989; Heyman, 1986; Mahoney & Suinn, 1986; Pinkerton, Hinz, & Barrow, 1987).

Although many of these concerns are common to the entire student population, unique pressures placed on the student-athlete serve to compound common concerns while creating additional ones. Differences between those who participate in athletics and those who do not have been noted by several authors, thus supporting the idea of athletes as students with special concerns and pressures (AIR, 1988; Etzel, 1989; Ferrante, 1986; Gordon, 1986; Schubert & Schubert, 1983; Sowa & Gressard, 1983). The student-athlete must be recognized first as an individual, second as a member of the academic community, and third as a participant in an extracurricular activity (Zingg, 1982). The common reference to athletes being students first and athletes second (Schubert & Schubert, 1983) neglects to take into account the varied personal/ social and developmental concerns of the individual (Tutko & Richards, 1971).

A "whole-istic" approach to providing counseling assistance to the student-athlete has support within the human development framework (Damon, 1983; Waterman, 1982). A life-development intervention program with a goal of educating the student-athlete in aspects of personal competence will enable him or her to do meaningful life planning, be self-reliant, and identify and effectively use coping resources (Danish, D'Augelli, & Ginsberg, 1984).

The developmental tasks that the student-athlete encounters affect not only academic issues such as career planning and graduation rates but also athletic and personal/social issues. An educational model of intervention and a human developmental framework for enhancing both athletic and personal development has been advanced by Danish and Hale (1981). These scholars support a philosophical position that views the individual as a whole person with changing needs and skills over time and in varied situations. This chapter discusses the results of an investigation using the Danish and Hale philosophy as its base and expanding it from which to develop a working model of counseling interventions for student-athletes.

There is some question as to the whole-istic concept existing on college and university campuses. The whole-istic program is seen as beneficial by athletic administrators but is not specifically available to most athletes (Bergandi & Wittig, 1984; Danish, D'Augelli & Ginsberg, 1984; National Association of Academic Advisors for Athletics, 1989-1990). The traditional model of counseling student-athletes appears to have begun as the special academic needs of recruited athletes became apparent. Problems that today's athletes face encompass athletic, personal/social, and career issues in addition to academic concerns. An alternate approach to the traditional structure would be to develop a model that could benefit the student-athlete in a variety of ways, including assisting in the adjustment to college life within the time constraints placed upon the athlete, increasing graduation rates, and preparing the student-athlete for life after college (Nelson, 1983; Rosenberg, 1982; Walter & Smith, 1986).

Based on a review of literature, discussions with over twenty professionals currently working with student-athletes, and the experience of this author as a teacher, coach and academic advisor, 45 components of a whole-istic model of counseling student-athletes were identified, and a relationship was found between the importance of the components and their existence at the experts' institutions.

METHOD

Evaluators. In developing the whole-istic model, the Delphi method was employed. Utilizing a series of questionnaires with controlled opinion feedback, the Delphi technique is designed to obtain the most reliable opinion of a group of experts. Characteristics of the Delphi method include the anonymity of responses, the ability to provide controlled feedback, and the provision of a statistical group response (Dalkey, 1969; Linstone & Turoff, 1975).

Experts were identified via a thorough review of related literature in the area of support programs for student-athletes, and consensus of recommendations from the heads of the National Association of Academic Advisors for Athletics (NAAAA), as well as from other experts within the field and the author's final informed judgment. All 10 of the evaluators possess their master's degree in a wide variety of disciplines such as English, college student personnel, clinical psychology, philosophy, and physical education. Doctoral degrees in counseling psychology, English, higher education administration, medieval literature, philosophy, and physical education/sport psychology are held by 60% of the panel. All of the experts currently work with student-athletes in higher education. In addition, their previous job experiences with student-athletes included prior positions within the academic advising area, academic counseling within the university at large, teaching in physical education and sport psychology, and psychological consultation with university and national teams.

INSTRUMENTATION

Based on a review of literature and contact with members of the National Association of Academic Advisors for Athletics, an initial list of 68 components of a whole-istic model for counseling student-athletes was prepared by the author. Three general headings were included within the whole-istic model: 1) academic, 2) athletic, and 3) personal/social. A fourth heading included general questions dealing with the location of the actual counseling program in the university structure and the use of university-wide support services.

The expert panel was asked to rate each component item using a Likert-type scale. The scale was designed to objectively tabulate responses ranging from 1 (*not important*) to 5 (*essential*). Each survey list mailed to the panel was designed to accommodate any additional component areas that an individual panel member wished to add to the model.

A second round of Delphi questionnaires containing the group mean for each item and each expert's original response for each item was mailed to each panel member. Each expert was asked to re-rate each item, as well as to write a justification for each item where his or her response varied significantly from that of the group. In Round II, experts were also able to rate new items that had been suggested by other panel members during Round I. In addition, experts were asked if each item currently existed at their institutions and, if the item did not exist, how feasible it would be to implement. Implementation ratings were also on a Likert-type scale ranging from 1 (*very difficult to accomplish*) to 5 (*very easy to accomplish*).

RESULTS

Components were accepted into the final model based upon a mean of 3.0 (i.e., *important*) or higher. Of those components retained in the final model, consensus was reached on 27 of the 45 components (see Table 1). Bipolar consensus (where the experts' responses on a question were at both ends of the scale, i.e., agreeing to disagreeing) was reached on three components whereas the panel had a wide range of responses on the remaining four components. Consensus was also obtained on 11 additional components except for one outlier who consistently ranked components as not important.

Rejected Components. Components with a mean rating score below 3.0 were not accepted into the final model. Although the rejected components included support services from all proposed areas, the largest single area rejected involved sport performance enhancement skills (e.g., muscle relaxation training, mental imagery training, biofeedback training, and hypnotic training), skills that are typically offered by educational and clinical sport psychologists.

Feasibility to Implement Components. The average degree of how important each component was to the model for counseling student-athletes was compared to the mean for how feasible each component would be to implement. The majority of the components accepted into the final model are currently in place at most of the experts' institutions. The schools that did not have certain components in place indicated that it would be easy to implement 9 of the missing components (e.g., non-academic minority mentoring program), difficult to implement 13 of the absent services for student-athletes (e.g., support services for learning disabled), while remaining neutral on 13 items (e.g., values and morals exploration and clarification).

DISCUSSION

The Delphi technique encourages both convergent and divergent responses (Cookson, 1986) and thus, it should be viewed as a decision-analysis rather than a decision-making tool (Turoff, 1970). In this study, bipolar consensus (*agreeing* to *disagreeing*) was reached on three of the final components: 1) written communication between the whole-istic program and the student-athlete's instruc-

Table 1
Final Model Components

Component	Mean	SD
Academic		
1. Help with academic major selection	4.7	.67
2. Tutorial assistance	4.7	.67
3. Support services for acquiring learning skills (i.e., note and test taking)	4.6	.97
4. Assessment of writing ability	4.4	.70
5. Assessment of learning disabilities	4.3	.67
6. Exploration of career options	4.3	.67
7. Support services for learning disabled	4.3	.99
8. Assessment of math ability	4.2	.63
9. Remedial work in reading	4.2	1.23
10. Remedial work in writing	4.2	1.23
11. Academic scheduling of student-athletes within academic departments	4.1	.99
12. Assessment of reading ability	4.1	1.20
13. Study table in P.M. after classes	4.1	1.05
14. Academic scheduling of student-athletes within office of academic advising of student-athletes	4.0	1.25
15. Remedial work in math	4.0	1.25
16. Study table available all day	3.8	.83
17. Written communication between holistic program & student-athlete's instructors	3.6	1.43
Athletic		
18. Counseling injured athletes	4.2	.63
19. Retirement from competition training	3.1	1.37
Personal/Social		
20. Counseling for drug users	4.8	.63
21. Drug Education	4.5	.71
22. Time-management education	4.4	.52
23. Eating disorders education	4.3	.67
24. Sanctions for drug use	4.3	1.06

Table 1
Final Model Component
(cont'd)

Component	Mean	SD
Personal/Social		
25. Sexually transmitted diseases education	4.3	.67
26. Goal-setting education	4.2	.63
27. Individual counseling sessions	4.2	.67
28. Nutrition education	4.0	.47
29. Pregnancy education	4.0	1.15
30. Communication skills education	3.8	1.13
31. Coping skills education	3.8	1.23
32. Education on the effects of athletic participation on personal development	3.7	.99
33. Decision-making skills education	3.6	1.17
34. Non-academic minority mentoring program	3.6	.70
35. Drug testing	3.5	1.43
36. Anxiety management training	3.3	.82
37. Values and morals exploration and clarification	3.3	1.42
38. Personality assessment	3.2	1.03
General/System		
39. Support of coach for whole-istic program	5.0	.00
40. Open communication between academic and athletic departments	4.9	.32
41. Recruit meet with academic department	4.4	.97
42. Staff whole-istic program with a combination of specialists with training in student development, physical education and counseling psychology	3.7	1.16
43. Staff whole-istic program with personnel trained in student development	3.5	1.35
44. House whole-istic program under one roof	3.2	1.75
45. Staff whole-istic program with personnel trained in counseling psychology	3.2	1.03

tors, 2) values and morals exploration and clarification, and 3) housing the whole-istic program under one roof. Proponents of written communication felt it assisted in the education of faculty about the unique concerns and needs of the student-athlete. Opponents believed that this contact led to a singling out of student-athletes, which could result in either preferential or discriminatory treatment. One opponent of values clarification believed that, although it is important, it should not be part of athletic programs, which already have too great an indoctrination to regimentation without questioning. This author believes that values clarification would, in fact, lead to less unquestioning regimentation on the part of the student-athlete. Other experts view values clarification as the essence of liberal education and student development as well as a necessary component in decision making. The follow-up telephone calls identified housing the whole-istic model program under one roof as a poorly understood question. Those in favor of this component understood the question to mean that support programs from all areas of campus would be employed in addition to services provided within the athletic-academic support unit. Those opposed to this component understood the question to mean that the programs would be providing all of the services within the whole-istic model themselves. Since this seemed impossible to have them based on the number of services, they were opposed to housing the model under one roof because they would not have enough time to provide all of the support areas.

No consensus was reached on four components (i.e., retirement from competition education, drug testing, personality assessment, and staffing the program with personnel trained in student development). Comments on retirement from competition assistance ranged from the belief that athletes must do some things on their own to the belief that the support unit needs to be committed to preparing the student-athlete for life beyond athletics. For those who have finished their athletic careers, developmental preparation, including assessment, career information, internships, and mentorship into an entry level career were recommended. Those who commented on the second component, drug testing, opposed it as a violation of personal rights and discrimination against student-athletes. However, the experts support programs in place at their institutions. Personality assessment, the third component, was a tool used by some but viewed by others as difficult to include in the program based on the training necessary to properly administer the testing instruments. The final component, staffing the program with personnel trained in student development, was supported by those who believe development is the central issue of the *student*-athlete. Training in cognitive, affective, social, and athletic development of the student-athlete is viewed as essential.

The remainder of the components received consensus on Round II. While using the midpoint of the Likert scale (*important*) makes intuitive sense, using the median of the actual mean ratings would add the following additional components to the final model: computerized study aids; training on working with the media; entry into professional sport training; assertiveness training; social-skills training (e.g., etiquette); team counseling sessions; a freshman student-athletes' required class dealing with assorted issues under the academic, athletic, and personal/social areas; communication skills education for coaches; education for coaches on understanding their personalities and their effect on their athletes' personalities; staffing whole-istic programs with generalists (i.e., trained in academic advising, athletic performance enhancement, and personal/social counseling skills); housing whole-istic program under many roofs in order to use established university resources for academic and personal issues such as academic planning, counseling centers and existing interventions like cognitive restructuring. The outlier respondent related during the follow-up telephone call that he believed components were not needed because admission practices should not allow ill-prepared students into the university at the outset. The fact is, however, that there are athletes on the campuses of many major universities with SAT scores hundreds of points below those of the rest of the student body (American Association of University Professors, 1990). This discrepancy can result in academic and related problems in other areas of the student-athlete's life that need to be addressed by a whole-istic support program. Unfortunately, this expert's focus on practices at his university affected the development of a model to be used in a wide variety of university settings.

Chi-square statistical analyses revealed significant relationships between the existence of academic, athletic, and personal/social components at institutions and their importance of inclusion in the final model. Overall, panel members who believed that components are more important were currently conducting those programs, whereas those who did not believe the components were important did not offer those services to the student-athletes.

Panel respondents moved towards the mean an average of 10.1 times (SD=4.45). No significant change overall was observed when the data were grouped by academic, athletic, personal/social, and general/system components. Based on the follow-up telephone calls, the lack of significant movement towards consensus may be due to experts basing their ratings of importance on what they currently do at their jobs. If the institutions have a component in place, the experts tend to perceive it as important and would rate it as valuable to the whole-istic model. If the component which included the performance enhancement skills is not in place, the panel was inclined not to see it as valuable to the model. In addition, some panel members felt that they do not have time to add components to their programs. They believed that any support services offered to student-athletes would involve their time, which was already extremely limited.

Implementation of the Model. The author believes this model could be implemented utilizing currently existing support services available on most campuses, with supplementation by consultants from off-campus when necessary. This, in fact, is what all the experts in the study were currently doing. For the most part, their traditional roles have been in academic support. Pressures from the student-athlete, the university, and society have thrust the experts into offering a variety of services, some for which they had no formal training. In implementing the final model, the head of the whole-istic program would need to spend a majority of time coordinating programs from within the unit, both from support services available on campus and from community resources. The panel members have an understanding of the support services currently available on their campuses and how to use many of these services to supplement the support program for student-athletes. However, they believe that they are providing the services needed by the student-athletes within the time they can humanly spend at their jobs.

Support for the Model. To succeed, the whole-istic model must have support from the administration, the faculty, and the athletic department staff. In support of Ferrante, Etzel and Pinkney's model (see Chapter 2), the panel agreed that to solicit support for the whole-istic program, the administration must believe not only that is the athletic department is one of the university's most important ambassadors but also that it can serve this function in a positive or negative way. Student-athletes who are pleased with their treatment become valuable alumni upon graduation. Those who perceive they have not been treated well fail to contribute in numerous financial and nonmonetary ways in the future. These same athletes are watched by the public during their competitive years via the press. How the athletes are portrayed by the press (i.e., as heroes to be emulated or idols accused of illegal activities) may affect university recruitment and contributions. To facilitate education and communication, one institution has its advisor for student-athletes meeting weekly in the provost's office with support service personnel from other campus offices.

Having faculty serve on the athletic council is viewed by the experts as one way to change the system from within. In support of the recent Special Committee Report on Athletics by the American Association of University Professors (1990), having an athletic association comprising faculty advise the student-athletes' support program leads to faculty understanding and support. Open communication is promoted and maintained by the student-athletes' support personnel when they offer breakfasts and lunches for the faculty, deans, department chairs, university academic counselors, and student-athletes, and an excellent communication opportunity is created by inviting these groups to attend athletes' award ceremonies.

Some of the experts believe that the whole-istic model would be a difficult concept for an athletic director to accept. It may involve changing philosophically from evaluating the advisor solely on student-athletes' eligibility to measuring success by other developmental measures of growth, but it would also require appropriate training and hiring practices among this group of support service personnel. Athletic directors and coaches are commonly viewed as high-control individuals who are very concerned with "turf" protection. At the outset, it is important for the advisor to communicate who he is and what the program will be like. Schools whose coaches are supportive of the advisor to student-athletes enforce mandatory meetings, seminars, and study halls and therefore ensure that the athletes attend these services. Where coaches and athletic directors want to control and are threatened by new ideas, advisors must move slowly and develop rapport. This may involve stepwise action directed toward gaining acceptance by the athletic director and coaches so that the advisor is then in a position to change attitudes towards and perception of the program of support for student-athletes. Educating athletic staff members about the helpfulness of services provided to student-athletes should be an initial goal. The coaches' endorsement is critical to the success of the athlete using the programs provided. The support of the coaches for the whole-istic model was the *only* component in the Delphi study that received a ranking of 5 ("*essential*") by all members of the panel.

Support programs on campus are critical to the implementation of the whole-istic model. Because of prior experiences, many campus agencies mistrust athletics. To facilitate a change in their views, advisors must create environments where the support units can succeed with the student-athletes. It is also important to let people in other support units know that the advisor to student-athletes is not trying to take over or duplicate the services they provide. Open communication between support units is essential. Student-athletes need roads into the bureaucratic system. In support of the service delivery model for student-athletes proposed by Ferrante et al, (see Chapter 2), many schools have liaisons in each campus support unit (i.e., career planning and placement, counseling center, student development, study skills center, campus academic advising center, learning skills center, registrar, financial aid, etc.). Although often accused of exercising too much control, these institutions believe the student-athletes must initially be directed to the liaison person so that in the future, they will know where and to whom to go for help. Most institutions believe in referring individuals to the support units and bringing the support unit personnel to the student-athletes when large groups are involved. Control is again the issue to ensure that the student-athlete is receiving the service. The philosophical question each program must address rests with the degree of control it will exercise over the life of the student-athlete.

Off-campus services may be used to augment campus support programs. Outside consultants such as psychologists, sport psychologists, media educators, and learning disabilities specialists are currently working with student-athletes. However, it is politically and fiscally prudent not to duplicate services already available to the student-athlete.

Housing and Staffing. Panel members' views on the question of where the whole-istic program should be housed and to whom its head should report were as diverse as the philosophies and practices of the schools involved in the study. Four respondents felt locating their office within the athletic department was important to serving the athletes, coaches, and athletic administrators. Four additional respondents wished to be housed in a student-athlete academic center that might consist of an office or a cluster of offices within the academic department or student life building or might be a free-standing building that house only advising to student-athletes. Brooks, Etzel and Ostrow (1987) have proposed that advisors employed by athletic departments may view developing a whole-istic counseling model as secondary to keeping athletes eligible. Certainly a whole-istic counseling model would both change and broaden the focus for many existing programs that support student-athletes at this time.

The American Association of University Professors (1990) has proposed counteracting the pressures in college sports that subvert the student-athlete's academic pursuits by removing all decision making that relates to the athlete's education from the financial incentives that affect the day-to-day operations of the athletic department. The benefit of housing services within or near the athletic area again appears to be one of control, control that student-athletes are getting what they need by literally walking them from place to place while being near enough to the coaches to deal with them at the same time. The remaining two experts preferred to house services in the academic affairs office or the counseling center under student development. One expert wished to report to the head of student life and one to the head of the counseling center, while one expert chose to report to the athletic director. Seven experts believed that academic credibility and protection come with reporting to the chief academic affairs officer (i.e., vice president or provost). One respondent felt that it did not matter who was reported to as long as the superior was honest and understood athletics. A lack of interest in and understanding of athletics and both the student-athlete and the coaching experiences, were the reason two experts did not want to report to the chief academic affairs officer.

Housing and line of reporting appear to be a reflection of philosophy, training, and experience. It may be important for recently hired or current advisors to student-athletes to consider a number of factors before deciding about any changes in these areas. If there is a question of academic integrity on the part of the office of advising to student-athletes at a particular institution, reporting to the chief executive officer may improve these perceptions. However, this author believes that the head of the proposed model for student-athletes should report to the head of the student life division. The question of service location appears to depend upon the actual physical layout of the campus. It is important that the director of the model and the utilized support services be easily accessible to student-athletes and to their coaches. At a particular institution, this may place the office for counseling student-athletes in or near an athletic facility, in or near residence halls, or in or near the office of student life.

Directing such a program will require a skilled coordinator who knows the student-athlete, who can make use of resources available both on and off campus, and who can draw student-athletes into using the services. Two experts believed that skills in systems consultation learned in conjunction with psychology or counseling psychology would facilitate bringing people together without having turf issues sabotage the success of the whole-istic program. This type of individual must be able to accept a peripheral position, thus allowing coaches and athletic directors control while providing the necessary support services.

Many experts believed that the educational background of the program coordinator was not important. What they believed is important is that the individual be sensitive to the needs of people at all levels (i.e., administrators, faculty, athletic administrators, coaches, and student-athletes) and is willing to work extended hours (60-70 per week). This author envisions that the type of knowledge these future service providers to student-athletes will need to have will involve not only academic areas but will also involve psychology and sport psychology areas. The make-up of the current panel of experts may have weighted opinions towards academic issues due to the experts' educational backgrounds and current job experiences. Perhaps performance enhancement skills such as mental imagery training, muscle relaxation training, biofeedback training and hypnotic training were discounted from the model due to a lack of knowledge on the part of the majority of the panel members, the belief that these services were not within their function and/or the belief that performance enhancement components did not fit within their institutional culture or were not essential to the primary purpose of the program.

Overall, the median for feasibility to implement the whole-istic model developed, at their respective institutions, was given a 3.75, with the 3 ranking meaning *neutral* and the 4 ranking meaning *easy to accomplish*. The reasons for the lowest three experts' rankings of 2 (*difficult to accomplish*) were time and facilities.

In summary, a whole-istic model designed to meet the need for counseling student-athletes in academic, athletic and personal/social areas was developed by a panel of expert service providers. Utilizing existing support programs available on university campuses, the whole-istic model will require minimum additional time and services if headed by a "systems-smart practitioner," that is, an experienced professional who understands the dynamics of the particular organization (A.P. Ferrante, personal communication, March 15, 1990). This individual needs to be skilled in working within the structure of higher education, with professionals from various backgrounds, and with a variety of agendas. The nature of the whole-istic model is such that the final listing of components is applicable to assisting the student-athletes on any campus of higher education. The goal of the whole-istic model is to mainstream people as much as possible during these critical developmental years, while providing the support necessary to assist them in meeting the unique challenges and pressures that they face as student-athletes (Kleiber, Greendorfer, Blinde & Samdahl, 1987).

Based on this research, it is recommended that the whole-istic model be implemented within institutions of higher education that are involved in supporting intercollegiate athletic programs. Student-athletes' concerns today are multifaceted. Although many issues fall within the academic realm, numerous others (e.g., finding personal fulfillment, learning communication skills, coping with injury) involve areas that traditionally have not been addressed in an organized fashion by support programs working with student-athletes. The student-athletes of today report that these areas are important to them (AIR, November, 1988; AIR, March, 1989a; AIR, July, 1989b; AIR,

August, 1989c; Bruno, 1989). By implementing the whole-istic model of support for the student-athlete, both the student-athlete and higher education will ultimately emerge as winners.

AUTHOR'S NOTE

The author wishes to thank the Delphi Committee:

Mr. Robert Bradley, University of Kentucky
Dr. A. P. Ferrante, The Ohio State University
Dr. Gerald Gurney, University of Maryland
Dr. Bruce Hale, Pennsylvania State University
Dr. Kate Halischak, University of Notre Dame
Dr. Chris Kennedy, Duke University
Ms. Elizabeth Kurpius, Indiana University
Dr. Richard McGuire, University of Virginia
Mr. Steve Milburn, University of Louisville
Mr. Fred Stroock, University of California, Los Angeles.

REFERENCES

American Institutes for Research. (1988). *Summary results from the 1987-88 national study of intercollegiate athletes.* (Report No. 1). Palo Alto, CA: Center for the Study of Athletics.

American Institutes for Research (1989a). *The experiences of black intercollegiate athletes at NCAA Division I institutions.* (Report No. 3). Palo Alto, CA: Center for the Study of Athletics.

American Institutes for Research (1989b). *Women in intercollegiate athletics at NCAA Division I institutions.* (Report No. 4). Palo Alto, CA: Center for the Study of Athletics.

American Institutes for Research (1989c). *Comments of student-athletes in the 1987-88 national study of intercollegiate athletes.* (Report No. 6) Palo Alto, CA: Center for the Study of Athletics.

American Association of University Professors (1990). The role of faculty in the governance of college athletics. *Academe*, January-February, 43-47.

Bergandi, T. A. & Wittig, A. F. (1984). Availability of and attitudes toward counseling services for the college athlete. *Journal of*

College Student Personnel, 25, 557-558.

Brooks, D. D., Etzel, E. F. & Ostrow, A. C. (1987). Job responsibilities and backgrounds of NCAA athletic advisors and counselors. *The Sport Psychologist, 1*, 201-207.

Bruno, J. E. (1989). *Developing a professional "standard of care" for academic advisors of student-athletes: Use of information based formative evaluation in academic support.* Manuscript submitted for publication.

Cookson, P. S. (1986). Charting the unknown: Delphi and policy Delphi strategies for international co-operation. *International Journal of Lifelong Education, 5* (1), 3-13.

Dalkey, N. C. (1969). *The Delphi method: An experimental study of group opinion.* The RAND Corporation, 7 (4), RM - 5888 - PR, 61.

Damon, W. (1983). *Social and personality development.* New York, NY: W. W. Norton and Company.

Danish, S. J., D'Augelli, A. R., & Ginsberg, M. R. (1984). Life development intervention: Promotion of mental health through the development of competence. In S. D. Brown & R. W. Lent (Eds.), *Handbook of Counseling Psychology* (pp. 520-544). New York: Wiley.

Danish, S. J., & Hale, B. D. (1981). Toward an understanding of the practice of sports psychology. *Journal of Sport Psychology, 3*, 90-99.

Etzel, E. F. (1989). *Life stress, locus of control, and sport competition anxiety patterns of college student-athletes.* Unpublished doctoral dissertation, West Virginia University, Morgantown.

Ferrante, A. P. (October, 1986). *Outreach programming for student-athletes: The problem, the need.* Paper presented at the meeting of the Southeastern Counseling Conference, Boone, NC.

Gordon, R. L. (1986). Issues in advising student-athletes. *NACADA Journal, 6*, 81-86.

Heyman, S. R. (1986). Psychological problem patterns found with athletes. *The Clinical Psychologist, Summer*, 68-71.

Kleiber, D., Greendorfer, S., Blinde, E., & Samdahl, D. (1987). Quality of exit from university sports and life satisfaction in early adulthood. *Sociology of Sport Journal, 4,* 28-36.

Linstone, H. A. & Turoff, M. (Eds.). (1975). *The Delphi Method, Techniques and Applications.* Reading, MA: Addison-Wesley.

Mahoney, M. J. & Suinn, R. M. (Summer, 1986). History and overview of modern sport psychology. *The Clinical Psychologist,* 64-68.

National Association of Academic Advisors for Athletics (1989-1990). *Summary of support programs for marginal students.* Unpublished manuscript.

Nelson, E. S. (1983). How the myth of the dumb jock becomes fact: A developmental view for counselors. *Counseling and Values, 27,* 176-185.

Pinkerton, R. S., Hinz, L. D. & Barrow, J. C. (1987, May). *The college student-athlete: Psychological consideration and intervention strategies.* Presented at the 65th Annual Meeting of the American College Health Association, Chicago.

Rosenberg, E. (1982). Athletic retirement as social death: Concepts and perspectives. In N. Theberge & P. Donnelly (Eds.), *Sport and the Sociological Imagination: Refereed Proceedings of the 3rd Annual Conference of the North American Society for the Sociology of Sport, Toronto, Canada* (pp. 245-258). Fort Worth, TX: Texas Christian University Press, 1984.

Schubert, G. W. & Schubert, A. F. (1983). A trilogy of academic concerns for the academic advisor of student-athletes: General advising; litigation; and NCAA Proposal Number 48. *NCADA Journal, 3,* 11-22.

Sowa, C. J. & Gressard, C. F. (1983). Athletic participation: Its relationship to student development. *Journal of College Student Personnel, 24,* 236-239.

Turoff, M. (1970). The design of a policy Delphi. *Technological Forecasting and Social Change, 2,* 141-179.

Tutko, T. A. & Richards, J. W. (1971). *Psychology of coaching.* Boston: Allyn and Bacon.

Walter, R., & Smith, D. E. (1986). Taking athletes across the academic finish line. *Educational Record, 67,* 41-44.

Waterman, A. S. (1982). Identity development from adolescence to adulthood: An extension of theory and a review of research. *Developmental Psychology, 18,* 341-358.

Zingg, P. J. (1982). Advising the student athlete. *Educational Record, 63,* 16-19.

CHAPTER 4

Understanding and Intervening with the Student-Athlete-to-Be

Dan Gould and Laura Finch

The authors discuss the need to intervene with student-athletes while they are still in high school and describe various methods of making the transition to college less difficult.

As athletics have become more competitive and lucrative throughout the century, athletes have turned to a variety of sources to aid performance. One of these sources is applied sport psychology, which is a field whose purpose is to help athletes achieve their sport objectives through educational techniques such as goal setting, relaxation training, and precompetitive and competitive mental plans.

Applied sport psychology in North America has a long and rich history, dating back to the 1920s. It has been only in the last fifteen years, however, that the provision of specialized helping services that attend to the personal-social needs of athletes has come of age. As demonstrated by recent survey evidence, over 20 U.S. Olympic sports now offer some form of sport psychological services to their athletes and coaches (Gould, Tammen, Murphy & May, 1989). Similarly, for the first time in its history the U.S. Olympic Committee assigned sport psychologists to the 1988 Olympic Games staff (Murphy & Ferrante, 1989). Finally, a recent issue [1990, 4,(2)] of *The Sport Psychologist* was devoted solely to issues involved in providing sport psychological services to professional athletes.

Although the growth of applied sport psychology is encouraging and long overdue, it is not without problems. Despite an estimated 25 million children participating in sport in the United States (Martens, 1986) and a substantial body of available youth sport psychological literature (Gould, 1987; Gould & Weiss, 1987), little attention has been paid to the developing precollegiate athlete. Instead, the focus has been and remains on the elite athlete, usually of college age. Additionally, most applied sport psychologists focus more of their attention on performance enhancement issues as opposed to the effect of sport participation on the development of the participant's total well-being (Gould et al., 1989).

Fortunately, there are signs that this state of affairs is beginning to change, particularly in regard to broadening consulting foci from merely performance enhancement issues to concerns focusing on total athlete development and well-being. For example, in recent years sport psychologists have given increased attention to issues such as athlete substance abuse (Tricker, Cook, & McGuire, 1989), eating disorders (Thompson, 1987), and career termination (Ogilvie & Howe, 1986). Especially encouraging is the appearance of articles emphasizing the need for helping professionals (e.g., psychologists, counselors, sports medicine specialists) to address the unique mental health needs of college athletes (Jordan & Denson, 1990; Pearson & Petitpas, 1990; Petruzzello, Landers, Linder, & Robinson, 1987) and the fact that Notre Dame, Pennsylvania State and Ohio State, among other universities, have hired full-time sport psychology counseling specialists.

The increased interest in counseling college student-athletes is not surprising given the developmental metatheory view of counseling (Steenbarger, 1990). This theory suggests that normal development is not free from turmoil and stress. Instead, normal development is characterized by struggles, turmoil, and stress, all of which are both normal and necessary for individual adaptation and growth. It is further suggested that these struggles are exemplified in college students because it is at this critical developmental stage that the young adult often leaves home for the first time, forms new identities, leaves old established friends, and makes new ones. College student-athletes are thought to experience additional struggles such as balancing athletic and academic schedules, not making the starting team, coping with physical injury, and retiring from active participation due to injury and graduation (Pearson & Petitpas, 1990).

The unique developmental crises experienced by college student-athletes suggest that it is important for counseling services to be initiated for collegiate athletes. However, helping professionals must adopt a long-term developmental perspective when working with the collegiate athlete. The collegiate athlete began participating in sport long before walking on campus and comes to the university with a unique individual history of physical and psychological athletic experiences. It is imperative that this history be understood and incorporated into the counseling process. More importantly, secondary school counselors and athletic leaders must be involved in the intervention process and informed of ways to prepare the potential collegiate athlete to cope effectively with the pressures, experiences, and normal developmental struggles that will occur in college. In essence, as recommended by Pearson and Petitpas (1990), primary prevention is needed.

This chapter is designed to help meet the primary prevention needs of college student-athletes by facilitating the counselor's understanding of the prospective collegiate athlete. It has two specific purposes: 1) to describe incoming collegiate student-athletes by examining their psychosocial development as interscholastic and youth sport participants, and 2) to recommend intervention strategies to be used with student-athletes-to-be.

CHARACTERISTICS OF THE
STUDENT-ATHLETE-TO-BE

Sport in America can be best thought of as a pyramid with a broad base and small, but high apex. It is estimated, for example, that 25 million children participate in competitive sport in the United States, with the majority being below the age of 12 years (Martens, 1986). Statistics from the State of Michigan's (1978) comprehensive study of children's sports also show that the majority of these children (85%) discontinue involvement by the age of 18. Hence, the college student-athlete-to-be has successfully progressed through this competitive system. Because of this progression it is safe to assume that the average entering college student-athlete has experienced a good deal of athletic success by trying out for and making high-caliber teams throughout his or her career. Moreover, collegiate athletes are in all likelihood the more successful participants from their high school programs. For these reasons, "being an athlete" and being a "successful athlete" form an important part of the prospective student-athlete's personal sense of identity.

Given the importance athletics and athletic success play in the identity of the student-athlete-to-be, most will enter college with expectations and dreams of athletic success, as well as of the rewards that accompany such success. In most cases, however, the prospective student-athlete will not have experienced major personal athletic failures during the scholastic years such as not starting or not being a successful participant.

It is also likely that the prospective student-athlete has earned much of status from his or her athletic participation. That is, a benefit of high school athletic participation and especially of successful high school athletic participation is the status it brings the adolescent. In the early 1960s, for instance, Coleman (1974) found that athletic participation was viewed as an important criteria for "leading crowd" status in the schools. In fact, the importance of the athletic status system was such that when forced into a choice, adolescents indicated that they would rather be successful athletes than scholars in the high school years. This same state of affairs holds true today as more recent studies (Feltz, 1978; Duda, 1981; Roberts, 1982) have replicated Coleman's original findings.

In summary, then, prospective collegiate student-athletes are individuals who have experienced substantial athletic success and involvement. It is also probable that these individuals will identify themselves through athletic success and participation because in the past this success has helped them gain status in the adolescent subculture. It is unlikely that such individuals have met with a great deal of athletic adversity such as sitting on the bench, not starting, or consistently performing poorly. Therefore, these individuals may not be prepared for some of these developmental challenges they may face for the first time in their collegiate athletic careers.

DEVELOPMENTAL OBSTACLES FOR THE STUDENT-ATHLETE-TO-BE

The entering student-athlete faces a number of situations which could turn into developmental crises that can serve as obstacles to individual development. These include readjusting athletic expectations, time management concerns, living adjustments, and coping with mistakes and adversity. Each of these is discussed below.

Adjusting athletic expectations. Because high school athletes who enter college have experienced a good deal of athletic success, they may have unrealistic athletic expectations. Prior to entering the university these athletes may dream of earning a starting position, winning the big game, achieving All-Conference or All-American honors, and/or becoming the stars of their teams. Seldom do they think about the fact that over 90% of those athletes that they successfully defeated or beat out to make the team in high school will not be competing in college (i.e., only the more successful high school athletes like themselves go on to college to participate in intercollegiate athletics).

Similarly, these student-athletes typically do not consider that they will be competing for starting berths against other athletes with up to four years more collegiate experience and that practices and games will be much more intense and demanding than they have ever experienced. It is quite likely, for example, that the typical incoming freshman athlete will need to adjust from being the star of his or her high school team to being a sub or scout squad player in college. She or he may also experience a good deal of frustration in practices as the adjustment is made to adapting to the higher caliber of play typifying college programs. In fact, incoming student-athletes may be coming to terms with "identity foreclosure" as they must adjust to a new collegiate athletic role out of the limelight. That new role may be as a nontraveling team member or as an NCAA proposition 48/42 athlete who for the first time life is prohibited from athletic participation for academic reasons.

Finally, this type of adjustment occurs in an environment where the athlete's previous social support system will not be directly available. Alternatively, those elements may be available (e.g., parents) but may not understand why or to what degree their own athletic hero or heroine may be having difficulties adjusting to collegiate competition. They, like the student-athlete, have never experienced such difficulties in the past.

Time management concerns. Like all other first-time college students, the student-athlete must learn to efficiently manage time. For many, it will be the first time in their lives that they are on their own and have to deal with making the majority of their own decisions. Although students look forward to being on their own they often make mistakes because of their lack of experience in this area. This may be especially difficult for the student-athlete who must deal with normal student time management concerns associated with academic and social involvements in an environment where two to four hours a day are devoted to athletic training. A number of classes may be missed because of team travel schedules, injury rehabilitation, and game preparations.

Living adjustment concerns. Like all students, student-athletes must adjust to a new living environment. They may have a roommate for the first time and experience varying degrees of homesickness. The student-athlete will also be attempting to meet and make new friends. Many of these experiences may be foreign to the student-athlete who as the high school athletic star was perceived by her or himself and others as a pillar of strength and center of attention.

Coping with mistakes and adversity. Even the most gifted entering student-athletes will find the first few months of college athletic participation a difficult period of adjustment. They are practicing and competing against a much higher caliber of player. They must learn new, more complicated offensive and defensive systems, and adjust to new coaches and teammates. In all likelihood this process will be a struggle. This does not mean the entering student-athlete is doomed to failure. Rather, most will successfully adjust to the new demands placed on them. Like the majority of maturing young adults, they will be able to adapt to the developmental challenges they must face.

Unfortunately, some athletes (especially those who judge their ability only on winning and losing) will have tremendous difficulty coping with the normal developmental process of mistakes and failure. For those who have such difficulty, their confidence will deteriorate, and their anxiety will increase.

The result will often be a decline in athletic and academic performance. In essence, the prospective student-athlete must be prepared to cope with this process of adversity. Helping professionals must be aware that this may happen in order to be of assistance.

In summary, as part of the normal transition from high school to college, the student-athlete will face any number of developmental crises. These may range from general concerns focusing on time management and living arrangements to sport specific concerns related to unrealistic expectations and the inability to cope with short-term mistakes and frustration. The student-athlete-to-be must be prepared to cope productively with and use these potential crises as opportunities for growth and development. Toward this end, helping professionals in high schools can play a central role in assisting these young men and women make the transition.

COUNSELING STRATEGIES FOR USE WITH
THE STUDENT-ATHLETE-TO-BE

Although it is highly desirable to prepare the student-athlete-to-be psychologically for the transition from high school to college, this is seldom done. If it is attempted, it is undertaken during the student-athlete's first semester on campus. A more productive approach involves preparing these young people for this transition in the junior and senior years of high school. This can be accomplished in several ways. First, high school counseling personnel can conduct special transition programs for those athletes who desire to participate in collegiate athletics. Second, coaches and athletic personnel can counsel their athletes regarding to these concerns. And, third, helping professionals should consider involving parents in such transition sessions in an effort to highlight the importance of the subject and educate a support source that will remain involved with the student-athlete throughout the collegiate experience. These interventions presume that these individuals understand the obstacles prospective student-athletes may encounter, have a willingness to involve themselves in primary-oriented interventions, and have the time to do it.

Regardless of the form taken to facilitate the transition from scholastic to collegiate athletics, a number of topics are critically important to discuss. These include perspective training, role of academics and athletics, goal setting training, time management skills, independence training, mistake and loss coping strategy facilitation, and stress management skills training.

PERSPECTIVE TRAINING

An important attribute, perspective training needs to be developed in student-athletes-to-be. Perspective training can best be viewed as the philosophical system of values that guides the thoughts and practices of the student-athlete, both on and off the field. Much as a philosophy of coaching determines every action of a coach (Martens, 1987), so to does the collegiate athlete's perspective on what it means to be a "student-athlete."

From an intervention standpoint, three issues are critically important to address in assisting the student-athlete-to-be to develop a healthy and productive athletic perspective: 1) an understanding of the role of academics and athletics, 2) realistic expectations of professional sport opportunities, and 3) the development of a positive mental attitude and outlook.

The role of academics and athletics. In recent years, college athletics has been the focus of increased criticism regarding the sacrifice of academic standards for athletic success (Purdy, Eitzen, & Hufnagel, 1982; Sperber, 1990). Frequent reports appear in the popular press regarding student-athletes who are given passing grades for courses they have never attended, senior athletes who have no academic majors, dismal graduation rates for student-athletes, and even reports of functionally illiterate student-athletes who have graduated from well-respected institutions of higher education. Although most attention is focused on these academic abuses at the collegiate level, they are not necessarily confined to that level. In some cases, athletically gifted scholastic athletes receive academic favors because of their athletic prowess. If this occurs, the student quickly learns that athletics are more important than academics and that as long as they are successful athletically, coaches and administrators will insure they will be taken care of academically even if this means circumventing the rules. To prevent such abuses, coaches, teachers and administrators need to convey clearly to student-athletes that academics are very important. Extracurricular activities such as sports are a privilege based on academic success, not a substitute for academics. This privilege will not be available if student-athletes do not consistently meet acceptable academic standards. Too often the young student-athlete becomes academically ineligible the week before the big game, but the suspension is postponed until after the game. This is often viewed as justifiable because in the end the student has been penalized for failure to adhere to academic standards. Yet by postponing the suspension, the student-athlete learns to assume that academics are less important than athletic contests. And, thus, the cycle of deteriorating academic standards for the athlete continues. In both the short and long run, this type of behavior on the part of instructors and administrators is a clear disservice to the student-athlete.

Developing an appropriate academic perspective involves more than penalizing the student-athlete for inappropriate behavior, however. It is imperative that coaches and administrators take an interest in their athletes' academic progress. Along with parents, they can have a major impact on the academic value system of high school student-athletes.

Realistic expectations of professional sport opportunities. One reason many student-athletes do not stress academics to a desirable degree is their erroneous assumption that they will go on to star in college and then make a successful transition to professional sports. Unfortunately, for the majority of athletes this is a myth. Ogilvie and Howe (1986), for instance, indicate that less than one percent of male college athletes go on to join professional basketball and football teams. Specifically, only 50 of the 15,000 male college basketball and 150 of the 75,000 college football players will go on to make professional squads in any one year. Moreover, because the average NBA and NFL career ranges from three to four years, betting on a career in professional sports is a very poor strategy and one that high school athletes must be made regularly aware of (Ogilvie & Howe, 1986).

Even fewer options exist for female athletes. Although professional opportunities exist for women in individual sports such as golf and tennis, few opportunities are available for women athletes participating in team sports. For example, because professional basketball leagues for women have failed financially in the United

States, the only current professional opportunities for female basketball players exist overseas. Moreover, these foreign teams are limited by regulations as to the number of Americans they are allowed on their rosters. Thus, both male and female athletes face exceedingly few professional sport opportunities after their collegiate eligibility is completed.

In order for aspiring college student-athletes to develop a realistic perspective regarding their athletic participation, counselors and coaches should have accurate statistical information available to present to them. Similarly, programs should be designed or videotapes developed in which former athletes whose collegiate and/or professional athletic dreams were shattered discuss the need to develop a strong academic base. It would also be useful if successful professional athlete role models emphasized the need for completing one's education. Finally, it is important to recognize that this kind of reality review does not have to be a brutal ending to what has been a long-term athletic dream. Rather, the counselor or coach might explain the need to plan for options in case a professional career does not materialize and the fact that outstanding high school athletes who have solid grades have many more scholarship offers and choices than athletes of equal caliber who do not excel academically. When this type of information is presented as a group program to all student-athletes in a category (e.g., sophomores), the appearance that someone thinks a specific student-athlete will never achieve a professional contract or tryout will be lessened.

Positive mental attitude. One of the most difficult perspective elements to instill in the prospective student-athlete is a positive mental attitude. Sport psychologists have emphasized the need for athletes to use positive affirmations such as "I am strong" or "I have practiced hard" (Bell, 1983; Harris & Harris, 1984). However, having a positive mental attitude means more than espousing a series of memorized positive statements. As Bell (1983) has indicated, it involves knowing oneself, being able to realistically appraise one's strengths and limitations, and realistically believing in one's ability. This is clearly an area in which the helping professional can be of assistance.

The athlete must also develop emotional control by learning how to deal with those situations which arise in athletics (and life) that may be seen as unfair. Situations such as bad calls from officials, unpopular coaching decisions, and injuries which sideline athletes before big games occur in sport. Over the course of an athlete's career, however, these negative events typically balance out with lucky breaks, favorable calls, and positive coaching decisions. When bad luck and inappropriate calls and decisions occur, athletes must learn to maintain emotional control and sustain motivation. This is especially difficult to accomplish when an athlete is in a slump or when the team is struggling. Many athletes lose control and give up in these situations. Hence, it is important that coaches and counselors discuss the role of luck in sport and how the athlete will sometimes face difficult and seemingly unfair situations. To help the athlete keep a cool head in these situations, psychological skills like relaxation and positive coping thoughts can be used. Additionally, the athlete must remind him or herself of the need to sustain motivation in these situations. Finally, coaches must continually remind the developing athlete of the need to maintain a realistic perspective when they face adversity and setbacks during competitions and practices.

GOAL SETTING SKILLS

An extremely valuable skill for any potential college student to learn, but especially the student-athlete, is goal setting. Systematic goal setting procedures are seldom taught to the student-athlete-to-be. Rather, it is assumed that athletes will automatically develop the ability to set goals as a byproduct of scholastic participation. Most athletes do learn to derive long-term general objectives like winning a championship, going on to play college sports, or making the varsity team. They often fail, however, to develop systematic goal setting principles that will assist them in their efforts to achieve these long-term objectives. It has been shown that utilizing goal setting in sport parallels goal setting procedures shown to be effective in other life situations (Gould, 1986; Locke & Latham, 1985). It has been recommended, for instance, that athletes set goals in measurable and behavioral terms, that difficult but realistic goals be set, that short as well as long-range goals be set, that goals be written out, that target dates for attaining goals be identified, that goal achievement strategies identified, and that goal support and evaluation be provided (Gould, 1986).

The problem does not come from the lack of appropriate goal

setting information to provide to the developing athlete. An abundance of information is available. Instead, the most difficult aspect of implementing goal setting with the prospective collegiate student-athlete is getting the individual to systematically set goals. Too often at the start of the season goal setting is discussed, and a number of goals are set. After the first few weeks of practice, however, there is little follow-up and goal evaluation. Hence, the student-athlete becomes frustrated or loses interest and discontinues the process. For the above reason, we have found that it is more effective first to expose goal setting information to athletes while they are in high school, then to set one specific goal with the athlete, monitor that goal over time, and provide evaluative feedback. After the athlete learns how to set and achieve one goal effectively, additional goals can be set. In essence, one must teach the student how to set and accomplish one goal before implementing goal setting on a widespread basis.

An especially difficult problem encountered when goal setting with athletes is their strong tendency to focus exclusive attention on outcome (e.g.,winning a game, beating an opponent), as opposed to performance or technique goals (e.g., personal improvement). Yet there is mounting evidence (Burton, 1989; Martens, 1987) that there are severe drawbacks to focusing sole attention on outcome goals. Specifically, athletes have only partial control over contest or event outcome and outcome goals are less flexible. Moreover, when athletes focus solely on contest outcome, it often results in increased anxiety (Martens, 1987).

In contrast, by emphasizing personal performance goals such as decreased times in track or increased shooting percentage in basketball, athletes are provided greater opportunities for individual success and corresponding increased confidence. Because they judge success and failure relative to their own ability and not solely on comparisons with peers, less skilled athletes are no longer doomed to failure. Their more skilled counterparts who can easily exceed the performance levels of their peers learn to compete against themselves and, in so doing, reach higher performance levels.

Lastly, when a total counseling perspective is considered there is great potential for teaching the life skill of goal setting through sport, where students are highly committed to achieving excellence and receiving clear performance feedback. After the student-athlete experiences the benefits of goal setting in the sport domain, teachers, coaches, and helping professionals can then work with the student to transfer these skills to other situations such as academic course work, time management, and personal-social development.

TIME MANAGEMENT SKILLS

As previously stated, time management is a key skill for the college student-athlete to develop. Few high school athletes, however, are given any training in time management. In fact, their athletic practices and contests are typically controlled and scheduled by their coaches. When coupled with many parents organizing their lives at home and their classes being tightly scheduled, it is no wonder that collegiate freshmen student-athletes may experience time management problems when left on their own. High school counselors can provide an important service to these prospective collegiate athletes by providing special sessions on time management and its importance in college.

FOSTERING INDEPENDENCE

Closely associated with the idea of time management is the need to help develop independence in the scholastic athlete. Coaches often pay lip service to the development of independence in their athletes, but when changes in the scholastic athletic system over the last three decades are scrutinized, it can be seen that athletes have been allowed to make fewer and fewer decisions. Gone are the days when a quarterback called his own plays, a gymnast developed her own routine, or a wrestler competed without his coach's continually yelling instructions from the side of the mat. Due in part to increased pressures to win, today's coaches make most of the decisions for the athlete, and hence, the athlete receives little independence training.

If interscholastic sport is to achieve its educational goals, the role of independence training needs to be discussed with coaches. Coaches must provide situations that allow athletes opportunities to make some of their own decisions, whether it is allowing them to call some of their own plays, have input into game or practice plans, and/or make team rules. Equally important, coaches must assist the athlete in this process by providing feedback relative to the appropriateness of choices made and ways to handle setbacks. This is certainly a less efficient process for the coach, but it is a proven way to enhance the potential for independent growth in the athlete.

Finally, independence training should not be confined to the playing field. Because of their influential status with their athletes, coaches can be invaluable in helping athletes develop independent behavior off the field. This can be accomplished by discussing the need to transfer athletic training discipline to the academic arena or the discipline needed to execute a complex offensive system effectively to refusing peer pressure to experiment with drugs. In essence, independence training is not "caught" by participating in athletics, it is "taught" by knowledgeable, caring coaches and helping professionals who systematically and continually emphasize it.

MISTAKE AND LOSS COPING STRATEGIES

Research and experience have consistently shown that young athletes' self-esteem is tied to their athletic success (Weiss, 1987). As previously mentioned, most entering freshman student-athletes will have experienced considerable athletic success. What they may not be prepared for, however, is the adversity they will face when making the transition from high school to collegiate athletics. Initially, mistakes and losses occur on a much more frequent basis in college than they did in high school and the athletes will need psychological skills to help them cope with such adversity.

Much has been written in the youth sports literature about the importance of providing positive experiences for the young athlete (Gould, 1986; Martens, 1990; Smith, Smoll, & Curtis, 1979). In fact, Smith and his associates (1979) have shown that a positive approach to coaching that emphasizes the frequent and liberal use of rewarding and encouraging statements is strongly associated with the young athlete's psychological development. Yet this does not mean that losing and making mistakes are not important learning tools for the developing athlete. Scholastic athletes need to be taught how to cope successfully with defeat, mistakes, and adversity.

An excellent way to teach appropriate coping responses to prospective collegiate athletes is to discuss the meaning of success and failure with them. Success must not be seen solely as winning or losing, but as the achievement of personal performance goals (Martens, 1990; Smith, Smoll, & Smith, 1989). Similarly, instead of viewing mistakes or losses as terrible, the coach or counselor can help the young athlete view mistakes and losses more productively—as building blocks to success. Undoubtedly, the young athlete will be frustrated after a loss or mistake, and this must be recognized. However, to grow, the young athlete must learn to analyze why the mistake or loss occurred, learn from it, and move on. It is irrational to dwell on errors and disappointments!

It has been our experience that the most productive means of teaching this coping orientation to young athletes is by having coaches discuss it with them at the start of each season. Then during the season coaches should repeatedly remind the athletes of the importance of implementing these procedures and reward them for using these techniques in frustrating situations. In addition, coaches should stop practices when players become frustrated and react poorly to mistakes, explain the coping orientation again, and encourage their athletes to employ it. Finally, those young athletes who repeatedly become frustrated and have difficulty shutting off negative thoughts that follow mistakes should be taught thought-stopping skills and realistic positive replacement affirmations. Referral to a helping professional is another useful option. Only through consistent, repeated, and systematic efforts will this coping orientation be learned by the developing athlete.

STRESS MANAGEMENT TRAINING

A final psychological skill for the student athlete-to-be to master is stress management. Fortunately, much has been written about stress and stress management training in athletics, and a profile of the young athlete who is at risk relative to excessive levels of stress is available (Gould, 1990b July; Scanlan, 1986). For example, Scanlan (1986) has shown that the at-risk young athlete who is most susceptible to heightened stress is high trait anxious (has a personality that predisposes him or her to view competition as threatening), has low self-esteem, has low personal and team performance expectancies, experiences less fun and satisfaction, and worries about failure and adult evaluation. These young people experience excessive stress in environments characterized by uncertainty relative to expectations of others, to their ability to perform, and to social evaluation. These high-stress environments are also characterized by the importance placed on competitive contest outcomes.

Fortunately, specific stress management techniques that can be used with these at-risk athletes and methods of conveying them have been identified (Martens, 1987). Cognitive stress management techniques focus on monitoring and controlling negative thoughts and increasing rational thinking, whereas somatic stress management techniques include progressive relaxation and biofeedback. Attempts must be made to identify prospective student-athletes who are susceptible to heightened stress and expose them to counseling and stress management techniques such as these.

SUMMARY

This chapter has emphasized the need to provide applied sport psychology and counseling services to the college student-athlete-to-be. By receiving primary prevention services such as perspective taking, goal setting, time management, independence, mistake and loss coping strategy, and stress management training, the prospective student-athlete will be better prepared to handle those developmental crises that characterize the transition from high school to college athletics. Hence, developmental crises such as readjusting athletic expectations, handling hectic schedules in an independent fashion, living on one's own, and coping with mistakes and adversity will become sources of growth and development, not of anxiety and depression, for the college athlete. Moreover, when severe problems do arise, the prospective student-athlete will be better prepared to handle them or seek appropriate professional assistance. College counseling services for student-athletes, then, must begin long before the collegiate athletic experience begins.

Regardless of when in the transition process counseling services for student-athletes are initiated, the individual needs of each athlete must remain paramount. Although the suggestions offered can be applied in most settings with most athletes, it is imperative that professionals involved in helping relationships with student-athletes remember the uniqueness of each individual student-athlete. Helping professionals must be knowledgeable of and sensitive to the influential role athletic participation has and will continue to play in the psychological development of these young people.

REFERENCES

Bell, K. (1983). *Championship thinking.* Englewood Cliffs, NJ: Prentice-Hall.

Burton, D. (1989). Winning isn't everything: Examining the impact of performance goals on collegiate swimmers' cognitions and performance. *The Sport Psychologist, 3,* 105-132 .

Coleman, J. S. (1974). *Youth: Transition to adulthood.* Chicago, IL: University of Chicago Press.

Duda, J. L. (1981). *A cross-cultural analysis of achievement motivation in sport and the classroom.* Unpublished doctoral dissertation, University of Illinois, Urbana.

Feltz, D. (1978). Athletics in the status system of female adolescents. *Review of Sport and Leisure, 3,* 98-108 .

Gould, D. (1986). Goal setting for peak performance. In J. M. Williams (Ed.). *Applied sport psychology: Personal growth to peak performance.*(pp. 133-148). Palo Alto, CA.: Mayfield.

Gould, D. (1987). Promoting positive sports experiences for children. In J. May & M. J. Asken (Eds.). *Sport psychology: The psychological health of the athlete.* (pp. 77-98). New York: PMA Publishing Corp.

Gould, D. (1990a). AAASP: A vision for the 1990s. *Journal of Applied Sport Psychology, 2,* 99-108 .

Gould, D. (1990b, July). *Stress and stress management in sport: Sport science implications for guiding practice.* Paper presented at the International Association for Physical Education In Higher Education World Congress, Loughborough, England.

Gould, D. Tammen, V., Murphy, S., & May, J. (1989). An examination of U.S. Olympic sport psychology consultants and the services they provide. *The Sport Psychologist, 4,* 300-312 .

Gould, D., & Weiss, M. R. (1987). (Eds.). *Advances in pediatric sport sciences: Behavior issues.* Champaign, IL: Human Kinetics.

Harris, D. V., & Harris, B. L. (1984). *The athlete's guide to sports psychology: Mental skills for physical people.* New York,NY: Leisure Press.

Jordan, J. M., & Denson, E. L. (1990). Student services for athletes:A model for enhancing the student-athlete experience. *Journal of Counseling and Development, 69,* 95-97.

Locke, E. A., & Latham, G. P. (1985). The application of goal settings to sports. *Journal of Sport Psychology, 7,* 205-222.

Martens, R. (1986). Youth sport in the USA. In M. R. Weiss & D. Gould (Eds.), *Sport for children and youth* (pp. 27-34). Champaign, IL: Human Kinetics.

Martens, R. (1987).*Coaches' guide to sport psychology.* Champaign, IL: Human Kinetics.

Martens, R. (1990). *Successful coaching.* Champaign, IL: Human Kinetics.

Murphy, S., & Ferrante, A. P. (1989). Provision of sport psychology services to U.S. Team at the 1988 summer Olympic Games. *The Sport Psychologist. 3* (4), 374-385.

Ogilvie, B. C., & Howe, M. (1986) . The trauma of termination from athletics. In J. M. Williams (Ed.). *Applied sport psychology: Personal growth to peak performance* (pp. 365-382). Palo Alto, CA: Mayfield.

Pearson, R. E., & Petitpas, A. J. (1990). Transitions of athletes: Developmental and preventive perspectives. *Journal of Counseling and Development, 69,* 7-10.

Petruzzello, S. J., Landers, D. M., Linder, D. E., & Robinson, D. R. (1987). Sport psychology service delivery: Implementation within the university community. *The Sport Psychologist, 1,* 248-256.

Purdy, D., Eitzen, D., & Hufnagel, R. (1982) . Are athletes also students? The educational attainment of college athletes. *Social Problems, 29,* 439-447.

Roberts, C.G. (1982). Achievement motivation in sport. In R. Terjung (Ed.), *Exercise and Sport Science Reviews* (Vol.10, pp. 236-269). Philadelphia, PA: Franklin Institute Press.

Scanlan, T. K. (1986). Competitive stress in children. In M. R. Weiss & D. Gould (Eds.), *Sport for children and youth* (pp. 113-118). Champaign, IL: Human Kinetics.

Smith, R. E., Smoll, F. L., & Curtis, B. (1979). Coaching effectiveness training: A cognitive-behavioral approach to enhancing relationship skills in youth sport coaches *Journal of Sport Psychology, 1,* 59-75.

Smith, R. E., Smoll, F. L., & Smith, N. J. (1989). *Parents' complete guide to youth sports.* Costa Mesa, CA: HDL Communications.

Sperber, M. (1990). *College sports inc.: The athletic department vs. the university.* New York: Henry Holt.

State of Michigan (1978). *Joint legislative study on youth sports.* Lansing, MI: Author.

Steenbarger, B. N. (1990). Toward a developmental understanding of the counseling specialty: Lessons from our students. *Journal of Counseling and Development, 68,* 434-437.

Thompson, R. A. (1987). Management of the athlete with an eating disorder: Implications for sport management team, *The Sport Psychologist, 1,* 114-126.

Tricker, R., Cook, D. L., & McGuire, R. (1989) . Issues related to drug abuse in college athletics: Athletes at risk. *The Sport Psychologist, 3,* 155-165.

Weiss, M. R. (1987). Self-esteem and achievement in children's sport and physical activity. In D. Gould & M. R. Weiss (Eds.), *Advances in pediatric sport sciences:Behavior issues* (pp. 87-119). Champaign, IL: Human Kinetics.

CHAPTER **5**

African-American Student-Athletes: An Example of Minority Exploitation in Collegiate Athletics

James Scales

Information about the experience of African-American student-athletes is presented. The author also provides survey data describing different developmental stages that members of this minority group pass through.

"Students choosing to compete in intercollegiate athletics face a unique set of challenges and circumstances as they make the transformation from high school to college. In addition to common issues associated with making the transition to college, such as living away from home for the first time, developing new social groups, and assuming responsibilities of self-discipline, student-athletes also face significant hurdles throughout the course of their college experience" (Jordan & Denson, 1990, p.95). The largest of these hurdles is considered to be the student-athlete's ability to balance an academic load with a schedule of practice and competition. This particular hurdle has become the focus of educational institutions, sports programs, administration, and the concerned public.

Why the focus and concern? There is a general feeling that student-athletes are exploited for their talents. Due to many misconceptions the relationship of race to sports, minority student-athletes appear to be the most exploited group. African-American student-athletes are the most visible and obvious example of this phenomenon. This chapter will explore why African-American student-athletes appear to be the most exploited group, what the issues and concerns of this group are, what has been done to assist these student-athletes in the mastery of other marketable skills, and what remains to be accomplished for minority student-athletes.

THE PARAMETERS OF EXPLOITATION

To understand the systematic exploitation of the African-American student-athlete, we must first understand the relationship of sports to the African-American community in general and to the African-American student-athlete in particular.

Race Relations. The minority community has witnessed some great advances by minority student-athletes in the sports arena, primarily in basketball, baseball, and football. This is not to say that African-Americans and other minorities are not making great strides in other areas such as business and industry. These areas are also showing significant statistical increases for minorities. However, the popularity of the American sports scene leads to more visibility in the media for the athletes.

Edwards (1983) states that the relationships between African-American and white athletes have been exemplary since the introduction of Jackie Robinson into professional major league baseball. Edwards goes on to say that to some extent this reputation has been deliberately fostered by skilled sports propagandists eager to project "patriotic" views consistent with the United States of America's professed ideals of racial justice and equal opportunity.

Such is not the case for minorities interested in a nonathletic way of life. In fact, in business and industry we do not hear much about the positive steps taken in the employment of minorities. Rather, we are more likely to hear about the injustices of an individual business or corporation.

The African-American community is led to believe in sports as an institution with great opportunities for the minority participant. Thanks to mass media and long-standing traditions of racial discrimination limiting African-American access to many prestigious occupations, the African-American athlete and student-athlete are much more visible to the youth of their communities than, say, African-American lawyers or doctors (Edwards, 1983).

Education and the African-American Student. A general complaint by African-American students and student-athletes is that many teachers assume they are academically substandard and are admitted to colleges and universities only because admission requirements are lowered to accommodate them. The academic potential of the African-American student is assumed to be low and that of the student-athlete even lower. The African-American student-athlete and the African-American nonathlete are also very much aware of the difficulties they will experience at the hands of educators and administrators who are poorly prepared for dealing with most minorities. African-American students enroll at predominantly white institutions, colleges and universities with curricula and support systems that were not originally designed with the minority student's needs in mind. Beyond being made to feel academically inferior, minority students can look forward to feeling isolated, alienated, and "pressured to alter their behavior and their view to fit into the white, upper-middle-class culture that holds sway there" (Lederman, 1989, p. A33).

We have invested large sums of money establishing student development agencies and training student development professionals. Unfortunately, special programs designed to support the diverse and often unique needs of the minority students are relatively nonexistent on today's campuses. John Thompson, Georgetown University's basketball coach, has been quite outspoken about problems surrounding the exploitation of minority student-athletes, who he believes should be better supported academically by their schools (Paterno, 1990).

Sports Misconceptions in Relation to Race. A prevalent misconception is that African-Americans, especially males, are physically superior to their white counterparts. The African-American athlete is considered a natural athlete with raw talent. Since coaches are pressured to win in order to keep their jobs and to bring in additional revenue for the institution, they look first for the natural athlete who can win a few games and bring prestige and revenue to the athletic program. However, the factors determining the caliber of sports performance are so complex and disparate that attempts to trace excellence to a single biological feature such as race are rendered ludicrous (Edwards, 1983).

Community Beliefs. Does anyone remember the last time an African-American lawyer returned to the neighborhood to visit? Can you remember the last time the media did a feature story on the return of an African-American doctor to the ol' stomping grounds? When was the last time an African-American undergraduate, returning to the "block," was applauded for academic achievement above the 2.5 grade point level? These people, and their successes, are lost somewhere in the pursuit of day-to-day living.

But what about the return of the athletic star whose athletic prowess has been successful and publicized? The younger generation of African-American students is very much aware of the hullabaloo we make over the return of this "conquering hero." These students are very much aware of where the family and the community place prestige and admiration. Young African-Americans begin to pursue similar accolades. The African-American family and their community tend to reward athletic achievement much more and much earlier than any other activity. This lures more young African-Americans into athletic career aspirations than the actual opportunities for sports success would warrant (Edwards, 1983).

Personal Image. Much has been said and written about the demise of the African-American male with most of it negative. However, some research has been able to shed a little light on why the African-American male student is attracted to the sports arena. Edwards (1983) suggests that sports are seen by many African-American male youths as a means of proving their manhood: "This tends to be extraordinarily important to Blacks, because the Black male in American society has been systematically cut off from mainstream routes of masculine expression, such as economic success and positions of authority" (p. 38-39). Research conducted by Nation and LeUnes (1983) upheld some of these same convictions. Their research indicated that through sports the African-American athlete: 1) was preoccupied with such factors as dominance, power figures, and exaggerated assertions of strength, 2) preferred power and toughness to mental prowess as the determinants of success, 3) was more likely to choose power figures as role models, 4) was more responsive to the exacting, imposing, rigid style of a disciplinarian, and 5) was more likely to ignore internal emotional and motivational referents and deal with each competitive proposition in isolation. This tough, machismo style is what is projected as the "red-blooded American" by the media and public alike.

It is fairly obvious that the misconceptions of race relations in the sports arena have been combined with the stereotypes of sports according to minority groups. This overrides a very inadequate education system located in a sports-crazed community that feeds off a weak personality system. The African-American student-athlete is in a very good position for exploitation and victimization. This is the problem as this author sees it. How is it viewed by the African-American student-athlete?

ISSUES AND CONCERNS OF
THE AFRICAN-AMERICAN STUDENT-ATHLETE

The question of what problems are of greatest concern to the African-American student-athlete has been addressed through several research efforts (Cohen, 1988; Henderson, 1988; Jordan & Denson, 1990; Lubell, 1988; Salles, 1988). Concisely, Daniels (1987) listed most student-athletes' concerns as problems with time management, precollege academic preparation, faculty expectations, institutional ambiance, peer relationships, health (injury) concerns, and financial concerns.

Time Management. The inability to balance the academic load with training and practice schedules is a problem. Coaches profess their support for student-athletes getting a good education, but do not adjust schedules accordingly. Faculty are often reluctant to alter their homework and assignment schedules to meet the needs of the student-athlete. To add to this difficult situation, there is little, if any, time for leisure activities.

Precollege Academic Preparation. This is a double-edged sword: the faculty member has low expectations of the student-athlete, whereas the student-athlete focuses the majority of his or her attention and effort toward becoming a better athlete. Both sides are content with the status quo.

Faculty Expectations. There are those faculty who have low expectations of the "jock" and will grade accordingly. However, there are also those faculty who push for academic excellence for all students and refuse to give the student-athlete any kind of a "break." In the latter situation, this becomes a frustrating dilemma for both the faculty and the student-athlete. To add to the student-athlete's confusion, some faculty are loyal to the institution to the point of excessive zeal. They may "grade easy" on student-athletes to protect their eligibility to compete.

Institutional Ambiance. The institution often becomes more interested in the revenue gained from athletic competition than in the welfare of the student-athletes who produce the revenue. In this situation the student-athlete is treated more like a possession of the institution than like an individual seeking an education and personal growth (Anshel, 1990). Also, administrators are slow to take steps to relieve the racial stereotyping done by the staff, students in general, and faculty.

Peer Relationships. This is an intriguing problem. A major issue, according to Jordan and Denson (1990), is the insufficient amount of time available for the student-athlete to establish and deal with relationships. The student-athlete misses out on a considerable number of the social and cultural events designed to promote personal and interpersonal relationships. African-American student-athletes find themselves associating with other student-athletes or living in isolation. Even though the student-athlete feels the necessity to maintain the "machismo" role, she or he expects to have satisfying relationships with others.

Health and Injury Concerns. An injury in high school could lead to no scholarship for college. Many African-American youth are not able to finance college without financial assistance (an athletic scholarship is the first choice). Also, in many professional sports, college visibility is a necessity. Injury in college could end in no offers from pro teams. Pearson and Petitpas (1990) discuss the more private effects of injury for student-athletes. Many student-athletes believe they must continue to work out even during the off-season to avoid injury by staying in good physical shape. This means that more time needs to be extracted from a very tight schedule that is now tight year round. Closely related to injury concerns is getting sick, which can also mean lost playing and practice time. Both of these results are perceived as threatening by student-athletes. Playing sick or hurt results in lowered performance that may be seen by pro scouts, which can also lessen chances for a pro tryout.

Financial Concerns. Not all student-athletes have the luxury of a four-year full scholarship. To make ends meet some student-athletes have to take on student work or off-campus jobs. This intensifies the time management problem as more time needs to be "squeezed from the turnip." Like any other student, student-athletes who must scramble to finance their education live a precarious day-to-day existence filled with additional worries and stress.

Along with these stated problems, there are other pervasive issues that need to be dealt with. There is the problem of finding study time and time to work with tutors. There is also the problem of receiving inadequate advising about curricula and majors. Advisors and counselors also appear to have stereotyped misconceptions and low expectations of the student-athlete (Henderson, 1988).

Last but not least, there is a problem that is very seldom addressed. The issues stated above and the very act of competition generate stress and tension. Student-athletes tend to be very competitive about their sports, and many medical studies have indicated that Blacks appear to experience higher levels of stress and tension than do their white counterparts (Lubell, 1988).

It is important to keep in mind that these concerns are only the tip of the iceberg. There is still much to be learned about the needs and concerns of the minority student-athlete and the impact of these needs on academic success, personal development, and athletic performance. "Black student-athletes (more than any other students) are placed in the middle of a credibility conflict between faculty who teach them, the administration which regulates them, and the community which finances much of the overall athletic program. The demands of class participation, homework assignments, practice schedules, intercollegiate competition schedules, travel schedules, public relations and personal relationships are viewed as Herculean tasks by student- athletes" (Daniels, 1987, p.160).

WHAT HAS BEEN DONE?

Many institutions are beginning to make meaningful attempts to recruit student-athletes with better academic skills and create an environment that fosters a recognition not only for the diversity of the minority student-athlete but also for all minority students. To encompass the full range of student development, administrators have made the following efforts: 1) created or strengthened multicultural development centers with staff specially trained in multicultural counseling, 2) urged students, faculty, and administration to attend programs designed to promote sensitivity to diversity, 3) urged faculty to include and approach issues of diversity from a more positive perspective in their classroom curricula, 4) encouraged minority and white student organizations to work together in planning and implementing cultural events, 5) urged the incorporation of multi-ethnic courses into the general curriculum—in many instances at least one course is a requirement for freshmen, and 6) made commitments to minority enhancement a part of the performance appraisal of faculty and staff.

These measures constitute a commitment to the development of all minority students. However, when we look at what has been done for the minority student-athlete, the list is somewhat shorter. In relation to the minority student-athlete, academic and athletic administrators now: 1) conduct seminars on the high school level to inform parents and student-athletes of academic requirements; in many cases, unfortunately, academic advisors are not involved in these seminars, 2) provide academic advisors and tutors for their student-athletes, 3) provide structured study halls for student-athletes, and 4) stress strict adherence to the National Collegiate Athletic Association's (NCAA) Proposition 48, which states the academic requirements a student-athlete must meet prior to being allowed to compete in intercollegiate sports activities on the Division I level. A later ruling by the NCAA established minimum academic criteria to be met by the student-athlete while actively engaged in such sports activities.

Much has been said and written about the perceived racial discrimination and other problems of the NCAA decisions (Allen,

1988; Daniels, 1987; Edwards, 1983; McCormick & Meiners, 1988). However, the purpose here is not to argue the pros and cons of the NCAA propositions. What is important to note is that an attempt is being made to improve the level of academic performance prior to allowing student-athletes to participate in intercollegiate sports activities. An attempt is being made to persuade student-athletes to maintain a respectable level of academic performance while participating in intercollegiate athletics.

In reviewing what has been done to support the successful achievement of the educational aspirations of the minority student-athlete, we note that the social aspects of the support have centered around cultural events while the academic support naturally involves "passing the class." The support systems are also designed to deal adequately with collective groups of students (i.e., African-American women's support group, football freshmen study hall) but inadequately with individual concerns. There are issues that can be worked on collectively with the student-athletes such as study skills or tutoring. However, there are other issues, such as personal problems or self-identity other than as an athlete, that may require individual attention from the student development professional. Another problem is that many of the support programs occur late in the athletic life span of the student-athlete. Note that many of the programs mentioned earlier take place as early as the freshman year in high school and as late as the senior year in college.

In many cases, the African-American student-athlete has started thinking about a "pro career" as early as the middle elementary years of sixth to eighth grade. There are now hundreds of elementary school districts that compete in organized athletics that include state playoffs. Therefore, by the time educators and sports administrators sit down to talk with student-athletes and their parents (usually at the beginning of high school), they have already missed approximately three years of that student-athlete's career and life planning.

In addressing what remains to be done, I propose a time sequence approach in which the stages are synonymous with the varying levels of education and athletic competition. The Early or Formative Stage would consist of grades six through eight. The Middle or Adjustment Stage is the high school period from freshman to senior. A Later or Life-Styling Stage covers the four years of higher education, and the Out-of-School or Readjustment Stage begins when the student-athlete has completed collegiate eligibility. I also propose that there are behaviors and characteristics inherent to each stage that need to be dealt with appropriately by educators, sports administrators, and student affairs professionals. These proposals could lead to better support and more resources for the student-athletes and their parents.

A PRELIMINARY STUDY OF
AFRICAN-AMERICAN STUDENT-ATHLETES

The purpose of this preliminary study was to investigate the plight of the African-American student-athlete and, as a result, to suggest measures that could be taken to correct or ease some of the negative effects of being a minority student-athlete. The data used to establish the behavior and characteristics of the stages are the result of a small survey of 154 African-American student-athletes (see Table 1) ranging from the sixth grade to post-higher education (several athletes did not go on to compete at the collegiate level).

The 43 students who were in the Formative Stage attended a middle school (grades six through eight) of 550 students located in a small midwestern city of 24,000. The school had an active sports program. All of these students were actively competing in interschool games and matches. The 52 students who were the high school sample (Adjustment Stage) attended a high school of 1,800 students in the same city and were competing at the scholastic level.

The 44 college student-athletes were attending a midwestern college of approximately 18,500 students. This NCAA Division I institution is an active member of an athletic conference with a full range of sports participation. Approximately half of these student-athletes were on various levels of scholarship support in football, basketball, track, softball, and swimming. The 16 respondents in the Readjustment stage were living in the same city and had completed their eligibility for participation in organized athletics at either the high school or college level. Respondents' results were subdivided by stage and by gender.

The survey instrument required written responses to the following items:

1. In what grade did you begin playing competitive sports?
2. Which sport, or sports, did you play?
3. Is your future goal to be a professional athlete?

4. If your answer to #3 is yes, what encourages you to be a professional athlete?

5. Approximately how much time, per week, do you spend out of class in order to play in a game (do not count time spent practicing after school or on weekends)?

6. How much time, per week, do you spend practicing after school or on weekends?

7. Rate your parents' support of your "athletic career" using the following scale:

   5 = Practice hard and try to make the pros.

   4 = Practice hard to be a good athlete and it is okay to be a "C" student.

   3 = Sports are okay but get an education just in case you do not make it in sports.

   2 = It does not really matter, the odds of making the pros are about as good as getting a job.

   1 = The chances of making the pros are negligible, get a good education and get a good job.

   0 = Forget sports altogether, get a degree and get a good job.

8. Have you given any thought to a future in something other than athletics? If so, what do you want to be?

Personal interviews were also conducted to allow the respondents to further explain their answers. The survey was conducted during the 1989-90 school year.

RESULTS AND DISCUSSION

Let us address what we can do as helping professionals for African-American student-athletes with the assumption that such efforts would generalize to other minority student-athletes. The results of the survey are suggestive: there appears to be a sequential staging of the concerns and issues of these minority student-athletes. The discussion of results and what the helping professional can do to address the situation in each stage will be presented in the same sequential manner.

Formative Stage (Grades 6-8). As early as the middle school years, the African-American student-athlete has indicated early signs of paying more attention to sports than to academics. The mean grade point average of 2.18 (Table 1) is marginal for college, and at least 6%

Table 1
Breakdown of Respondents by Stage, Race, and Sport

Stage	Formative	Adjustment	Life-Styling	Readjustment
N	43	52	44	16
Males	28	30	26	12
Females	15	22	18	4
Mean GPA Males	2.00	2.13	2.15	2.10
Mean GPA Females	2.36	2.41	2.67	2.39
Baseball Softball M/F	5 / 3	3 / 5	3 / 5	3 / 3
Basketball M/F	6 / 7	12 / 10	9 / 6	2 / 1
Football	13	12	10	7
Swimming M/F	0 / 2	1 / 5	0 / 1	0 / 0
Track M/F	4 / 3	2 / 2	4 / 6	0 / 0

of class time (4.8 hours) was missed due to athletic competition (Table 4). Of the 43 African-American student-athletes in this group, 26, or 60.5% implied developing aspirations of becoming a professional athlete (Table 2). The dominant factors influencing this decision were money (42.3%), power (19.2%), and peer pressure (15.4%). Parental influence (Table 5) ranged from *It's okay to be an average student (30.8%)*, to *Practice hard and try to make the pros (50.0%)*. Personal interviews presented such issues as high interest in being known as an athlete, being famous, having a lot of money (one million dollars was

Table 2
Aspirations of Becoming a Professional Athlete

Gender	Formative Stage		Adjustment Stage		Life-Styling Stage		Readjustment Stage	
	Yes	No	Yes	No	Yes	No	Yes	No
Males	20	8	25	5	25	1	11	1
Females	6	9	1	21	2	16	0	4

considered a low wage), meeting girls, and getting released from school. The African-American student-athletes electing not to pursue athletic careers stated that sports required too much of their time for leisure, study, and class. Several of these students also commented that the coaches and other people made them act in a manner with which they were not comfortable. They (the students) did not like these kinds of people (the coaches) and did not want to be like them. The African-American nonathletic students saw student-athletes as brash, rude, crude, too loud, ignorant, academically poor students, and as socially undesirable.

Note that as early as the sixth grade, African-American student-athletes were exhibiting behaviors that would not be addressed for at least another three years. Intervention should be made at this stage, instead of after the student enters college. Of course, intervention during the school year would pose some problems as many school districts do not have a very large complement of counselors.

However, there is another opportune moment in which helping professionals can work with student-athletes at this age level. Many student-athletes will attend sports camps during the summer break. Camps present a golden opportunity not only to improve the athletic prowess of the participant but also to address the educational, social, and personal concerns of the student-athlete. At least once a day during a sports camp, the minority student-athlete should be able to discuss educational and career aspirations, especially with African-American role models who may have been student-athletes but are now pursuing other careers.

Much too often at sports camps, we gain the minority student-

Table 3
Factors Influencing Decision to Become a Pro Athlete

Factor	Formative Stage		Adjustment Stage		Life-Styling Stage		Readjustment Stage	
	M	F	M	F	M	F	M	F
Money	9	2	8	--	10	--	8	--
Power	5	--	5	--	2	--	3	--
Fame	2	--	5	--	2	--	--	--
Parents	1	1	1	--	3	--	--	--
Peers	3	1	6	1	--	--	7	1
Free	--	--	--	--	--	--	--	--
Educ.	2	0	1	1	--	--	--	--

athlete's attention through presentations by well-known college and/ or professional athletes. It is vitally important that young African-American student-athletes have some exposure to role models who are "no longer athletes" but successful in nonathletic careers. This acquaints them with the other, more common side of the career picture ex-student-athletes in "nonprofessional" careers when competition is over. The use of these ex-athletes as career role models also enhances several other aspects of the program: student-athletes can be introduced to professionals in nonsport, noncompetitive careers.

The importance of having a sound education when the professional or collegiate sports career comes to an end can be brought out. Examples of noncompetitive careers found in sports settings are statisticians (strong math skills), broadcasters (oral and written communications), coaches and trainers (usually teaching degrees), managers (business backgrounds), and public relations personnel (strong skills in journalism, advertising, or management).

African-American student-athletes seldom realize until much later in life that they can remain in a sports environment even though they may not be involved in professional competition. At the same

Table 4
Hours Spent Out of Class Competing(C) or Practicing(P)

Gender	Formative Stage		Adjustment Stage		Life-Styling Stage		Readjustment Stage	
	C	P	C	P	C	P	C	P
Males	8.3	10.8	9.4	11.7	11.3	13.5	12.5	14.0
Females	3.7	5.7	4.2	7.5	9.4	11.3	10.2	11.0

time, we can introduce and discuss the NCAA propositions, their requirements, and their relationship to the career and life planning of the student-athlete. For life planning the African-American student-athlete should begin to take a realistic look at the role an education plays when the professional sports career comes to an end—as a result of being injured, being competitively forced out, or retiring. Even if one retires a millionaire, it takes an educated person to manage a million dollars. These facets of a career must be planned for, much as they are planned for in any other career.

A third and vitally important aspect of the sports camp should be programs dedicated to personal development. These support programs should be directed toward both student-athletes and their parents. The parents need to be built into the system as a strong support in the educational, athletic, and personal growth of the minority student-athlete. Here is where the helping professional comes into focus since she or he is trained to provide this type of programming. Adding even more strength to the program is the use of a helping professional who is, or has been, a student-athlete.

Professional development workshops should introduce the minority student-athlete to the expected personal-social rigors of being a student-athlete. All student-athletes need to begin to develop coping skills for dealing with identity problems (student versus athlete), pro versus retiree, peer pressure, ethnic identity and the role of the African-American athlete in society, parental pressure/conflict, and the range of emotions connected with winning and losing. In their own ways, at this stage, minority student-athletes have to deal with these issues and concerns, and, in many unfortunate instances, they inappropriately deal with these stresses.

Table 5
Parental Support for a Professional Athletic Career

Stage	5	4	3	2	1	0
Formative	13	8	3	2	--	--
Males	13	4	2	1	--	--
Female	4	1	1	--	--	--
Adjustment	11	6	3	4	2	--
Males	11	6	3	3	2	--
Females	--	--	--	1	--	--
Lifestyling	27	9	3	1	1	1
Males	13	9	3	--	--	--
Females	--	--	--	--	1	1
Readjustment	8	3	--	--	--	--
Males	8	3	--	--	--	--
Females	--	--	--	--	--	--

For the African-American student-athlete, the inability to cope with and adjust to the situation is sometimes stereotyped as negative behavior attributed to the racial group and, therefore, dismissed without developmental assistance being considered. In return, many of our African-American student-athletes develop a negative attitude towards the "white man and his world" and never really recover from nor learn to cope positively with the frustration and tasks that need to be handled.

In summary, the helping professional can play a very important role in affecting the educational, personal, and social growth of the budding minority student-athlete. An important and practical point to keep in mind, though, is that the helping professional may have to take his or her skills and assistance outside the school building. The support programs presented here do not fit nicely into an already crowded school day, and we do not want to take a select group of people out of class when they are already missing valuable class time.

Adjustment Stage (High School.) By the time the African-American student-athlete enters the ninth grade, she or he exhibits further manifestations of the behaviors identified during the Forma-

Table 6
Other Career Choices

Factor	Formative Stage		Adjustment Stage		Life-Styling Stage		Readjustment Stage	
	M	F	M	F	M	F	M	F
Yes	8	2	2	8	9	15	0	4
No	20	13	28	14	17	3	12	0

If So, What?

Artist - 2	Optometrist
Babysitter	Psychologist
Biologist	Receptionist
Cook/Chef	Scientist
Dancer	Secretary
Engineer - 3	Secretary, Legal
Geologist	Teacher
Housewife - 2	Teacher, French
Interior Decorator	Truck Driver - 2
Lawyer	Veterinarian - 2
Mathematician	X-ray Technician - 2

Undecided - 19

tive Stage. In Table 1 we notice that the minority student-athlete shows a slight increase in GPA (2.27) with at least 6.8% (5.44 hours) of class time missed due to athletic competition (see Table 4). Of the 52 African-American student-athletes in this group, 26 (50%) were considering professional athletics as the career of choice (see Table 2). The dominant factors influencing this choice (see Table 5) were money (30.8%), peers (26.9%), and power/fame (19.3%). The range of parental support included the same categories as those expressed in the Formative Stage; *It's okay to be an average student* (23.1%) to *Practice hard and try to make the pros* (42.3%). Personal interviews presented such issues as fear of not measuring up to the expectations of peers, family, and self; interest in substances that improve performance; interest in the social use of drugs and alcohol; desire to belong but not having enough time; and fear of subpar athletic performance that could lead to nonselection by colleges and/or professional teams.

Interestingly, several minority student-athletes stated that they placed more trust in their coaches, for discussing and planning their futures, than they did in teachers and counselors. The African-American student-athletes who had decided against pursuing professional sports careers stated as their reasons that there are no pro sports for women, the level of competition had become too rigorous, they had other career plans, and they were already recuperating from potential sports-ending injuries.

The African-American student-athletes at this stage showed manifestations of the same characteristics and behaviors of the respondents included in the Formative Stage: low (but passing) GPA, high level of desire to become a professional athlete, feeling that they have a chance to make a lot of money, and parental support that leans more towards athletics than academics. On a personal level, their concerns were clearly related to those of the Formative Stage: fear of not being able to measure up to self-expectations and the expectations of others, performance pressure, and desire to be socially accepted even though there is very little time for social interaction.

In contrast, the respondents in this group have identified someone to talk with concerning future plans. However, this person did not appear to be the person to confide in about personal issues. Also missing from the personal interviews were references about ethnic identity and/or racial problems. A possible explanation is that these students are putting more of their time into being better athletes. Being "better than the rest" is the way in which these students wish to be identified. The issue during this stage is to identify one's major area of competition and be the best in that sport in order to be noticed by college, amateur, and/or professional scouts.

But let us look at what we have here: a perfect opportunity to make the system work in terms of supporting the African-American student-athlete. The minority student-athlete often feels more comfortable working and talking with the coach or the coach's staff. It would appear fairly obvious that a good way to provide support and assistance to the student-athlete is through this same coach and staff. Why not include the athletic staff in academic preparation, counseling, student development, personal development, and discipline? We conduct student conferences that will generally include parents, teachers, and, sometimes, counselors or the school administration. Why not include the coach and staff? If the student-athlete is utilizing the coach and staff for guidance and assistance, why not network these services through the athletic department?

Likewise, coaches need to network with teachers, counselors, and administrators to enhance the prospects of their student-athletes receiving, understanding, and benefitting from the offered services. Teachers and coaches could work together in: 1) highlighting the importance and impact of an education above and beyond the NCAA requirements, 2) establishing study and tutorial sessions, 3) scheduling tests and assignments around athletic events, and 4) preparing the student-athlete for the adjustment to college.

African-American student-athletes responded that they performed better academically when instructors and coaches conferred about their behavior in the classroom. For these student-athletes, there was an expectation that the coach would not allow them to participate in athletic events if classroom performance was reported as poor. Active participation by the athletic staff in the academic pursuits of the student-athlete may be the missing link in encouraging the minority student-athlete to continue to pursue a meaningful and useful education. The message that can be sent to the student-athlete by this shared effort is that it is acceptable to be a student-athlete as long as you are also a real student preparing for unforeseen circumstances that could limit the athletic career (i.e., a career-ending injury).

Counselors/advisors and the athletic staff should share the burden of assisting the student-athlete to adjust to the emotional, personal, and social rigors of being a minority student-athlete. At present, this is an underutilized support area due to the shortage of trained student development personnel at the secondary level and the demand placed on an already crowded school and class schedule. In addition, this is an area of support in which African-American students, in general, and African-American student-athletes, in particular, do not seek assistance. In that respect, if an athletic staff member has already gained the respect, trust and confidence of the minority student-athlete, then she or he can play an important role in encouraging the student-athlete to use the services of the helping professional.

Helping professionals may also find that they are more effective when they leave their sanctuaries and go to the office of the coaching staff in order to speak with the student-athlete. We must keep in mind that the student-athlete may feel more comfortable in familiar surroundings initially. Helping professionals may also find it very helpful to use a more directive approach when working with the minority student-athlete.

The student-athlete lives in a highly structured environment. It is somewhat frustrating and confusing to attempt to adjust to an unstructured event (e.g., a counseling session) on a moment's notice. Helping professionals can use the existing structure to deliver effective service. For example, the student-athlete follows an established scheduled of practice, class, and study during the season. This schedule is usually maintained even during the off-season. Why not use these set-aside practice time slots for organized study sessions, tutorial sessions, and/or personal development workshops during the off season? And, if student-athletes are willing to spend a little extra time, the helping professional could also use the time for individual or group counseling sessions.

The helping professional can also provide assistance outside the school environment. At present there are numerous community agencies that provide academic and personal growth support for the African-American student. These agencies are very valuable to coaches of high school athletes as these agencies generally provide support services after the school has closed for the day and practice is over. The big problem is that if the coaching staff were able to get the student-athlete to attend these sessions, she or he would invariably find that there are very few helping professionals available to provide assistance. We need also to keep in mind that the minority student-athlete at the Adjustment Stage needs more in-depth help. These student-athletes are beginning to look at what to do with the rest of their lives. They want, need, and deserve factual "real world" information.

In comparison to the earlier Formative Stage, which is highlighted by working with the African-American student-athlete to understand herself or himself in relation to athletics and education, the Adjustment stage asks the young person to look realistically at what is required and make the appropriate adjustments. Of paramount importance during this stage is that the student-athlete feels that it is certainly all right to be an athlete but there are educational and personal hardships and barriers that will have to be dealt with. The adjustment should be accomplished through the networking of services by helping professionals, administrators, and the athletic department.

Life-Styling Stage (College). Overall, the grade point average (see Table 1) continued to improve (2.41), and at least 9.3% of class time (4.45 clock hours/based on a 12 credit hour load or 36 clock hours per week) was missed due to athletic competition (see Table 3). Of the 44 student-athletes in this group, 27 or 61.4% had made the decision to try for a professional career in athletics (see Table 2). The dominant factors influencing this decision (see Table 3) were money (37.1%), peers (29.6%), and parents (11.1%). Parental support continued to range from *It's okay to be an average student* (33.3%), to *Practice hard and try to make the pros* (48.1%). Personal interviews found such issues as not enough time for social activities; not enough time for studies; more emphasis on succeeding in competition than in academics; feeling treated more like equipment than as humans; little tolerance by coaches for personal problems; negative stereotypes (racial) by coaches and teammates; fear of not meeting expectations of coaches, fans, peers, and parents; fear of not making the pros; and fear of drug/substance dependency. Those students electing to drop out of athletics stated they did so because of they were unable to compete at a higher level of efficiency, being fed up with harsh treatment and ridicule by teachers and coaches, and unable to substantially recover from a possible career-ending injury.

The African-American student-athlete is offered more support during this stage than in any of the other proposed stages. Most educational institutions provide student development services in the areas of counseling (academic, personal, and career), job placement, tutoring, mentoring, and cultural diversity. Many of these same institutions also provide special services for the disabled (temporary due to injury), women, and minority groups. In addition, special programs and seminars are offered to address such issues as how to study, manage time, cope with test anxiety, and deal with procrastination, personal relationships, health and nutrition, and cultural diversity. All of the aforementioned programs and services are open to the entire student body. Or are they?

Generally, these programs and services are offered during the scheduled operating hours of the institution (8 a.m. to 4 p.m.), during prime-time evening hours (6 to 8 p.m.), or on weekends. These normally are the hours in which the student-athlete is not available. Student affairs professionals need to work more closely with the athletic department staff in setting up programs and services at a time more convenient for the student-athlete. For example, counseling, tutoring, and advising can be made available during scheduled study hours, or workshops and other programs can be presented during these same hours. Of utmost importance, the athletic staff needs to know who their support personnel are. A referral network needs to be established through which an immediate response can be made to the needs of the student-athlete. Progress consultations should include the student-athlete.

During the off-season, many of the programs could be offered as weekend retreats that allow the participants to continue to work together and support each other as a team. The student affairs professional need not be a minority even though the use of minority staff provides role-modeling. Keep in mind, however, that due to the services requested and/or the nature of the program, race and/or gender may become strong factors in determining student affairs support.

Another area of concern that needs to be addressed by student affairs/developmental professionals is the training of the helping professional. Counselor training is currently being expanded to include counseling minorities, women, and the disabled. Actually, training is provided for working with any categorical breakdown of clientele except the student-athlete. The general feeling is that the training received for working with minorities and the training received for working with women prepare the counseling trainee for working with the minority student-athlete. There is merit for part of that reasoning, but there are problems and issues that are unique to being a student-athlete. The trainees are not being prepared to deal with those issues. For this preparation, one must enter a program of sports psychology.

At one time or another, virtually all helping professionals come into contact with minority student-athletes and their problems. At that time, counselors try to assist the minority student-athletes utilizing traditional strategies and techniques that may not work well with these particular clients. We need to develop the special skills for working with the minority student-athletes much the same as we develop the skills for working with issues of cultural diversity, gender, or sexual orientation.

At present, the American College Personnel Association's Council for the Advancement of Standards for Student Services/Development Programs (CAS) has established competency standards in all areas of student development except athletics. Of relevance to this counseling area is the stereotype that the best helping professional for a minority student is another minority. There are several reasons why we need to modify this assumption. First, the area of student development is critically short of educationally qualified minority professionals. If we follow the aforementioned assumption, we would seriously overload the schedules of the minority professionals.

Second, there are even fewer minority helping professionals available outside the educational institution. Therefore, minority student-athletes need to understand that they will receive that same service and support from a majority helping professional as they would from a minority.

Third, majority helping professionals can serve as role models for minority student-athletes and assist them in making the adjustment to the environment of the white American. This is not to say that the minority student affairs/development professional is not needed. Rather, the point to be noted is that the minority helping professional should not be solely burdened with the plight of the minority student-athlete and chiefly responsible for providing solutions. Minority student-athletes and their adjustment are supported by the programming involvement of many different helping professionals.

In summary, the Life-Styling Stage needs a more concerted effort by both student affairs professionals and the athletic department staff to 1) make existing programs and services more available for all student-athletes, 2) generate programs and services that directly address the needs and concerns of the minority student-athlete, and 3) make the student-athlete more available to take advantage of existing programs and services. It is also apparent that there is a need for the development of competencies in working with minority student-athletes during the training, licensure, and/or certification of the helping profession trainee.

Readjustment Stage (College). This group was composed of African-American student-athletes who completed high school and either did not attend college or entered college, played out their period of athletic eligibility, and then dropped out of school. These students had a mean grade point average of 2.24 (see Table 1) with at least 12.5% (10 hours) of class time missed due to athletic competition (see Table 4). Of the 16 minority student-athletes in this group 11, or

68.7%, had considered professional athletics as their career choice (see Table 2). Table 3 indicates that the dominant factors influencing this choice were money (72.7%) and power (27.3%). The range of parental support (see Table 5) was the same as the earlier three stages with a somewhat different emphasis: *It's okay to be an average student* (27.3%), and to *Practice hard and try to make the pros* (72.7%). Personal interviews revealed a myriad of issues and emotions including 1) anger at self for not working harder to be more successful in their chosen sport, 2) anger directed at the coaching staff for perceived lack of training and not enough playing time, 3) disappointment in not attaining the professional level, 4) frustration and stress as a result of unemployment or employment in a low-level blue-collar job, 5) perceptions of nonselection due to racial discrimination, and 6) fear of the unknown— "All I know is sports." The 5 group members choosing not to go into professional sports careers stated they chose this path because 1) there were no professional teams in their area of activity, 2) they did not want to compete any longer, and 3) they were recovering from a career-ending injury.

Not much attention or assistance is provided for persons in this stage. In essence, these minority student-athletes are experiencing difficulties similar to the nonathletic, midlife career changers. The significant difference is that the midlife career changers have completed a number of successful years of education or training in a particular career field and, with little or no additional training and education, can make the transition to a modified or new career field with relative ease. However, the minority student-athlete may also be faced with making the personal adjustment from being a "big man or woman on campus" to being an ordinary member of the community. Helping professionals must have the necessary skills to deal with career change and help build the coping mechanisms needed to support role transitions (Pearson & Petitpas, 1990).

Of prominent importance is the helping professional's ability to assist the ex-student-athlete in coming to grips with, and rechanneling in a positive, constructive manner, the feelings of anger, frustration, anxiety, disappointment, failure, inadequacy, identity, and perceived racial discrimination. Unfortunately, the services of the helping professional will seldom reach the ex-student-athletes since they often exit the educational environment and return to their communities. This exit can happen immediately at the termination of athletic eligibility.

Even if the individual remains in the institution as a student, there is little, if any, follow-up networking performed by the student affairs personnel and coaching staff. It becomes the responsibility of the ex-student-athlete to request assistance, and she or he probably has not been made aware of its existence. Student affairs professionals need to establish follow-up programs that maintain contact with the student-athlete after competitive eligibility expires; encourage the student to remain in school to pursue a meaningful career; network the student into the available programs, services, and support, or network existing services in the surrounding community if the choice is to leave school.

GENDER DIFFERENCES

Until now, we have surveyed what needs to be done for minority student-athletes by sequential stages. If we go back and look at the results within stages by gender, we find some discernible differences that could aid the helping professional in concentrating efforts to provide assistance.

Grade Point Average. Reported as a total group, the grade point averages appeared to be respectable or average (see Table 1). However, isolated by gender, there were distinct differences. Among the males, there was no discernible difference in GPA from the sixth grade through completion of some level of higher education. The males started the stages right at the "C" level (2.0 on a 4.0 scale) and ended up not much higher at 2.15. Once these young men made the decision to compete in the sports arena, academics were set aside. It is important to note that these student-athletes met the NCAA requirements during each stage. However, good jobs and graduate school are not readily open to the average student. Females started the stage sequence at a much higher grade level (2.36) and finished at a more respectable level (2.67). Usually, female minority student-athletes are well aware of the unavailability of professional sports for women and will therefore spend more time academically preparing themselves to compete on the job market or go on to graduate or professional school.

Selection of Sport. Ninety-eight percent (98%) of the male respondents chose those sports clearly dominated by minority student-athletes—basketball, football, baseball, and track (Edwards 1983). The male minority student-athlete virtually eliminates himself from any chance of being successful in other areas. Note also that these sports are generally viewed as being the most prestigious: they have an obvious connection to professional athletic opportunities and, as much discussed, offer very large paychecks at the professional level. The minority female student-athletes were distributed throughout the collegiate sports generally funded for females: softball, basketball, swimming, and track. At present, these sports do not have a large professional foundation in the United States.

Professional Athletic Aspirations. Within this category, the number of males who were seeking professional sports careers was at a level of over 90% throughout the stages (see Table 3). Females were more likely to disregard being a professional athlete as a potential career choice. Again, the reason for the female lack of interest in a career as a professional athlete could be that as she progresses through the stages, she becomes more and more aware of the virtual nonexistence of professional sports opportunities for females and comes to the realization that she must prepare herself for other career endeavors.

Parental Support. Nine female student-athletes chose to consider professional sports careers (see Table 3). Four (44.4%) of these respondents reported that their parents would like them to practice hard to be good athletes and that it was okay to be an average student. Forty-five male student-athletes chose to consider professional sports careers, and 13 (55.6%) reported parental support similar to that of the 4 females. Within the family support system, it appears that the emphasis is placed on athletics as the key to success and education is a distant second. Note that in Table 3, only four 4 student-athletes (2.6%) indicated they would consider using athletics as a means to pursue an education (attaining scholarships to pay for school). It should also be noted that 3 of these four students were female.

Other Careers. There were 48 (19 males and 29 females), or 31% of all respondents, who chose or were looking for a career outside of professional sports. Nineteen of the 48 respondents (39.6%) had no idea what they wanted to do as an alternative career. The remaining 29 student-athletes chose science (6 students), technical careers (5), engineering, fine arts, medical, office/clerical (3), education and home economics (2), and human services and legal careers (1). Only

2 of these 48 (4.2%) student-athletes reported interest in continuing on to professional or graduate school.

Carey (1990) wrote that Black [student] athletes say sports help them get better grades and stay in high school. But a survey funded by Northeastern University and Reebok International (Carey, 1990) revealed that many of these same student-athletes have unrealistic expectations in terms of making a professional team. As Lapchick has noted (in Carey, 1990) it has been difficult to get African-American student-athletes to focus on alternatives to sport.

The survey we have been discussing for the past several pages adds impetus to the whole notion of unrealistic expectations but does not totally agree with the statement that athletics has led to better grades. The Stages survey also indicates that there is a much larger problem among minority males than among females. The plight of the African-American male is presently being studied and diagnosed by many national agencies and helping professionals. General consensus is that the problems of the African-American male student-athlete should be considered as another facet of the myriad of problems of this select population.

SUMMARY

To assist in maximizing opportunities for the African-American student-athlete and other minority student-athletes, the following recommendations are made for the helping professional:

1. Attain the skills necessary to address the unique problems of being a student-athlete.
2. Be prepared to deal with issues and concerns considered to be unique to special populations; for example, issues relating to race, gender, or sexual orientation.
3. Begin the process of educational orientation and career awareness at an early period in the sports activities of the student-athlete, preferably in middle school.
4. Consult with student-athletes, coaches, teachers, and administrators to determine the needs of the student-athlete and develop programs and services to meet those needs.
5. Generate programs and services that can be used before, during, and/or after school hours.
6. Create a network of program and service support, delivery of

service, evaluation of service delivery, and follow-up.

7. Play a dynamic role in presenting useful, valid information during workshops, seminars, or group sessions.

8. Support and/or participate in sports camp activities.

9. Consult and network with community agencies to coordinate services and assistance for the ex-student-athlete.

10. Work from the standpoint that it is all right to be an athlete as long as the student-athlete gives consideration to education and other career alternatives.

In providing assistance to the minority student-athlete, the helping professional need only refer to the competency and performance statements provided by the Department of Counselor Education, University of North Texas (Engels & Dameron, 1990): the professional counselor 1) is able to define and recognize the needs of multicultural and specific populations and respond to such needs with effective interaction or appropriate referral, and 2) develops, maintains, and provides effective counseling, guidance, consultation, organization, and administration skills and expertise appropriate for a school setting.

REFERENCES

Allen, W.B. (1988). Rhodes handicapping, or slowing the pace of integration. *New Perspectives, 18,* 19-24.

Anshel, M. H. (1990). Perceptions of Black intercollegiate football players: Implications for the sport psychology consultant. *The Sport Psychologist, 4,* 235-248.

Carey, J. (1990, November 16). Study: Prep athletes misled by pro dream. *USA Today,* p. 2C.

Cohen, G.L. (1988). *Sports psychology and the coach.* Institute For International Sport. Kingston, RI: The University of Rhode Island.

Daniels, O.C.B. (1987). Perceiving and nurturing the intellectual development of black student-athletes: A case for institutional integrity. *Western Journal of Black Studies, 11,* 155-163.

Edwards, H. (1983). The exploitation of black athletes. *AGB Reports, 28,* 37-48.

Engels, D.W. & Dameron, J.D. (1990). *The professional counselor: Competencies, performance guidelines and assessment.* Alexandria, VA: American Association for Counseling and Development.

Henderson, G. (1988). Advising black student-athletes. *NACADA Journal, 6,* 3-11.

Jordan, J.M., & Denson, E.L. (1990). Student services for athletes: A model for enhancing the student-athlete experience. *Journal of Counseling Development, 69,* 95-97.

Lederman, D. (1989, February 15,). On a campus that's almost all white, black athletes and non-athletes struggle to cope with isolation. *The Chronicle of Higher Education,* p. A33-A36.

Lubell, A. (1988). Blacks and exercise: Part 2, prescribing exercise to black Americans. *Physician and Sports Medicine, 18,* 168-171.

McCormick, R.E., & Meiners, R.E. (1988). Sacred cows, competition, and racial discrimination. *New Perspectives, 18,* 47-52.

Nation, J.R., & LeUnes, A. (1983). A personality profile of the black athlete in college football. *Psychology: A Journal of Human Behavior, 20,* 3-4.

Paterno, J. (1990, November). Exploiting student-athletes defeats colleges' purposes. *USA Today, 119,* p. 26-27.

Pearson, R. E., & Petitpas, A. J. (1990). Transitions of athletes: Developmental and preventative perspectives. *Journal of Counseling and Development, 69,* 7-10.

Salles, G.A. (1986). The exploitation of the black athlete: Some alternative solutions. *Journal of Negro Education, 55,* 439-442.

CHAPTER **6**

Career Strategies for Student-Athletes: A Developmental Model of Intervention

Kathleen Riffee and Dennis Alexander

Career development assistance is an important service that can be beneficial to student-athletes throughout life. The authors discuss related developmental issues and present a model for effectively providing career counseling to this unique population.

Student-athletes with exceptional athletic ability represent a special segment of the collegiate population (see Chapter 1). Being elevated to a status of specialness encourages student-athletes to pay a great deal of attention to their physical abilities and athletic skills at some cost to other aspects of their development as people. Because they spend so much time involved in sport-related activities, there is a real need to actively pursue career development issue with student-athletes to show them that there are other future options.

Both Erikson's (1963) psychosocial developmental stages and Chickering's (1969) developmental vectors (or tasks) are relevant to the career development of student-athletes. However, Super's (1957) theory of career development perhaps most effectively casts such thinking in usable terms for the helping professional who becomes involved in working with the career development of student-athletes. Zunker (1990) has a brief and very readable summary of Super's theory.

The college student-athlete should be involved in Super's exploratory stage and actively accomplishing the career development tasks of crystallization and specification. The early decision to pursue an athletic career may shortchange these tasks for the student-athlete, but Super's focus on the importance of the self-concept in career planning offers some ideas on helping student-athletes broaden their career horizons. Although student-athletes are firmly defining their self-concepts through their athletic participation, active career planning and a more holistic view need to be encouraged as part of the student-athlete's career development during the critical years of late adolescence and early adulthood.

PERSONAL CONSIDERATIONS RELEVANT TO CAREER DEVELOPMENT SELF-ASSESSMENTS

The issues that collegiate student-athletes must consider as they address preparation for a career include three critical areas. First, there are general personal considerations that most individuals examine whether they are student-athletes or not (e.g., interests, values, and experiences). Then there are those personal considerations that are unique to student-athletes (e.g., athletic talent, physical ability, and a long-term commitment to a special focus). Second, they must deal with linking academic preparation to a career and with maintaining athletic eligibility while making satisfactory progress toward a college degree. Finally, there must be an integration of personal considerations and academic progress into information student-athletes gather about occupational options. This integration is important as they try to transfer their skills into professional or elite amateur sports careers, into careers related to sports, or into careers unrelated to sports.

Sources of information about the career decisions that we make tend to come from a variety of places. However, one of the most important should be from self-assessments that we make over the course of our lives (Steele & Morgan, 1990). From childhood throughout adult life, we receive, adjust, and assimilate information about our career potential many times over. For people with athletic ability, this information is often heavily influenced by physical achievements in their chosen sport(s). Also, idolized childhood sports figures from the media and playground affect self-assessment.

Ideally, early career exploration and development involve a broadening of self-awareness relative to talents, values, abilities, and interests, with exposure to models of successful careers in the young person's immediate environment. Unfortunately, for many student-athletes, role model examples and sources of career information are limited to relatives or others who an individual may somehow come in contact with or observe through the media.

Another factor that impacts career planning is the nature of the decision-making strategy that one acquires. Many pieces of information about a person's skills, abilities, values, and interests are repeatedly processed over time. Feedback about these factors is sometimes provided by external sources (i.e., from others) and sometimes by internal sources (i.e., from oneself). As young people evaluate information about themselves in different ways, they weigh advice about their pursuit of various career options. This pattern of decision making appears to be commonly used by young people with athletic potential at various stages of their personal development. Early career decision making is often heavily influenced and overshadowed by feedback obtained from a student-athlete's sport-related experiences and a limited range of experience in other life areas of potential endeavor.

One aspect of career development that has received considerable attention is the role that self-concept plays in the development of career plans and potions (Osipow, 1973). However, little research has been directed at identifying the factors of the self-concept that influence the career decisions that student-athletes make. Athletic prowess is one factor that shapes the self-concepts of many student-athletes because of the successes they have experienced using their physical skills. Over time, these young people often learn to define themselves as athletes.

Intellectual and social development are also critical factors that influence the career development process. As student-athletes mature and develop, so much attention is often placed on the acquisition and refinement of athletic skills that intellectual and social skills can be shortchanged. As student-athletes strive to maximize physical potential within their sport, the time demands of achieving this goal can very often detract from developing intellectually and socially. Kennedy and Dimick (1987) note that because of this many student-athletes may be less mature than nonathletes from an educational and career perspective. Frequently, student-athletes are escorted through a system where many of the decisions about their education, athletic schedule, and social life are made for them by influential others like coaches. Usually, intellectual and social pursuits must compete for the limited time remaining after athletics to make independent choices and decisions.

Self-Management. Another area that reveals how well student-athletes make these personal adjustments is the extent to which they achieve self-management. Student-athletes must learn to manage 1) the often extreme demands on their time, 2) the self-discipline required to strive to be the best in their sport, and 3) the personal sacrifice required to delay gratification under various stressful conditions.

The pressure to win is often communicated to student-athletes by coaches through messages that encourage commitment and dedication to the student-athlete's sport. For college student-athletes, the management of their sport-related activities, academics, and social life is even more critical. Many athletic programs attempt to assist the student-athlete through the stringent and programmed management of their time. This approach commonly takes the form of participating in daily scheduled events that student-athletes are required to attend (e.g., classes, study halls, practice sessions, meetings, training table). Unfortunately, this "protective" stance and directive involvement in the student-athlete's life may be seen as intrusive because it does not promote the development of independent self-management skills that usually prove critical throughout life.

Self-discipline is one aspect of performance that good coaches attempt to develop in their athletes. However, the development of self-discipline, one of the functional, transferrable skills that student-athletes can take with them from athletics to other areas of life, requires persistent attention. Unfortunately, the obvious and desirable connection is rarely made by student-athletes.

The self-discipline required to achieve academic success is another related area that requires special attention. Identifying academic strengths and weaknesses as well as developing the willingness to invest the time and energy necessary to address those academic weaknesses is one of the most compelling challenges faced by student-athletes. Gratification from a college education is often found in the financial reward of a job or in the nonmonetary rewards of finding a career that provides personal satisfaction and a sense of accomplishment. Frequently, student-athletes are tempted to solve career concerns by forgoing the completion of their degree to pursue the monetary rewards of a professional or elite amateur sport career. Consequently, the development of alternative long-term career objectives and life plans is commonly overlooked or bypassed. Learning to delay gratification is a life skill that is unfortunately often overlooked even though it is critical to meeting the challenges of both life and career planning.

Very often the rewards from energy expended on sports participation and on academic pursuits are not immediately evident. Consequently, many individuals give up on one or both prematurely. The energy spent on training and physical conditioning requires much practice and persistence. Typically, the time required for such activities along with that required for travel and competition is extracted from any leisure time student-athletes would have if they were not participating in athletics. This is often considered the price they must pay for the privilege of participating in their chosen sport(s). Some student-athletes are able to defer leisure time and effectively manage their combined responsibilities. For others this time is often stolen from the time available for schoolwork and sleep.

Values and Interests. Personal values can significantly influence many life choices including the career choices a person makes (Figler and Figler, 1984). The rewards that appear to make life worth living are often the things closely related to our values and are the basis of those values. Often the ways in which we are socialized strongly influence the values we acquire in life. Some of the values are realized through visible, tangible accomplishments. Other values are those that have a more subjective quality to them and can determine the degree of perceived satisfaction with oneself and others.

Student-athletes may participate in individual or team sports. Those who are involved in team sports often learn early through sports participation the value of cooperation with their teammates. The reliance on others and the importance of cooperative effort are essential ingredients for success in team sports. Individually, student-athletes are trained to give and expect their best. Similar individual effort is expected from their teammates. In the planning of a career, it is important for student-athletes to consider the importance and relevance of such values learned from athletic participation that can shape the quality of their later lives. The transfer of these important qualities learned from athletics is something that should be emphasized to student-athletes when they are considering careers and life planning.

When choosing a career, interests are usually considered to be the most critical factors in later satisfaction with work. For nonathletes, athletic interests are usually satisfied through avocational pursuits and leisure activities. For collegiate athletes, it is important to consider both athletic as well as nonathletic interests in planning and preparing for future career options. Information about a student-athlete's interests needs to be explored systematically from a variety of perspectives.

Various computer applications such as the System of Interactive Guidance Information (SIGI+) (Educational Testing Service, 1988) and DISCOVER (American College Testing Service, 1988) as well as other instruments such as the Strong Interest Inventory (Strong, Hansen, & Campbell, 1985), the Self-Directed Search (Holland, 1985), and the Kuder-DD Occupational Interest Survey (Kuder & Diamond, 1979) can assist student-athletes in understanding the nature and pattern of their interests. These tools may subsequently help generate lists of occupations and other related information that may help fulfill identified interests. These lists can be further used to explore occupational information and options.

Comparative Assessment. Additional exploration in which student-athletes must engage is a realistic evaluation of themselves in comparison to others. That is to say, comparative evaluations such as the ease and style of social interaction, mental performance and team leadership skills all have relevance to and influence on the career decisions which people make and implement.

Social skills have an important impact on many interactions student-athletes have with others during their collegiate years. Whether with coaches, advisors, teammates, the media, or important others student-athletes have a definite need to develop the communication skills necessary to interact successfully with others in their lives. They also need help appreciating the many different roles they have to handle. From these interactions, micro-communication skills are learned and refined over time. Listening, negotiating, and articulating thoughts and feelings are just a few of the skills that are readily transferable into many if not all work settings. Helping professionals who work with student-athletes may wish to encourage them to take courses in speech and communications to develop these useful skills, or to work on their development within the context of a counseling relationship.

Successful athletic performance is a blending of mind and body unparalleled in many other activities or careers. Most student-athletes recognize the importance of mental preparation, rehearsal, and training required to successfully perform in their chosen sport. Athletic participation requires an incredible amount of mental discipline to handle the many aspects of competition and training. Although much of the raw ability that student-athletes possess is innate, in most cases athletic skill and discipline have to be refined by coaching and experience over the years. Coaches typically want athletes who are able to exhibit and maintain the strongest sense of determination under difficult circumstances. The discipline required to perfect athletic skills on the field is the same discipline one exercises in the learning and perfecting of job skills in work settings.

The positive and disciplined mental attitude required to overcome injury or cope effectively with coming from behind in competition is important in athletics. This kind of disciplined thinking is something that often requires considerable development. Such discipline and toughness are skills and assets that are valued in the work environment. Furthermore, as student-athletes compare themselves with their peers and their opponents, they can clearly rate themselves as to the quality of their performance and determination in these areas. Student-athletes need to know that these skills and mental attributes are valuable and applicable to academics, career planning, and future life endeavors. Helping professionals are in a good position to encourage and assist student-athletes with refining these skills and translating them into career and life planning for future use.

The final assessment for career development is the identification and development of leadership skills. Effective team leadership is characterized by consistently high levels of achievement and maintenance of exceptional standards of performance in various aspects of one's sport. Usually the recognition of leadership within any team sport is rewarded by being selected as a team captain or representative. As an athlete evaluates career options, team leadership attributes and experience should be taken into account when various careers are being considered. Leadership ability and experience are clearly an advantage for the student-athlete who is making the transition from the athletics and the university to the world of work. Employers commonly seek out graduates with ability and experience who may quickly be able to assume responsibility for themselves and others in their work setting. Student-athletes should be encouraged to seek out such opportunities for personal growth that will likely benefit them in the short (athletics and college) and long runs (career and life).

ACADEMIC ADVISING ISSUES
RELATED TO CAREER DEVELOPMENT

The academic issues that confront collegiate student-athletes occur as early as the student's high school years. Minimum academic standards, as specified by the National Collegiate Athletic Association (NCAA, 1990), are required of student-athletes, prior to collegiate enrollment, in order for them to practice, compete, and receive athletically related financial assistance at any Division I or II institution. The specifics of NCAA Bylaw 14.3 (freshman eligibility) are as follows:

1. A minimum of 11 units of college preparatory core courses, which must include at least:
    a. 3 units of English
    b. 2 units of Mathematics
    c. 2 units of Social Sciences
    d. 2 units of Natural Science (including at least one laboratory)
    e. 2 additional units.
2. A minimum of a 2.00 grade point average in the 11 core classes.

3. Minimum scores on standardized college entrance examinations specifically either a combined score of:

   a. 700 on the Scholastic Aptitude Test (SAT) or,

   b. 18 on the American College Testing exam (ACT).

The purpose of this regulation is to provide general evidence indicating that the student-athlete has at least a chance to make the academic progress necessary for success in college, and it is hoped, for many occupational options. There are other NCAA requirements that have a direct relationship with the career development process. NCAA Bylaw 14.5, the satisfactory progress requirement, regulates the eligibility of the student-athlete for practice, competition, and financial assistance. According to the NCAA (1990), eligibility for financial aid, practice, and competition at an institution shall be governed by the rules of the respective conference, if any, of which the institution is a member. Any existing conference regulation governs a student-athlete's eligibility for practice, competition, and financial aid. To participate in organized competition after one year of residence or after the student has participated in one year of competition, eligibility is based on the student's existing academic record.

To compete at this point, the student-athlete must have earned a minimum of 12 semester or quarter hours for each of the previous academic terms of enrollment or have completed 24 semester or 36 quarter hours since the beginning of the prior fall term. In addition to earning the minimum number of credits per term, each student-athlete must meet the requirement of designating a specific program of studies that will lead to a specific undergraduate degree by the beginning of the fifth semester or seventh quarter of enrollment (junior year). With regard to the quality of academic work, Bylaw 14.5.2.1.1 indicates a strong component of the satisfactory progress requirement. This regulation specifies a student-athlete must maintain a cumulative grade point average that places him or her in good academic standing as defined by the individual institution. It should be noted, however, that at many institutions the status of "good standing" is below what is required to graduate.

Most of the research that has been done linking athletic participation and the career-planning process has shown a negative relationship. Kennedy and Dimick (1987) suggest that student-athletes may be unprepared to take advantage of one of the most highly valued aspects of the collegiate experience--the initiation and development of viable and appropriate career plans. It has also been suggested that the development of educational skills, career planning, and academic progress is hampered by athletic participation (Lanning, 1982; Sowa & Gressard, 1983). Yiannakis (1981) found that since most of the collegiate student-athletes spend their time daydreaming about their sport, they are not as attuned to educational and career plans as they could be. Most studies have found that those student-athletes who are most negatively affected are male scholarship athletes participating in revenue-producing sports (Purdy, Eitzen, & Hufnagel, 1982). Blann (1985) found similar results, noting that freshman and sophomore male student-athletes did not formulate mature educational and career plans as did their freshman and sophomore nonathletic counterparts.

When considering the academic strengths relevant to the career planning process, Shiflette and Galante (1985) recommend the formulation of realistic occupational goals. Nelson (1982) and Wittmer, Bostic, Phillips, and Waters, (1981) all discuss the connection between academic success, realistic choice of major, and satisfaction with that major. An assessment of current academic strengths is necessary in any attempt to begin the search for realistic occupational choices. Information that may be available and useful include the core curriculum of college preparatory courses, the level of achievement in those courses, performance on college entrance SAT/ACT exams, high school class rank, and the quality of that high school (Shiflette and Galante, 1985). It is vital to determine individual academic strengths to begin successful career planning (Question and Answers, 1987). Knowledge of specific academic strengths and needs supports the formulation of specific, reasonable, and appropriate career options.

Once an individual assumes the role of a college student-athlete, an assessment of current academic needs is essential to begin the initial steps of the career decision-making process. Skills directly related to academic success go beyond reading and writing abilities and include skills needed in athletics. Student-athletes must be proficient in many diverse learning and developmental skills to succeed in their sport. Many of these skills learned through sports training and competition have a great deal of carry-over to the classroom and the career development process. Goal setting is one such skill that is taught through athletic participation and is transferable to a number of nonathletic pursuits, such as career planning (Question and Answer, 1987). Due to the strict time constraints and demands experienced by collegiate student-athletes, living in the here-and-now is often the reality. This leads to a failure to formulate long-range career goals. Therefore, Shiflette and Galante (1985) recommend that goal setting be done in both 5 and 10 year plans. Nelson (1982) concurs, stating that collegiate student-athletes need assistance with the formulation of long-range realistic goal setting.

Decision making is another developmental skill that is vital to athletic performance, to academic success, and to overall development of the individual. Shiflette and Galante (1985) suggest that the structured nature of the collegiate athletic environment lends itself to a lack of decision making skills outside of the sports arena. Brede and Camp (1987), Lanning (1982), Edwards (1986), and Wittmer et al (1981) are just a few of the authors who express the need for athletic department intervention programs to address the formulation of decision-making skills, which they feel are necessary both during and after the collegiate experience. The structured, busy life style of the student-athlete greatly reduces the number of decisions that have to be made, and a decision-making approach may be both relevant and developmental for the student-athlete. Dilley (1968) presents counselor actions that facilitate student decision making skills. His suggestions offer a supportive approach to counseling student-athletes for both career planning and decision-making. Career development may be delayed or even ignored by the student-athlete because of these skill deficits, not because it is undervalued or unwanted.

Intervention programs must also address the exceptional demands of the athletic life style and the conflicts it presents with other important aspects of student life (i.e., academics, career development, social living). The development of time management skills can assist a student-athlete in adequately meeting these demands. A high priority must be placed on assisting student-athletes in the management of the little time allocated for nonathletic pursuits (Lanning, 1982). Time management is not only a skill necessary for academic success: it is the number one skill necessary for college survival (Whitner and Meyers, 1986).

The developmental skills of goal setting, decision making, time management, as well as others such as stress management and effective communication skills, are not only necessary for the promotion of academic success. But addressing these tasks will also probably decrease academic pressures, improve graduation rates, and assist with the formulation of appropriate career options (Shiflette & Galante, 1985; Winston & Miller, 1987). The focus of intervention programs directed toward the development of these skills should be developmental and preventative in nature and should build on the strengths of the individual student-athlete (Wittmer et al, 1981).

Knowledge of self is an important task of the career development process. The purpose of this chapter thus far has been to illustrate that the establishment of self is much more complex than most student-athletes realize. To formulate a comprehensive picture of self, a variety of characteristics are included. Psychological considerations both of self-assessment and comparative assessment, in combination with an overall academic assessment, are necessary before a person can advance in the career planning process. Once an individual has knowledge of who he or she is, as well as an understanding of his or her abilities, values, interests, and experiences, the next step is to advance the development of realistic career options. The specific steps of the career development process are outlined later in the chapter.

Many researchers have investigated the relationship between academic success and the career-planning process. Nelson (1982) reported a study that investigated the effects of career counseling on academic achievement and choice of major. She hypothesized that appropriate counseling would improve the academic performance, increase realistic choices of majors, and therefore result in higher degrees of expressed satisfaction with student-athletes' career direction. She found that participants in early career counseling produced higher grades, had more changes in major, and expressed higher degrees of satisfaction in their majors. Lower attrition rates were observed for those who demonstrated the ability to set realistic occupational goals.

The collegiate student-athlete's identity often is so wrapped up in the athletic role that there is a definite need for increasing knowledge of career options beyond the world of sports. Nelson (1982) suggests that student-athletes may be helped by involving them in the exploration of the following three primary developmental tasks: 1) understanding one's self-assessment of individual interests, abilities, values and experiences, 2) narrowing future career opportunities i.e., looking at trends in the job market, major degree requirements, specific job responsibilities, rewards, and alternatives, and 3) preparing a resume and cover letters, implementing the actual job search, and learning interviewing skills.

Intercollegiate student-athletes have several barriers to overcoming their career development that the helping professional needs to be aware of in the planning process. The resources available to the student-athlete usually focus on the maintenance of eligibility for competition and performance enhancement. Brooks, Etzel, and Ostrow (1987) reported that the typical athletic department counselor has a master's degree and an athletics background. These counseling professionals spend less than 20% of their time dealing with the career-related issues of student-athletes. Both Lanning (1982) and Remer, Tongate, and Watson (1978) point out that although student-athletes are often thought of as an overprivileged part of the student body, in reality they receive very little help with either career development or personal problems.

CAREER DEVELOPMENT MODEL

The following is a career development model that is appropriate for the intercollegiate student-athlete population. The model stresses an individualized approach that research indicates is most effective. Most colleges provide several sources of occupational information for student-athletes to explore aspects of themselves relevant to career planning. Though the model provided is a comprehensive approach to career planning for a special population, it must be stressed that each student-athlete also should be encouraged to use any services that are available to the general student body. The model is designed to serve as a supplement to already existing services. Many of the programs and workshops could be facilitated by experts in the career development field already employed by the institution. Since the student-athlete feels a sense of isolation from the general student body, providing isolated services would only add to an existing problem.

Pre-Freshmen. A model of a formalized career planning program for student-athletes should begin while the student is still in high school. During the athletic recruiting process, a career development specialist can intervene and begin the systematic process of career decision making. Following Super's model of vocational developmental tasks (Zunker, 1981), students at this age are typically in the stage of "crystallization", where the primary objective is the formulation of a career goal. The tasks at hand for the helping professional are the dissemination of academic information and an evaluation of the academic profile that can be used to explore academic majors. During a campus visit, the prospective student-athlete could have the opportunity to meet with a member of the faculty or an academic advisor who specializes in a relevant academic area of interest to outline the requirements of specific academic programs and to discuss potential career opportunities after graduation. This time might also be used to discuss the importance of academics and the exploration of career options.

A variety of printed information can be distributed to provide information on academic programs and support services. The prospective student-athlete should also meet with a member of the athletic department advising staff to evaluate academic materials and outline appropriate academic options. An evaluation of transcripts, standardized test scores, and recommendations can be used as discussion tools to outline academic directions that are appropriate to the student-athlete's ability and preparation. A person who has tak-en two years of high school mathematics and scores a 230 on the math portion of the SAT may have a difficult time if he or she wishes to pursue a program in engineering. Though it is not good practice to discourage a student's irrational goal, a counselor might want to take this opportunity to discuss other majors which are related to the individual's primary interest.

Freshmen. During the freshman year, students are typically still in the crystallization stage of Super's model. The primary objectives at this level still center on the process of career exploration and goal setting. The focus should be on development as a college student and the assessment of occupational interests, abilities, skills, and values. A specific, systematic method of achieving these tasks is through the formulation of a structured course, in which each freshman student-athlete could enroll on a credit basis. The course (entitled "Options") addresses relevant topics of student development and career exploration. The first phase, student development, addresses specific developmental tasks that are appropriate for freshmen. Topics include goal setting, decision making, time management skills, stress management skills, and effective communication (Riffee, 1990). The second phase of career exploration addresses the assessment of occupational interests, skills, experiences, values, information about the world of work, identification of appropriate occupational options, research on those occupational options, narrowing of occupational alternatives, and introduction to available career information resources (Harris-Bowlsbey, Spivack, & Lisansky, 1986).

Sophomore. Once the student-athlete progresses into the sophomore year, a more specific method of career exploration occurs. According to the model by Super, students at this stage are making their way into the specification stage. The primary foci are on specific decision-making skills, the formulation of appropriate career goals, and the designation of an academic major, as the student-athlete moves from broad preferences toward more specific plans. The method of addressing these foci is to provide a variety of workshops and seminars. Specific topics of these programs might include the self-concept of the student-athlete, stereotyping in employment, interviewing for occupational information, developing a career action plan, and co-op or internship opportunities. The nonathletic student may not be subjected to this type of immediacy in choosing a major. However, intercollegiate student-athletes, because of academic eligibility regulations, must designate specific areas of study by the beginning of their third year of residency. If a student-athlete is still undecided at this point, he or she must be regularly encouraged and supported through the decision-making process.

Junior. The goals of the junior year involve the pursuit of coursework in the major area of study and the formulation of practical experience options. Students are grappling with either the specification or implementation stages of Super's model. A primary focus is for the individual student-athlete to formulate specific plans of gaining practical experience through co-op or internship programs in a designated major. Since the time demands of a collegiate student-athlete far exceed those of the nonathlete, it is important that the athletic experience in no way deter an athlete from gaining this valuable experience. Even though student-athletes are accustomed to structure, directive interaction, and hands-on experience, these assets will be difficult to use in the career development process (Sowa & Gressard, 1983). Experiences such as cooperative placements, volunteer work, and career exploratory courses may be limited to summer break, yet they are still an important aspect of the career development process. Workshops and seminars that might be helpful at this juncture include internship opportunities, job search skills (e.g., job information, employment letters, resume writing, and interviewing skills), graduate and professional school information, and establishment of a placement file.

Senior. Once a student reaches the senior year, Super's task of implementation is the stage of note. The objectives of intervention at this point include the discussion of various transitions or options available at this time, the development of a specific career action plan, and the establishment of long-term goals. A study of the postathletic career adjustment of elite athletes was documented by Svoboda and Vanek in Ogilvie (1987). These athletes had made a commitment to their sport as children and continued their participation into early adulthood. The findings reported that 17% of these athletes stated that the transition from sport participation to nonparticipation was uneventful. The remaining 83% admitted to a variety of social, vocational, and psychological conflicts. One of the most common stressors was the conflict between maintaining high athletic performance while addressing the career development process. Many indicated that it was impossible to respond to both demands. An academic course that could be offered for credit to seniors might consider the variety of transitions available to the student-athlete population. "Transitions" would address common characteristics of the athletic termination experience, as well as three specific options available upon completion of the senior year. The first transition is the passage into graduate or professional school. At this time, topics of importance include researching appropriate options, making contacts, gaining academic information, obtaining letters of reference, the application process, follow up, and the establishment of a placement file. A second transition is direct entry into the job market. Developing job search skills (e.g., gaining job information, obtaining letters of employment, resume writing, developing interviewing skills, and establishing a placement file), and how to survive in the job market (i.e., networking, mastering your function, learning from your evaluation, long- range planning for promotions) are important areas of concentration. The other transition after or during the senior year involves those who enter the world of professional sports. Topics of importance include the professional contract, the selection of an agent, basic financial management, and goal setting for reentry into school to complete graduation requirements. This transition is most often the transition that receives least attention. A cooperative relationship with the professional sport franchises and/or the professional sports agent involved will make for a much smoother transition.

Alumni. Alumni student-athletes are also an often overlooked segment of the population, and just like seniors, they evolve through a variety of transitions. A select few proceed from a career in professional sports (successful or unsuccessful) back into an undergraduate program for the purpose of graduation. Interventions necessary at this point include contact with the student-athlete's faculty or academic advisor to audit the requirements necessary for graduation. It is also important to research possible NCAA and other grants available to those returning to school, review the goal setting process, and set specific guidelines for degree completion. Similar steps would be taken for those who make the transition from the job market back into an undergraduate program for the purposes of graduation. Still others make the transition from the job market back into graduate or professional school programs. Topics relevant for this type of transition are similar to those previously mentioned.

Ongoing Services. A resource designed to address the specific career development needs of the collegiate student-athlete population needs to maintain a variety of ongoing services. A career library is essential for these student-athletes to obtain printed information that would be beneficial to the career development process. Types of information might include relevant books, pamphlets, occupational information files, references and resources, catalogs, and brochures that are accessible and useful to the student-athlete population. A computerized guidance program such as SIGI-PLUS or DISCOVER would provide a student with a wealth of career information, assessments, and strategies. Facilities that address the interviewing process would also be seen as beneficial during the job search and interviewing portion of the transitions made by a student-athlete.

Kennedy and Dimick (1987) suggest to athletic department administration that by recruiting and accepting student-athletes into the university community, they are accepting students with diverse abilities and deficiencies. Some may be disadvantaged in areas critical to the educational process. Athletic administrators must acknowledge their responsibility to compensate for these potential deficiencies by providing, if not requiring, measures to address the developmental process. However, the responsibilities do not rest solely on the administrators. Interventions with student-athletes need to involve the personal investment of the individual student-athlete. Student-athletes must be encouraged to take part in an ongoing fashion as active participants. Isolated, highly structured, hit-or-miss approaches such as career assessment or computerized counseling resources will do little to involve the student-athlete. A career development model such as the one presented in this chapter provides an ongoing, personalized approach for the student-athlete's developmental process of career planning.

REFERENCES

American College Testing Program (1988). *DISCOVER* (Computer program). Hunt Valley, MD.

Blann, F. (1985). Intercollegiate athletic competition and students' educational and career plans. *Journal of College Student Personnel, 26*, 115-118.

Brede, R., & Camp, H. (1987). The education of college student-athletes. *Sociology of Sport Journal, 4*, 60-62.

Brooks, D., Etzel, E., & Ostrow, A. (1987). Job responsibilities and backgrounds of NCAA Division I advisors and counselors. *The Sport Psychologist, 1*(3), 200-207.

Chickering, A. (1969). *Education and identity.* Washington, D.C.: Jossey-Bass.

Dilley, J. (1968). Counselor actions that facilitate decision-making.*Personnel and Guidance Journal, 16,* 247-252.

Educational Testing Service (1988). *System of Interactive Guidance Information(SIGI-PLUS)* (Computer program). Princeton, NJ.

Edwards, H. (1986). The black "dumb jock": An American sports tragedy. *The College Board Review, 131*, 8-13.

Erikson, E. (1963). *Childhood and society* (2nd ed.). New York: W.W. Norton.

Figler, S. & Figler, H. (1984). *The athlete's game plan: For college and career.* Princeton, NJ: Peterson's Guides.

Harris-Bowlsbey, J. Spivack, J., & Lisansky, R. (1986).*Take hold of your future*. Iowa City: The American College Testing Program.

Holland, J. (1985). *The Self-Directed Search*. Odessa, FL: Psychological Assessment Resources.

Kennedy, S., & Dimick, K. (1987). Career maturity and professional sports expectations of college football and basketball players. *Journal of College Student Personnel, 28*, 293-297.

Kuder, G., & Diamond, E. (1979). *Kuder-DD Occupational Interest Survey General Manual*. (2nd ed.). Chicago: Science Research Associates.

Lanning, W. (1982). The privileged few: Special counseling needs of athletes. *Journal of Sport Psychology, 4,* 19-23.

National Collegiate Athletic Association (1990). *1990-91 NCAA Manual*. Mission, KS: Author.

Nelson, E. (1982). The effects of career counseling on freshman college athletes. *Journal of Sport Psychology, 4*, 32-40.

Ogilvie, B. (1987). Counseling for sports career termination. In J. May & M. Asken (Eds.), *Sport psychology: The psychological health of the athlete* (pp. 213-230). New York: PMA.

Osipow, S. (1973). *Theories of career development*. Englewood Cliffs, NJ: Prentice-Hall.

Purdy, D., Eitzen, S., & Hufnagel, R. (1982). Are athletes also students? The educational attainment of college athletes.*Social Problems, 29*, 439-448.

Questions and answers. (1987, Spring). *Journal of Career Planning and Employment*, 24-25.

Remer, R., Tongate, F., & Watson, J. (1978). Athletes: Counseling the overprivileged minority.*Personnel and Guidance Journal,56*, 626-629.

Riffee, K. (1990).*The effectiveness of a treatment designed to address the academic autonomy of varsity intercollegiate student-athletes*. Unpublished doctoral dissertation. The Ohio State University, Columbus, OH.

Shifflette, B., Galante, F. (1985). A career development model for college athletes. *Journal of College Placement, 45,* 27-29.

Sowa, C., & Gressard, C. (1983). Athletic participation: Its relationship of student development. *Journal of College Student Person-*

nel, 24, 236-239.

Steele, J., & Morgan, M. (1990). *Career planning and development for college students and recent graduates*. Lincolnwood: VGM Career Horizons.

Strong, E., Hansen, I., & Campbell, D. (1985). *The Strong Interest Inventory*. Stanford, CA: Stanford University Press.

Super, D. (1957). *The psychology of careers*. New York: Harper & Row.

Whitner, P., & Meyers, R. (1986) Academics and the athlete. *Journal of Higher Education. 57*, 659-672.

Winston, R., & Miller, T. (1987). *Student developmental task and lifestyle inventory manual*. Athens, GA: Student Development Associates.

Wittmer, J., Bostic, D., Phillips, T., & Waters, W. (1981). The personal, academic, and career problems of college student athletes: Some possible answers. *The Personnel and Guidance Journal, 60*, 52-55.

Yiannakis, A. (1981). *Manipulative socialization in intercollegiate athletics: Some initial observations*. Paper presented at the American Alliance for Health, Physical Education, Recreation and Dance, National Convention, Boston, MA. (ERIC Document Reproduction Service No. 238 175).

Zunker, V. (1981). *Career counseling: Applied concepts of life planning*. Monterey, CA: Brooks/Cole.

Zunker, V. (1990). *Career counseling: Applied concepts of life planning* (3rd ed.). Pacific Grove, CA: Brooks-Cole.

CHAPTER **7**

Student-Athletes and Time Management for Studying

James Pinkney

Time management is perhaps the most important skill for college students—a skill athletic participation both helps and hinders. Several useful suggestions are provided to assist student-athletes to maximize their limited time available to study.

Time management is often approached with a didactic presentation of basic concepts such as Lakein's (1974) organizing, listing of tasks, prioritizing, and analyzing how time is spent. Unfortunately, the student-athlete's college experience presents some problems for this direct approach. A brief review of that experience suggests a different way of helping student-athletes find more practical ideas for managing their study time during their college experience.

First, student-athletes are so time constricted and over scheduled by the demands of their sport that they don't really have much free time. This is especially true for tasks like studying that may be perceived as peripheral to sport and winning.

Second, student-athletes already know how to manage time. They are rarely late a single minute for practice, team busses, team meetings, or any event related to athletics. The true issue is getting them to manage time for less valued tasks such as studying. Student-athletes, like anyone else, only have time management problems with things that are not perceived as enjoyable.

Third, if student-athletes do have free time away from their sport, numerous options are more attractive and appealing than to spend time studying. They are social targets because of their high visibility on campus, and other students seek them out for many reasons. Personal relationships may have a high priority because sport-related commitments restrict the time available for such relationships just as sport restricts the time available for studying.

Finally, playing time and winning are the coin of the realm at the collegiate level of competition. Time management for studying may be viewed by the student-athlete as a matter of merely maintaining eligibility to compete in his or her sport. The excellence the student-athlete pursues in athletics does not automatically transfer to the classroom—the minimum time needed to stay eligible may be the student-athlete's target for studying.

These facts of life for student-athletes work against traditional time management programming, but such facts do not equal student-athletes being unwilling to manage their time for studying. These facts do mean that programming needs to be altered to meet the unique demands of the student-athlete's collegiate experience. The following issues must be considered as basic in helping student-athletes change their time management behavior for studying: 1) the programming has the coach's overt approval, 2) time management programming does not insist on more time being given to studying, 3) the programming fits the student-athlete's reward system, and 4) the resource person has an obvious understanding of what student-athletes experience.

THE PROCESS OF BECOMING A
RESOURCE FOR STUDENT-ATHLETES

The coach's approval is critical to reaching student-athletes. He or she controls playing time, large chunks of the student-athlete's time and energy, and determines how important the task of studying is to the student-athlete. Without coaching support the resource person remains an outsider of little consequence, an added demand with undetermined relevance to the student-athlete's reward system. The time needs to be invested to explain and justify how what the resource person will do with the student-athletes will contribute to the success of the team. This means meeting coaches, attending practice, dropping in on study hall, and having administrative support to invest time during working hours in being with student-athletes.

Student-athletes are constantly asked to keep their grades up to protect their eligibility. Unfortunately, the most frequently offered advice is to spend more time studying. This does not fit well with a straight forward reward system. For most student-athletes the only thing more important than the chance to compete is winning. Get the playing time, get the win, and everything else will work out.

The less something relates to this reward system (like time management for studying), the lower down in the student-athlete's priorities it will be. Time management for student-athletes needs to be reframed from something irrelevant to winning and presented in a way that relates to the student-athlete's sense of competition and reward system. Ferrante (1989) noted that student-athletes actually have four major roles: 1) student, 2) athlete, 3) public performer, and 4) developing adult. This means they go through what all students go through, but they must also meet the demands of personal sacrifice and public performance. These two demands are met in a pressure cooker called intercollegiate competition. Studying can easily be discounted or avoided in a busy, public life style simply by labeling it as a private matter of little importance.

This time management for studying program does not ask student-athletes to increase the time spent studying. The program is presented as a concept most student-athletes are familiar with, efficiency of effort. The program makes two basic assumptions about student-athletes and studying. First, they already study about as much as they are willing to study. More time will not be given to studying without clear proof that the extra time will pay off in better grades and protected eligibility. To ask for more time is to lose credibility by repeating often heard advice that has been consistently ignored in the past.

Second, efficiency of effort makes sense to people who work at their chosen sport for long hours every day. In a physical sense, getting the most out of practice with minimum effort is a highly desirable goal for student-athletes. The time management program is presented as needing the same amount of time for studying, but resulting in A's and B's rather than D's and C's. The message is that how you study is more important and productive than how long you study.

Theoretically, the program fits the support and challenge approach encouraged by reflective judgment concepts (Kitchner & King, 1981; Knefelkamp & Slepitza, 1978; Welfel, 1982). Support is provided to the student-athletes by being a familiar resource, reframing studying into the student-athletes' athletic framework and rewarding them for the time they do give to classes and studying. The challenge throughout the program is for each participant to figure out what will work for him or her and what in the program will save time and effort. The program also works to make immediate sense to the student-athletes through the use of concrete examples from sport and practice.

TIME MANAGEMENT FOR STUDENT-ATHLETES

The actual program is organized into three parts and takes between 60 and 75 minutes, depending on questions and interaction with the student-athletes. The first 20 minutes are directly used to support the student-athletes' current efforts to study and present studying longer as an unsubstantiated idea that may or may not produce better grades. The next ten minutes cover basic time management concepts ending with a "pop quiz" of the multiplication table. The rest of the time is given to presenting differential study techniques, relating the techniques to specific courses, and answering questions brought up by the student-athletes.

Throughout the program the concept of efficiency of effort is brought up. Effective examples from the student-athletes' own experience are used to reinforce this concept. For example, is reading a page three times because you are tired efficient? How well will a person do on a biology test if she or he studies German to get ready for a biology test? Will running backwards improve your free throw shooting? What do your coaches have you do in practice?

BASIC TIME MANAGEMENT CONCEPTS

There are some concise and informative resources about managing time for studying. Weigand (1974) presents studying by subjects such as science, math, and English. Lengefeld's (1986) brief fifty-minute book has excellent tips on studying and has been a helpful, quick review. A more comprehensive resource is the master student book by Ellis (1985), general study tips, or Haynes' (1987) book on personal time management. Unfortunately, many student-athletes will not go directly to such resources, so the program presents some basic concepts as a starting point.

Time management is primarily an attitude problem since few people have time management problems with things they enjoy doing. Student-athletes have no problems getting to a game on time, going on a date, or chatting with friends. They do have problems with writing papers, staying caught up in classes, and studying. Thinking about managing time for something is admitting that the activity is not fun, unvalued, boring, or any combination of negative reactions.

It is a mistake to equate studying with the time spent doing it since there are many ways to mismanage study time while thinking that something is being accomplished. What does a student-athlete learn from not solving a calculus problem after two hours? Is it studying to read the same page three times because he or she is not interested in learning what is on the page? How much concentration and memory are active at the midpoint and second half of a marathon study session the night before a test?

It can be difficult for student-athletes to understand the time-related consequences of their behavior and the demands made of them. For example, there is an away game on Saturday. The team leaves at 1:00 p.m. on Friday, and with the excitement of winning, no studying is done until Monday morning at 8:00 a.m. when the student-athlete's first class starts. What has happened in a time management sense is that 67 hours from the weekend have been unavailable for studying. This means that 100% of the student athlete's studying must be forced into the 60% of the week that remains at least potentially available for studying. If practice, social interaction, sleep, and other activities are considered, there actually is little time for studying that student-athletes can squeeze from an often hectic season-long schedule. Student-athletes (and students) make an erroneous assumption about time management and studying: that about an hour is the minimum time needed to study. Anything shorter will be unproductive for studying. This assumption is particularly damaging for student-athletes.

First, it means the only time a student-athlete can study is after practice in the evening. This forces studying to occur when the student-athlete is fatigued and likely to be offered far more enjoyable options. The evening is an inefficient time to master new material when feeling dog-tired after three or four hours of intense physical activity. Second, this assumption wastes a frightening amount of time because the students believe that little can be gained from studying when only a half-hour or less is free. A final concept for this part of the program is the fact that all time is equal. An hour is always sixty minutes, and every minute is sixty seconds. But all time is not equal in terms of opportunities for having fun. On any college campus there are more enjoyable things to do, but these are possible and more likely after 6:00 p.m. In the evening, a student-athlete can go to movies, have dates, hang out with friends, enjoy a pizza—the list of options is endless. Better yet, buddies and girl/boy friends are free and also looking for recreation. Studying quickly loses importance as more attractive options become available. At 6:00 a.m. the opposite is true. Nightclubs are closed, friends are asleep or looking to start a day of classes, and it is actually hard to find fun things to do. It does not make sense to most student-athletes to do all their studying when they can have fun, but they have not considered alternative strategies. They do agree that most of the day they are killing or filling time rather than having a good time. In fact, casual student conversations often center on two topics: what did you do last night or what are you planning to do tonight?

The presentation of basic time management concepts ends with a pop quiz. Student-athletes routinely begin to tune out at this announcement, and it is only when several of them have correctly answered questions about the multiplication table they do pay attention to find out what is happening. This pop quiz leads to the heart of the program, differential study techniques. The fact that right answers are given makes a useful point. Why is it that you remember something you have not studied for years?

DIFFERENTIAL STUDY TECHNIQUES

Most of our student-athletes have only one way to study—they put their material on a desk or table, sit down, and proceed to study as long as they can stand it. Or until a friend or the television offers a better option. No, student-athletes do not feel efficient or particularly effective about this kind of studying, but that is how studying has always been done. Besides, everyone else studies the same way: it is just that some can do it longer or better than other students. Yes, student-athletes know the frustration and discouragement of being bored silly while studying, but no one has offered them a better way to go about it.

This part of the program is based on the reasonable assumption that what you study should, to a large extent, determine how you study. Good grades are like winning, more likely to happen if you adjust your game plan (studying) to what the competition will let you do best. There are different ways to study, and efficiency suggests some study techniques are better for some courses and have some advantages for the student-athlete. These are strange ideas for most student-athletes. Why do student-athletes get right answers to questions about a multiplication table when they have not studied it for years? In part because of how the table was learned in the first place.

Flash Cards. Everyone remembers the challenge of the teacher holding up flash cards and the fun of being right. Flash cards as a study approach have some unique advantages for busy student-athletes. The cards can be used anywhere and, given even a few minutes, let the student-athlete immediately study. Flash cards also give the student-athlete a form of studying that takes place in brief periods that are normally wasted or ignored. Flash cards also mean the student-athlete does not have to commit blocks of evening time to a course being studied with cards. As the flash cards are made, the student-athlete becomes more involved with the material. Best of all, flash cards automatically streamline test preparation for tests. As cards are learned, and learning reinforced, they are pulled from the deck being studied. This means test preparation thus becomes efficient since the time is being used exactly where it is needed, on the material that has not yet been learned. Personal experience with flash cards provides a helpful anecdote. I used them when I took Chinese in 1981. Not only did the cards result in high test scores, but much of the studying was also done during prime-time television commercials.

Flash cards have been used successfully by students in foreign languages, anatomy, art history, biology, and other courses where terminology and definitions are important. Cards are not particularly useful for problem courses, philosophy, or courses where application of principles is important. Flash cards are easy for student-athletes to relate to because of the importance given to repetitions or "reps" in their practice for sports.

It is important that student-athletes understand that flash cards are not the solution for every course. A good tip is to have the student-athlete ask the instructor's feelings about a flash card approach to studying for the course. This forewarns the student-athlete if there is a potential problem. It also opens up the possibility of the instructor directly coaching the student-athlete on how best to study for the course. Student-athletes are very practiced in relating to coaches and expect coaching in performance situations, which is what a classroom certainly is.

Continuity Tracking. For this approach the student-athlete is asked to consider committing a small amount of time to a course, say twenty minutes a day. The important point is that he or she commits that time every single day. Most student-athletes are amazed to learn that in the average semester twenty minutes a day adds up to over thirty hours a semester. This is considerably more time than might otherwise be committed to reading for a single course.

If twenty minutes a day seems unreasonable, the same idea can apply to a number of pages per day. The student-athlete can read the syllabus for a course, add up the number of pages that will be covered, and divide that number by how many days remain until the final exam. The result is how many pages a day will keep the student-athlete on track to get it all done. For an undergraduate course (except some English courses or courses with unusual expectations), the number of pages needed per day will be six or fewer. Anyone can handle five or six pages a day without disrupting his or her life.

Student-athletes have reported that continuity tracking seems to work best when the twenty minutes or six pages can be associated with some everyday event. Just before or after lunch, before going anywhere in the evening, before practice, and before going to bed have been times that have been successfully used. The important issue is that continuity tracking occurs everyday to gain the advantages of this approach to studying, and there are several advantages.

The short time frame of continuity tracking means that the reading always occurs with good concentration. Twenty minutes of almost anything can be focused on without stress or boredom. The fatigue and loss of attention associated with cramming or marathon studying are avoided. The daily exposure to the material jogs the memory and slows down forgetting. The student-athlete keeps up with where the instructor assumes he or she is in reading the text. This means the instructor can be approached as an asset rather than as a threat who will ask if the current material has been read. Again, large blocks of evening time are not used, so the penalty of missing out on friends and fun is avoided.

My experience with continuity tracking for a course in information science illustrates these advantages. At no time during the semester did the textbook leave my office except when I took it to class. There was no time to study or cram for any of the three tests or the final. No social events, athletic games, exercise, or television programs were missed because of the course. But the textbook was always open and on my desk. Over the course of a day, pages would be read or reviewed: the end result was an "A" for the course. Continuity tracking is ideal for courses with a known amount of reading where factual information is going to be learned.

Taped Studying. Student-athletes are asked if they like to listen to music, enjoy bull sessions with friends, do not mind lectures but get bored reading, or enjoy having coaches tell them how to do something better. Some student-athletes are far more comfortable and effective with information presented in a form that allows them to listen rather than read. For whatever reason, some student-athletes dislike reading, hate to take notes, and avoid learning much from higher education's traditional style of read and remember.

For student-athletes who have an audio preference, taped studying may be a far more efficient way to study. Taped studying has the student-athlete replace traditional note taking with a recorder. The student-athlete tape records materials such as brief summaries, concepts definitions, and other information worth remembering. This audio record of notes is then available for review at a later time. The night before a test the student-athlete's own voice reminding him or her of what was important may be the most potent recall stimulus for efficient learning.

Taped studying can be particularly efficient for courses that use essay tests. The note taking process of recording what is important actually requires that student-athletes do exactly what they will have to do for the test—in their own words, convince the instructor that they understand the content and have covered the reading. This is a form of direct practice because the student-athlete is telling himself or herself how to remember things that are important. All student-athletes recognize the importance of practicing and that its direct relationship to winning. They may not like it, but they realize that without practice they won't play. And many student-athletes have already proved that if you do not "practice" for courses, you may not play because of poor grades.

Sunshine Studying. Do student-athletes practice at midnight? Are games scheduled for 7:00 a.m.? Of course not. That would be inconvenient for coaches and spectators as well as disruptive for student-athletes. Practice is scheduled for afternoons or early evening for very practical reasons. The student-athletes have finished classes and can concentrate on what they are doing and games are played on weekends or in the evening because fans work. Sunshine studying, or the art of timely convenience, takes advantage of the fact that there is little going on early in the day.

Any studying that gets done before 5:00 p.m. is efficient in a unique way: it will not cost the student-athlete fun. Better yet, the number of distracting options open to the student-athlete is far smaller than during the evening hours when most students assume they should study. It is also the time when the student-athlete is fresh, before being physically tired by long hours of practice. During the day friends and acquaintances are busy with their own schedules and are unlikely to be readily available as they will be in the evening.

Although student-athletes may not think of themselves as early birds, neither are they true night owls. It is simply that in the evening diversions do not require the same concentration that studying does. This creates the illusion of being more alert at night. It is certainly worth a try to see if sunshine studying might actually be more efficient for some courses. Student-athletes might seriously want to consider studying for problem-oriented courses such as math and science during the daytime.

A good reason for this is that very little assistance is handy in a residence hall or at the study table at 11:00 p.m. If the student-athlete gets stuck on a problem at that hour, study time will be wasted since there is no one to resolve the problem in a way that promotes understanding the material. The best time to study for a problem solving course is when the instructor has office hours or a graduate assistant/tutor is known to be available.

Sunshine studying lets the student-athlete do problems when a resource can be quickly accessed to figure out something. Student-athletes need to know that it is not really studying to work on a problem for two hours, not solve it, and quit in frustration. It is efficient studying to use resource people in a timely fashion—during the day when resource people are available to help the student-athlete understand the material and concepts.

Reading Instructors. Student-athletes read all the time, but not necessarily books. They read "keys", behavior, situations, and other student-athletes' intentions. "He takes a deep breath before throwing a fast ball," "She always claps her hands before spiking down the line," and "He looks at every receiver except his primary one" are examples of the kind of reading that student-athletes do and for which they receive rewards. In athletic competition there is a dramatic advantage in correctly guessing what your opponent is going to do. It makes sense to student-athletes that correct guessing is also an advantage in the classroom where test performance will determine the grade.

Reading instructors is a learnable skill once the clues and cues are known and understood for a particular instructor. It is a universal student maxim that what goes on the blackboard is important and needs to be in one's notes. There are other cues that the student-athlete can begin to look for in lectures by an instructor. The idea of reading instructors also reinforces and accents the importance of going to class and attending regularly.

Student-athletes are encouraged to use their knack for reading in the classroom. In fact, it should be easier than reading opponents because the instructor is not trying to hide his or her intentions. Instructors want their students to understand what is important and give several signals that certain material should be remembered. Student-athletes are well trained to capitalize on this if their athletic reading skills can be reframed for the classroom.

Repeating something verbatim is not an indication of the instructor's senility. It gives the students time to write it down. Most instructors know that the surest way to capture student attention is to move closer to the students—physical proximity draws student attention like a magnet. Raising the voice or slowing the cadence are both ways of making information stand out. Writing on the blackboard is still the most tried and true way of alerting students to the importance of information. Student-athletes need to know, though, that blackboard information is usually a shorthand symbol of the original information and some explanation is needed. Otherwise, by test time the actual comment in the notes may be cryptic to the point of worthlessness. Student-athletes, like anyone else, will do better when they have actively tried to figure out what is important to the instructor. Everyone does well on a test when she or he know what will be asked. A good example is what happens when students face their first driver's license examination—the sixteen year olds frantically ask the seventeen year olds to make their preparation goof proof because the license is so important to them. A suggested resource for problem courses is Weigand's (1974) chapters on how to study math and science.

EVALUATIONS AND CONCLUSIONS

Many of our student-athletes are excellent time managers, but for their sports rather than for studying. A time management program needs to focus on helping them translate their time management skills into the classroom. Ferrante's (1989) description of the academic semester as a season-long series of games (tests) is an excellent example of this kind of translation. Given the student-athlete's time compressed life style, asking for more study time is typically unproductive; the time is not there without sacrificing more important or more pleasant alternatives.

This approach to time management for studying assumes that the reasonable way to help student-athletes study effectively is to appeal to their well-honed understanding of the concept of efficiency of effort. A possibility is that as grades improve and student-athletes prove they can win in the classroom as well as on the field or court, they will increase their commitment to studying efficiently. Since this approach is not exhaustive of flexible ways to study for different courses, another possibility is that student-athletes may develop their own study techniques that work for them personally. The importance of flexibility in how studying is accomplished is supported by recent student evaluations. Between 1986 and 1989, the program was presented to students who were not student-athletes. Evaluations were completed following the program with encouraging results. The students were members of a sorority (11), freshmen in orientation courses (46), and students who were seen in small groups for time management at the university counseling center (55).

The 112 students who completed the program evaluation thought the length (60 minutes) was "about right" for 90% of the students. Over 93% agreed with the assumption that students know how to manage time but don't do effective time management for studying. The program was reported as interesting (90%), making good points (93%), and well presented (92%). All of the students (except for one) would suggest a friend attend the program, and 59% would strongly recommend attendance by a friend.

The only change in the program was not focusing examples on athletics and the student-athlete's collegiate experience. The content and basic assumption remained the same. Perhaps a radical idea is to assume that student-athletes learn skills from athletics that can be translated not only into the classroom but also into programming for students in general. After all, time pressure and having trouble studying are universal student concerns. It would be a far departure from "football physics" and the stereotype of "dumb jocks" who are just sliding by to maintain their eligibility. The above evaluation would certainly suggest that much of the program makes a great deal of sense to students who have to compete in the classroom.

REFERENCES

Ellis, D. B. (1985). *Becoming a master student* (5th ed.) Rapid City, SD: College Survival.

Ferrante, A. P. (1989). Glory or personal growth? The plight of the student-athlete, *The ECU Report, 20*(2), p. 6.

Haynes, M. E. (1987). *Personal time management.* Los Altos, CA: Crisp Publications.

Kitchner, K. S., & King, P. M. (1981). Reflective judgment: Concepts of justification and their relationship to age and education. *Journal of Applied Developmental Psychology, 1*, 89-111.

Knefelkamp, L. L., & Slepitza, R. (1978). A cognitive-developmental model of career development: An adaptation of the Perry scheme. In C. A. Parker (Ed.), *Encouraging development in college students* (pp. 135-150). Minneapolis: University of Minnesota Press.

Lakein, A. (1974). *How to get control of your life and your time.* New York: Nal Penguin.

Lengefeld, U. A. (1986). *The fifty minute study skills program.* Los Altos, CA: Crisp Publications.

Weigand, G. (1974). *How to succeed in high school.* Woodbury, New York: Barron's Educational Series.

Welfel, E. R. (1982). The development of reflective judgment: Implications for career counseling. *Personnel and Guidance Journal, 61,* 17-21.

CHAPTER 8

Student-Athletes and Test Taking: Some Serious One-On-One

James Pinkney

The author discusses the mastery approach to learning and test-taking strategies readily adoptable for use by student-athletes.

The relationship between student-athletes and test-taking is a curious one. On the one hand, they are tested all the time and do very well. On the other hand, they often take tests with little concern or preparation and do poorly. A quick look at student-athletes testing well but also testing poorly can easily explain this anomaly.

Student-athletes take tests extremely well—on the field, in practice, under game conditions, or when the coach is around. They are committed to success and make a large personal investment in performing well. Practice, repetition, weight training, constant thought about how to anticipate, and active learning about their sport all contribute to successful (and very public) testing in the arena of athletic competition.

The classroom is a vastly different story for many student-athletes. The necessary preparation is not as obviously relevant to personal goals. There may be little value given to intellectual achievement, either by the student-athlete or by significant others. A low standard of success may be acceptable or implied. The effort, time, and concentration that collegiate sports require can seriously detract from time available for studying and classroom performance. There are real barriers to student-athletes doing well on classroom tests.

This chapter offers a rationale for improving test performance in the classroom, the process of conceptualizing a one hour program on test-taking skills, some ideas on helping student-athletes get ready to do well on tests, and some tactics for taking classroom tests. The rationale is based on Bloom's (1968; 1976) mastery learning concepts. The ideas and tactics are taken from personal experience with test taking and counseling with both student-athletes and students in general.

MASTERY LEARNING AND THE STUDENT-ATHLETE

A major focus of mastery learning is the use of tutoring and formative testing (a check to see how well the student has mastered necessary material) before a test for a grade is given. This focus aims to uncover deficits in learning that can be corrected as part of the process of mastering classroom content. Bloom contends that such an approach guarantees the "prerequisites of learning" before students are expected to learn additional and more difficult material or be tested for a grade on material assumed to be learned. Mastery learning essentially aims to help students understand both their strengths and those areas that need more attention.

Bloom's thinking has been supported (Kulik, Kulik, & Bangert-Drowns, 1990) and challenged (Slavin, 1984; 1987). There has been a consistent effort to evaluate mastery learning, but the most damaging drawback was brought up by Arlin and Webster (1983): the cost-effectiveness of using tutors and formative tests. Both tutors and formative tests are expensive for general classroom use, no matter how well learning is promoted. Even though many collegiate athletic programs use tutoring (Brooks, Etzel, & Ostrow, 1987), this passing acquaintance with mastery learning does not address some critical issues for student-athletes and studying.

Mastery learning has more to offer than simply making tutors available to student-athletes who are then left to their own devices when tests come around. Some transfer needs to happen between the student-athlete's strengths in sport performance and what is needed to do well on classroom tests. Much of what the student-athlete does and learns in sport can be turned into academic assets.

For example, tutoring is really a form of focusing attention on what is important and of directing effort to what needs to be learned. It is a preparation for the upcoming test, but a form of prediction as well as of preparation. Where does more need to be done to be ready for a test? Formative testing is by its nature a kind of practice. What is needed for the real test the instructor will use for assigning grades? Finally, student-athletes learn from their sports, but they are not encouraged to transfer that learning to their academic collegiate experience. Nor are they told that they have acquired skills that can be translated into successful test taking.

DEVELOPMENT OF A TEST-TAKING PROGRAM

In January, 1985, one of the East Carolina University Athletic Department's academic counselors requested a presentation for the basketball team on test taking. It was agreed that some modification of traditional test taking would be needed to hold the team's interest and help team members improve their grade point averages. The academic counselor also wanted an assistant coach to attend. The presence of the coach would verify the importance of the test taking presentation and let the student-athletes know that the coaches were serious about grades.

The presentation was conceptualized as having to meet some facts of life that student-athletes live with: 1) the presentation would have to be an hour or less because it could only be scheduled after practice, 2) the content needed to fit into the players' frame of reference, 3) concrete examples would be most productive, and 4) ideally, the presentation would encourage more effective studying. The counselor intended to encourage the student-athletes by acknowledging the barriers to classroom success that their dual roles created, approving their past efforts to meet course requirements, and explaining how athletic skills would improve test-taking skills if a translation could be made.

The presentation was divided into two parts, getting ready to do well on a test (not just pass it) and actual test-taking tactics to use when taking a classroom test. The second part focused on multiple choice and essay tests as the two most commonly given in a college setting. About forty five minutes of content were planned, with the remaining time for questions and problems with specific courses.

Test anxiety was not included because of a lack of time and because research findings on the topic have been inconclusive. Kirkland and Hollingsworth (1980) found that most studies where test anxiety was reduced (about two-thirds of the time) did not report an increase in test scores. Hembree (1988) reviewed over 500 studies on test anxiety and agreed that a clear relationship between test anxiety and test performance has not been shown. Since the presentation was intended to improve grades (eligibility is a constant battle for student-athletes), the content was limited to information likely to have an immediate effect. In fact, most students quickly reveal that test anxiety is a symptom rather than a problem when they are asked a simple question: "Would you care about being anxious if you were getting an A?" An answer of "No" means the problem is somewhere else, probably in their preparation for tests.

PROGRAM CONTENT: GETTING READY FOR A TEST

Preparation. Tests will not be passed if students have not been exposed to the material. Unfortunately, the student-athlete's time commitments to sport often result in preparing for a test in the least productive way—cramming. Cramming is a form of massed practice with notable drawbacks for test-taking. It encourages forgetting, does not truly stamp in the material learned, requires the student-athlete to study beyond his or her limit of good concentration, and results in learning that is alarmingly temporary.

Our student-athletes resist or ignore advice about studying and test- taking if the advice asks for more time. They simply do not have more time to give to an unvalued task. At heart most student-athletes realize that cramming is a risky short-term approach to learning.

Not cramming means material must be read well ahead of the test. Since most of what is read will be forgotten, it must be reread the night before the test anyway. Why prepare ahead of time if the studying is wasted by forgetting? Student-athletes are encouraged to consider a way of banking the time put into studying by using a technique that improves studying and preserves information learned, well in advance of the test.

The student-athletes were asked to make a simple deal:Don't read a page and leave it without first writing down a question. For every page read, the student-athlete is compiling a record of something that may turn up on the test. Every page is read with a goal: get something to record. After about twenty minutes, most students unknowingly drift from reading to learn the material into reading just to say they finished. Then, students are no longer preparing for a test; they are just going through the motions of preparing.

Creating the list of questions page by page keeps the student-athlete focused on getting something out of what is being read. This improves concentration and produces a usable record, the list of questions, of what was covered. The night before the test the prepared list becomes highly productive in a way that all student-athletes understand. It allows the student-athlete to practice for the instructor's test.

Practice. Preparation is not practice in the same way that a good night's sleep may prepare one to attempt a marathon, but a good night's sleep will not improve your overall speed or endurance. Student-athletes understand that practice improves performance and is a necessary part of competitive athletics. Practicing may not be as much fun as competing, but it does help performance. Practice for a classroom test makes sense to student-athletes who have seen their athletic performance improve through practice and repetition.

The list of questions generated while reading the material adds minimal time to the student-athlete's studying. In fact, the night before a test, the list will return some of the time used to create it. The student-athlete can set an alarm clock for fifty minutes and take a practice test that will not be graded by the instructor. The practice test will tell the student-athlete exactly what needs to be reviewed— the questions that could not be answered on the practice test.

If the student-athlete includes a page number with each question, then only two things can happen on the practice test. Either a question is remembered, or the student-athlete knows exactly where to find the answer. The practice test allows the traditional cramming time, the night before, to be an organized review focused on what needs to be accomplished for maximizing the test score; the student-athlete can review information he or she is not sure of before being asked about it for a grade. At the same time, this is more efficient than trying to reread (hopefully reread) everything the student-athlete will be responsible for on the instructor's test.

Student-athletes are well prepared by their sport to appreciate the value of practice. Practicing for a classroom test makes sense to them, especially if the practice does not increase their preparation time. In fact, a practice approach that also improves concentration is hard to ignore. After the instructor's test has been taken, the list of practice questions is useful in a different way. The practice test then becomes a tool for predicting what material is important to the instructor and therefore important to the student-athlete.

Prediction. The student-athletes were encouraged to have their practice tests with them when they took the instructor's test. Immediately after a test, most students have almost total recall of what was on the instructor's test. This recall quickly fades since the tendency is not to think about a test once it has been finished. In a few hours many of the items will have been forgotten and are no longer available to the student-athlete. An instructor's test is the best blueprint obtainable for what subsequent tests will be like and what the instructor will ask on those tests. The instructor's test is an academic version of the game plan with which student-athletes are so familiar.

An excellent investment in grades for the student-athlete is to take a few minutes immediately after the instructor's test to check how many questions on the practice test appeared on the real test for a grade. This provides an estimate of how predictive the student-athlete was in getting prepared for the real test. A high percentage of practice questions on the instructor's test means the student-athlete is well attuned to what the instructor considers important.

A low percentage means some analysis is needed. How does the instructor's test differ from the practice test? Are the items more specific or do they have a different focus? Did items include material the student-athlete may have ignored on the assumption the information was not important to the instructor? Graphs, tables, and examples are things that are easy to speed past as unimportant. The important point is to do the analysis immediately after the graded test to take advantage of the recall before it fades.

Practice and prediction are two skills student-athletes are familiar with in their sports. Translating them into preparation for classroom tests will give the student-athlete more control over getting ready for a test. The effects on concentration and efficiency make sense to student-athletes who know that they do not do a particularly good job of studying but also know that they do an excellent job of preparing for their sports.

PROGRAM CONTENT: TEST-TAKING TACTICS

This part of the program focused on changing how student-athletes actually take tests. The issues covered are 1) how student-athletes typically take tests, 2) the problems their test-taking approach creates, and 3) alternative tactics to improve their test scores. Only multiple-choice and essay questions are considered because of the one hour time restriction. These are the two most commonly used formats for college tests. The advantages of preparing with practice and prediction are reinforced as part of the test-taking tactics. A pop quiz is given to illustrate some of the concepts used in modifying their test-taking tactics.

Test-Taking by Recognition. Student-athletes generally come out of high school with a recognition strategy for multiple choice items. This is a reactive approach to test taking that accepts the multiple-choice item as is, a question with five response options. Basically, student-athletes read the question, then look through the response options to try to recognize the right answer. In high school this strategy works because tests are straightforward and stick closely to what the teacher presented. At the more competitive college level, tests are better constructed, and more is expected of the student-athlete than just listening. At the college level recognition presents two major problems that reduce classroom test scores for the student-athlete.

Problems with Recognition. The first problem is that recognition encourages misunderstanding the question because speeding through the question to get to the response options seems reasonable. But how likely is a right answer if the test taker is thinking of the wrong question? Most student-athletes have known the frustration of getting back a test with wrong answers even though the right answer is obvious. Speeding through the question promotes this phenomenon.

A recognition tactic also means the student-athlete accepts the instructor's challenge to figure out the right answer from carefully designed options that mask that right answer. A generic example illustrates the problem:

Question: ?

Response Options	*Instructor's Challenge*
a) Silly	
b) Sort of wrong	*Zone*
c) Almost right	*of*
d) Right	*Confusion*
e) Wrong.	

For a student-athlete who has just learned new material, the zone of confusion represents a considerable challenge: "Can you figure out the confusion and get the right answer even though you are not sure?" Basically, the student-athlete elects to go one-on-one with an instructor who knows much more than any of the students about the course content. While this may seem unfair, it is a reality of multiple-choice tests. After all, a test is supposed to find out who really knows the material and who just has a passing acquaintance with it.

At this point in the presentation, a pop quiz is used to provide a concrete example of some basic concepts. The quiz (see Figure 1) has two radically different kinds of questions. The first four questions are about home phone numbers (student-athletes always get these right), and the other four are cryptoquotes (student-athletes never get these). A concrete structuring resource was developed to avoid frustration (see Figure 2).

The quiz and structuring resource demonstrate some important facts for test-taking effectiveness. First, information we can spontaneously recall (like our own phone number) is recalled correctly. The mere fact that it is spontaneously recalled almost guarantees that it is correct. Otherwise, we admit we do not have the information and

Please attempt to answer all questions. You have five minutes for both parts, and you are allowed to guess. Additional instructions for Part 2 are below.

1. How many digits are to the right of the
   dash in your home phone number? _____
2. What is the third digit of your home phone number? _____
3. Add together the last two digits of your phone number: _____
4. Square the first digit of your phone number: _____

Part 2.

The remaining questions are cryptoquotes. There are only two rules for cryptoquotes: a letter cannot stand for itself, and a letter must stand for the same thing throughout the quote.

5. QYW RKDI VWECRK CROW JWRJDW FWQ DRCQ TK
   QYRNFYQ TC LWPENCW TQ'C NKZEOTDTEV QWVVTQRVI.
6. RVN QNAAKH RVOR'F ZNOT OSKETY RVN VKZN XF OAHOMF
   RVN AXQN OTY FETFVXTN KQ FKZN AKYBN.
7. SKU GUXWUS HZ GVXXUGG QA RQZU QG DAHFA HARI SH
   SKHGU FKH KEMU AHS GVXXUUYUY.
8. MWOLBW EDW ABHFK KXAXEHP TPLTS JHY XFYEHPPWK
   HE EDW MHFS, XE JHY EDW ELTS LO EDW ELJF.

Figure 1. East Carolina University Counseling Center academic support series test-taking pop quiz.

---

either guess or dismiss the question. Not knowing something does not hurt with friends, but in a test situation it costs the student-athlete points.

Second, if we are not prepared for a question, it is unlikely that we will get it right. This is even less likely during a test situation when built-in confusion is part of the response set from which the student-athlete must choose. While student-athletes may not like the quiz, they do agree with both of these facts.

Finally, the structuring resource demonstrates that even apparently hopeless questions can be clarified to where there is a chance of getting the right answer. In fact, Kozoil (1989) suggests that such resources are critical for any student who studies and attempts homework long after the actual classroom lecture. If student-athletes created their own structuring resources, then their involvement with the course content would increase and their studying would be even

The following pointers are examples of the kind of thinking that goes into solving cryptoquotes. With practice you would also start to notice other rules and pointers that work for you.

1. Is there a letter that is noticeably most frequent?
   (High probability that it is "e")

2. Are there any apostrophes with letters after them?
   (identify as "s," "t," "d," or "m")

3. Do any word group patterns fit a unique word?
   (i. e., 1231 = that, 12_1_2 = people)

4. What is the punctuation?
   (Words after a comma are often "and," "but," "said")

5. Could any of the three letter groups be "the?"
   (the first three letter group or a repeated three letter group is often "the")

6. Does any three letter group have a repeated letter?
   (as in "all," "odd," "see," "too," "or ill")

7. Is any letter group embedded in a longer one?
   (It may give clues for additional letters in the longer one)

8. Any letter that only occurs once in the whole quote
   (Usually "x," "q," "z," "j," or "k")

9. Any restricted domain such as author or soure?
   (The field of possibilities is less in a restricted domain)

Figure 2. **East Carolina University Counseling Center academic support program series cryptoquote structuring resource.**

more effective. The list of questions that constitute the practice test might be viewed as a structuring resource to streamline retrieval of forgotten information on the night before a test.

Test Taking by Recall. Student-athletes do not try to fail in the classroom, but their reward system can make classroom success seem less important to them (Ferrante, 1989; Lanning, 1982). At this point a question is asked: "How would you like to take tests as if you were being tested on your phone number?"

A recall tactic is presented as a more effective alternative to recognition. Technically referred to as response generation (Crocker & Schmitt, 1987; Millman & Pauk, 1969), this tactic is very easy to implement and offers some major advantages over recognition for the test-taking student-athlete. Recall is used by covering the response options *without looking at them*. If the student-athlete can spontaneously recall an answer for the question, he or she just uncovers the response options and finds the spontaneous answer. The recalled answer is right otherwise it would not have been recalled without help.

The recall tactic avoids the instructor's built-in zone of confusion and has some additional advantages. The tactic also gives the student-athlete a meaningful estimate of how adequate the preparation has been. If 70% of the questions are answered by recall, then preparation is on the mark. A lower percentage suggests that either too little time was invested or that the focus of what the student-athlete thought was important differs from the that of the instructor. But the focus can now be analyzed and adjusted.

The other major advantage of a recall tactic is in the student-athlete's confidence about those questions that are not recalled. It is far more threatening to finish a test in which you have no clues as to how you are doing than to finish one in which you have some known percentage of correct answers before you have to start sweating. Perhaps the most important advantage is that a recall tactic gives the student-athlete control over preparation, practice, and prediction. Studying effectiveness becomes something that can be realistically evaluated and adjusted.

Tactics for Essay Tests. Essay questions are presented as an entirely different kind of task from the multiple choice question. Student-athletes are expected, in their own words, to demonstrate a command of the course content. This can be especially difficult because student-athletes may not understand all that is being asked. The critical concepts presented for essay tests are differentiating what the student-athlete is asked to do, organization, the instructor's mood while grading an essay test, relevance, and brevity.

Pauk (1984) defines 34 key words that are used in essay questions, and all of them require a different approach in order to fully answer the question for maximum points. The student-athlete who hopes to survive an essay exam by simply recalling a few remembered concepts will be penalized. Pauk also notes that a study of over 100 instructors found that much of what went into their grading of essay exams may not be known to student-athletes. For example, more than 85% of the instructors considered reasoning ability important to the quality of an essay answer. Just knowing the material was not enough, what has been done with what the student-athlete has learned also needs to be part of an essay answer. The student-athlete needs first to circle the key word that differentiates the form of the answer being asked for.

The key word helps the student-athlete figure out exactly what is expected by the instructor. For example, "List the causes of the American revolution" means a numbered, brief statement of why the Revolution happened. This is a much different task from "Discuss the causes of the American Revolution." When instructors create essay questions they have an ideal answer in mind. This ideal includes both content and form. Matching the instructor's ideal answer is an important part of scoring on an essay test.

Organization is important because of how essay tests are graded. Most instructors grade across the class in an effort to be fair. This means the student-athlete's answer to question one will be compared to everybody else's answer to question one. Organization, attention to grammar, and legibility improve the readability and score of an answer. Organization also supports better recall of related content and thoughts about the content.

Grading an essay test is a trial for most instructors, especially since they know that if they had given an objective test, the grading could have been done by a computer. Instead, hours are needed to go through each test, answer by answer. How generous, forgiving, or understanding an instructor's mood will be after six hours of reading essay answers is conjectural. Their patience with sloppy handwriting, fuzzy reasoning, poor grammar, and irrelevant information can be expected to steadily deteriorate. It is to the student-athlete's advantage to realize that the more thoughtful and precise the essay answers are, the easier it is to avoid irritating the instructor during five or six hours of grading.

Relevance is a matter of understanding what the instructor expects. This expectation is usually indicated by the key word and the amount of space provided. Lengefeld (1986) has a brief but pointed statement of things to avoid that are damaging to relevance. Padding (bull), weak development (isolated facts), and choppiness (lack of transitions to help the instructor) all contribute to making an answer seem irrelevant to the question.

Brevity is not only the soul of wit, it is also a kindness to the instructor who must grade an essay test. Ellis (1985) points out that repeated or rephrased questions, long-winded sentences, and un- supported opinions all lengthen an answer without adding anything. Unfortunately, instructors know when their time is being wasted by a student or student-athlete who is just filling space with the hope of extra points.

An essay test is an exercise in creativity and recall under pressure. Student-athletes can benefit from realizing that essay tests require forethought and planning as part of the preparation. As mentioned elsewhere (see Chapter 7), a tape recorder may be a good way to practice for essay tests since it has the student-athlete doing exactly what the essay test will require, that is, convincing the instructor in the student-athlete's own words that he or she is familiar with the content and has thought about it.

CONCLUSIONS

Test taking is a painful experience for many student-athletes, partly because they use a recognition strategy for multiple-choice tests and a casual approach to essay questions. The response of student-athletes to a presentation on test taking has been largely positive because study time is not the focus. Instead, the presentation offers ways to change their test-taking preparation and strategy.

The presentation was developed to meet some constraints often found in programs for student-athletes: lack of free time, unwillingness to invest more time in studying, and an unusual frame of reference for test taking. A basic assumption of the presentation is that student-athletes learn excellent skills from their sports but fail to translate those skills into the classroom. This assumption seems supported by the evaluations given the presentation by students in general.

Over the past three years the presentation has been evaluated by just over 100 students. The following results seem very positive: 88% found the presentation interesting; 95% felt good points were made; and 91% thought the content was well presented. In terms of what the students would tell a friend, 92% would recommend friends attend the presentation. The remaining 8% would suggest that friends attend if they had time.

Perhaps it is time for helping professionals to stop worrying about student-athletes in football physics or basket weaving, and start thinking about how to translate well-developed skills and qualities learned in sports into the classroom. After all, the classroom test is a contest and our student-athletes are great competitors who love to win.

REFERENCE

Arlin,M., & Webster,J.(1983). Time costs of mastery learning. *Journal of Educational Psychology, 75,* 187-195.

Bloom, B. S. (1968, May). Master learning. *Evaluation Comment, 1(2),* p. 2.

Bloom, B. S. (1976). *Human characteristics and school learning.* New York: McGraw-Hill.

Brooks, D. D., Etzel, E. F., & Ostrow, A. C. (1987). Job responsibilities of NCAA division I athletic advisors and coun-selors. *The Sport Psychologist, 1,* 200-207.

Crocker, L., & Schmitt, A. (1987). Improving multiple-choice test performance for examinees with different levels of test anxiety. *Journal of Experimental Education, 55,* 201-205.

Ellis, D. B. (1985). *Becoming a master student.* Rapid City, SD: College Survival.

Ferrante, A. P. (1989). Glory or personal growth? The plight of the student-athlete. *The ECU Report, 20 (2),* p. 6.

Hembree, R. (1988). Correlates, causes, effects, and treatment of test anxiety. *Review of Education Research, 58,* 47-77.

Kirkland, K., & Hollingsworth, J. G., Jr. (1980). Effective test taking: Skills-acquisition versus anxiety-reduction techniques. *Journal of Consulting and Clinical Psychology, 48,* 431-439.

Kozoil, M. E. (1989). The cognitive Doppler. *Journal of Educational Development, 13,* 14-16.

Kulik, C. C., Kulik, J. A., & Bangert-Drowns, R. L. (1990).Effec-tiveness of mastery learning program: A meta-analysis. *Review of Educational Research, 60,* 265-299.

Lanning, W. (1982). The privileged few: Special counseling needs of athletes. *Journal of Sport Psychology, 4,* 19-23.

Lengefeld, U. A. (1986). *The fifty-minute study skills program.* Los Angeles, CA: Crisp Publications.

Millman, J., & Pauk, W. (1969). *How to take tests.* New York

McGraw-Hill.

Pauk, W. (1984). *How to study in college.* Boston: Houghton Mifflin.

Slavin, R. E. (1984). Master learning and student teams: A factorial experiment in general mathematics classes. *American Educational Research Journal, 21,* 725-736.

Slavin, R. E. (1987). Mastery learning reconsidered. *Review of Educational Research, 57,* 175-213.

CHAPTER **9**

Drugs and the College Student-Athlete

John Damm

Substance abuse and drug testing are major concerns of those who work with student-athletes. The author provides an overview of the issues surrounding these problems and shares information about effective intervention options.

Not long ago, college athletes were among the most revered people in this country. Physically, mentally, emotionally, and spiritually they represented ideals that many emulated. The so-called "All American" clean-cut image was associated with the college athlete for decades. Given their life styles and larger-than-life status, many people assumed they were not susceptible to the vices that plague the average person. Consequently, Americans were shocked when they saw that many of their idols had feet of clay where drugs and alcohol (among other things) were concerned.

One need only read the popular press to appreciate the extent to which drug use has apparently been a problem for college student-athletes. For example, Tommy Chaikin, a former University of South

Carolina football player, underwent treatment in a psychiatric hospital because of his steroid use (Chaikin & Telander, 1988). University of Southern California quarterback Todd Marinovich was recently arrested on charges related to his cocaine use; he subsequently entered a drug rehabilitation hospital. Len Bias died after one-time cocaine use (Neff & Selcraig, 1986). The University of Alabama lost two players in 1986 because of alcohol-related problems (Murphy, 1988). Many people shake their heads and wonder what has happened to these young people. "Certainly this was not a problem seventy years ago." Maybe, maybe not.

Are today's student-athletes somehow inferior to their predecessors? This is probably not the case. People have been altering their moods with drugs for thousands of years. Athletes have been using drugs to improve their performance since the first Greek Olympic games: drug use in the college athletic arena is not a new phenomenon. Rather, society's awareness of the problem has become greatly increased. Today's student-athlete is probably not psychologically, emotionally, or morally weaker than yesterday's athletes. Some would argue that due to the exceptionally stressful nature of their lives these athletes are more susceptible to certain problems such as drug use than non-athletes. Many of us forget or are not aware of the fact that student-athletes are developing young people first, students and athletes second. As a result, they experience many of the same problems that most of us encounter.

The purpose of this chapter is to examine drug use among college student-athletes today. The nature and prevalence of drug use, drug education versus drug prevention programs, drug testing programs, and recognition of drug abuse/addiction are discussed. The chapter finally ends with a discussion of on-campus drug education/treatment programs available to student-athletes.

DEFINITIONS OF DRUG USE

It is helpful to consider drug use as a type of behavior. As such, there are currently five types of behaviors that have been used to characterize most drug use. These behaviors were first described by the National Committee on Marijuana and Drug Abuse in 1972 (Ungerleider and Andrysiak, 1984). The most common is "experimental" use: (early, occasional) drug use that is motivated by peer pressure and curiosity that leads to initial explorations with available drugs. It simply means taking a drug to see what the effects will be. The next most common form of drug use is "recreational." Individuals use mind-altering chemicals in this way experience no adverse effects from this behavior (e.g., the athlete who drinks alcohol socially but does not experience problems related to his or her alcohol use).

The third form of drug behavior is "situational" or "circumstantial" drug use. This involves the taking of a drug for a specific purpose. Students or truck drivers who take amphetamines or caffeine to stay awake all night fit into this category. This type of use also refers to the "Sunday syndrome", which has been described as high-dose amphetamine use on game days by (primarily) professional football players.

The fourth type of drug use behavior is considered to be drug "abuse" (rather than drug use) and is called "intensified" drug use. This behavior usually consists of daily drug use that impairs functioning on the job, in school, in sports, and interferes with one's interpersonal relationships.

Finally, the fifth category of drug use behavior is so-called "compulsive" drug use. This is a pattern in which most of the individual's waking hours involve the recurrent cycle of obtaining money for the drug, getting the drug, using the drug and experiencing its effects.

Ryan (1986) has offered a useful definition of drug abuse: "Taking a drug in doses that substantially exceed the optimum dose to produce a desired effect, either at one time or repeatedly is abuse" (p.213). Ryan's definition of intensified drug use (drug abuse) is generally consistent with the description of psychoactive (i.e., mood-altering) substance abuse as described in the *Diagnostic and Statistical Manual of Mental Disorders, 4th edition, Revised,* (Spitzer & Williams, 1987). This behavior is described as a maladaptive pattern of psychoactive substance use indicated by the following: 1) continued use despite knowledge of having a persistent or recurrent social, occupational, psychological, or physical problem caused or exacerbated by the drugs, or 2) recurrent use in situations in which use is hazardous (e.g., driving while intoxicated), and 3) some symptoms persisting for at least one month or occurring repeatedly over a period of time.

From these descriptions it is easy to see how these behaviors can be differentiated from moderate drug use and how drug abuse can be damaging to the student-athlete. It can increase the probability of diminished academic and athletic performance and psychosocial functioning. With the advent of drug testing, such behavior may also jeopardize continued participation in intercollegiate athletics. Drug use can cause student-athletes problems in multiple areas of functioning (e.g., school work, sport performance, physical health) and can potentially worsen problems they are attempting to deal with, perhaps leading to the opposite results of those they were first seeking.

Student-athletes are susceptible to experiencing the entire continuum of drug use behaviors. Risk taking is characteristic of young people of this stage of their lives, thus we can expect that they have experimented with drugs. Additionally, the stressful life-styles of student-athletes, isolation, and peer pressures may prompt them to change their moods through drug use. This requires that helping professionals who work with them carefully consider individual differences in behaviors. Generalizations about drug use should best be avoided. It is sometimes difficult to define the extent or nature (use, abuse, addiction) of the student-athlete's drug use. This population presents unique characteristics that can make diagnosis problematic.

PREVALENCE OF DRUG USE AMONG COLLEGE STUDENT-ATHLETES

Despite the considerable attention that has been paid to the use of drugs by student-athletes, we do not have a much hard data in 1991 for several reasons. First, valid, reliable drug use information has been notoriously difficult to obtain. Drug use is a highly personal topic that many people are wary of discussing. Evans, Hansen and Mittlemark (1977) discussed the problem of obtaining reliable data concerning drug use through self-report measures among young people. Student-athletes must be concerned about disclosing information related to their possible drug use because of the many potential problems it may cause (e.g., loss of athletic eligibility, suspension from the team or school, expulsion). Student-athletes may lose playing time, status on the team, or suffer public embarrassment. Obviously, these students face serious consequences if their drug use is problematic. Alcohol use is likely to be reported more honestly than is use of illicit drugs such as cocaine and marijuana. The extent of their use is another factor. The student-athlete who uses the drug socially is more likely to produce a valid report than is a student-athlete who is experiencing drug-related problems because minimization and denial are likely. To compound this problem, student-athletes are often immature which may sometimes lead them to falsely believe that their sport-related prowess entitles them to special privileges such as the use of drugs. This combination of minimization and privilege only fuels student-athletes' belief that they "can handle it themselves."

It is estimated that over one million athletes in the United States are currently taking anabolic steroids (Duda, 1986). To give this figure some perspective, the number of steroid users was greater than the total estimated number of heroin addicts (0.5 million) and "crack" users (0.5 million) (Taylor, 1988). In regard to college student-athletes, empirical studies of steroid use are relatively new, and therefore little information is available.

Systematic studies of steroid use among college athletes have been conducted by a small number of researchers (Dezelsky, Toohey, & Shaw, 1985; Toohey, 1974; Toohey, 1978; Toohey and Cox, 1971). The general findings indicate that approximately 20% of college student-athletes appear to use anabolic (muscle building) steroids. Although this may seem a small percentage, when one considers the total number of student-athletes participating in intercollegiate athletics across the country (i.e., several hundred thousand). One can see that thousands of student-athletes may be using this drug.

In terms of other "ergogenic" (i.e., performance enhancing), drugs, researchers have noted that 24-28% of college athletes apparently use amphetamines. Clearly, these are high percentages given the large number of student-athletes in the United States. These numbers are not significantly different for nonathletes. In general, athletes and nonathletes tend to use all stimulants (e.g., cocaine, amphetamines, caffeine, over-the-counter diet pills) similarly and in essentially equal proportions.

Unfortunately, the literature concerning the effectiveness of these drugs as performance enhancers is inconsistent (Cooter, 1980a, 1980b; Eichner, 1986). In reviewing the literature, one can build a case for either the effectiveness or the impotence of these drugs in improving sport performance. Although the literature does not provide definitive statements concerning the ergogenic properties of these drugs, this issue is secondary to student-athletes' beliefs about the ability of these drugs to improve their performance.

Despite the inconclusiveness of research findings, student-athletes' opinions or personal experiences with ergogenic drugs seem to be the key factor in their decision relative to the utility of these drugs. Therefore, it may be futile to tell student-athletes about the results of various studies when they are convinced that the drug may help or is helping to improve their sport performance. Thus, student-athletes may ignore or discount people who present data-based evidence indicating that drugs are ineffective performance enhancers. Information on health risks associated with drug use can also be minimized or denied because the concerned helper has already lost credibility with the student-athlete.

In terms of recreational drug use, the usage patterns of college athletes are essentially similar to those of non-athletes. Studies by Toohey (1978) and Toohey and Corder (1981) suggest that college student-athletes and nonathletes use marijuana at approximately the same rates, that is 73% and 63%, respectively. The same studies reported no significant differences between collegiate athletes and nonathletes in their use of alcohol. The use of alcohol was reported by 91% of college athletes and 90% of nonathletes.

Similar studies have been conducted by a variety of researchers (Bell & Doege, 1987; Duda, 1984). For example, at the request of the National Collegiate Athletic Association, the College of Human Medicine at Michigan State University investigated the drug use in five men's and five women's sports. Student-athletes from six Division I, three Division II, and two Division III colleges and universities were included in the study (Anderson & McKeag, 1985). The drugs inquired about were alcohol, amphetamines, anti-inflammatory pain medications, anabolic steroids, barbiturates and tranquilizers, marijuana and hashish, minor pain medication, psychedelic drugs, smokeless tobacco, and vitamins and minerals. The following percentages of respondents reported using particular substances during the preceding 12 months: alcohol, 88%; marijuana, 37%; smokeless tobacco, 20%; cocaine, 17%; amphetamines, 9%; anabolic steroids, 4%; and tranquilizers, 2%.

Most studies have revealed that essentially similar proportions of college athletes and nonathletes use a variety of the same drugs. The only exception is anabolic steroids, which athletes have been found to use more than nonathletes. These findings raise two important issues. First, they address primarily the percentage of individuals using drugs, not the frequency or circumstances of actual drug use. The data give a general indication of the numbers of college athletes involved in drug use, but they do not indicate how much or how often these drugs are used. Secondly, it should not be assumed that drug use is not a problem among college athletes. Drug abuse cuts across all socioeconomic categories and is a considerable problem in this country. The fact that the percentage of athletes involved in drug use is not different from the percentage of college nonathletes, lends credence to the notion that we need to view student-athletes first as people.

College athletes are a unique group who are as likely as non-athletes to abuse drugs, and apparently more prone to abuse certain drugs (e.g., steroids). If people use drugs as a means of coping with stress, student-athletes have various reasons for using them. They may feel pressures from coaches, peers, instructors, parents, press, fans, and intimates. College athletes face many challenges that most people do not encounter. Student-athletes are required to spend a large percentage of their day involved in sport-related activities. They must also attend to their academic responsibilities, and they are required, like nonathletes, to be at least average students. Depending on the nature of their sport, the level of competition, and their skill level, student-athletes face additional and considerable stress that many other people neither appreciate nor understand. (See Chapter 1.)

Most people use drugs to enhance or cope with some aspect of their daily lives. Certainly, if one is looking for an excuse to use drugs, student-athletes easily can come up with reasons for using drugs (e.g., reduce pain, cope with stress, avoid responsibilities, obtain instant gratification have fun with the little free time they have, fit in with peers). However, rationalizations and excuses are not licenses for student-athletes to use or become addicted to drugs. Nevertheless student-athletes often do so; they are moreover, overtly and covertly encouraged to do so by societal messages and the athletic culture. Indeed, Lipsyte (1985) observed:

> There is no argument that drugs pose at least as serious a health problem in major league sports as they do in most high schools. By the time they have made the pros, most athletes have been given so many pills, salves, injections,

potions by amateur and pro coaches, doctors and trainers, to pick themup, cool them down, kill pain, enhance performance, reduce inflammation, and erase anxiety that there isn't much they won't sniff, spread, stick in or swallow to get bigger or smaller, or to feel good.(p. 613)

Additionally, Wadler and Hainline (1989) have noted that:

Drug use has become an accepted aspect of everyday living. Coffee awakens the morning, cigarettes buffer the day, alcohol smoothes the edges. Sedatives mellow, cocaine enhances,psychic and physical aches and pains seek relief in a swallow or injection. Drug use by the athlete is but a part of this intricate and self perpetuating web.(p. ix)

Because college student-athletes are vulnerable to drug-related problems just like anyone else, it is essential that coaches, trainers, and helping professionals be aware of the nature and extent of this problem. They should be equipped to recognize drug use/abuse and make appropriate recommendations and referrals when necessary to help these people in a timely and confidential manner. All too often the student-athlete is not viewed as a person, rather as an object or a performer. Accordingly, their problems are often minimized or ignored by those who are not concerned about these student-athletes' personal welfare. Some individuals who work with student-athletes may have their own agendas that do not always coincide with student-athletes' best interests. The physical, emotional, and mental health of student-athletes should be a primary concern of coaches, trainers, counselors, and others involved with them on a daily basis. As such, drug abuse is an issue that must be a concern for everyone.

RECOGNIZING DRUG USE

The first step in helping a student-athlete with drug-related problems is recognition of drug abuse symptoms. The student-athlete will probably not be the first person to admit experiencing such a problem. Therefore, it is crucial that individuals involved with them be able to identify the signs of drug abuse.

Most people can readily identify an individual who is blatantly intoxicated or high on drugs. However, the symptoms of drug abuse and drug use are sometimes subtle. Identification of the abuser can be difficult even for the trained professional. Individuals working with student-athletes should be aware of signs that may indicate drug use and abuse and, it is hoped, be able to provide assistance and referral.

Generally speaking, drug abuse is a possibility when observable changes occur in the student-athlete's behavior, mood, appearance, concentration or performance over time. Other noteworthy changes include problems in interpersonal relationships, a shift in associations to individuals who condone or use drugs, and unwarranted challenges to authority figures. A list of common indicators for drug use or abuse is summarized in Figure 1.

An in-depth personal interview to determine if the student-athlete is experiencing problems with or engaging in drug use should be conducted by a trained professional. Coaches, trainers and counselors in general do not need to be drug abuse experts. However, they should be generally knowledgeable about the indicators of drug abuse (see Figure 1). The majority of these signs can be registered through direct or indirect observation of the student-athlete by anyone who has regular contact with the individual. It should be noted that a college student-athlete who is abusing or addicted to drugs will not necessarily exhibit the majority of these indicators. Drug abuse may be a possibility when three or more of these changes are noted.

When drug abuse is suspected in the student-athlete, referral should be made to a trained professional (e.g., drug counselor, physician, psychologist) who can confirm or deny its existence. This referral preferably should be made not only to a trained expert with experience in the substance abuse counseling, but also to a person with an understanding of the college student-athlete population. Expertise as a drug counselor only may not be as effective an intervention tool as referral to a resource person who also has an appreciation of student-athletes' unique life-styles and needs. The professional who is well trained in both areas will more likely be able to help the student-athlete, given the professional's ability to understand and work on the presenting concern within the context of the student-athlete's unique situation.

Although useful, this approach will also present some difficulties.

1. Relationships with others
    a. Increased arguments
    b. Challenges to authority
    c. Isolation
    d. Changes in circle of friends
2. Antisocial behaviors
    a. Lying, conniving
    b. Stealing
    c. Aggressive behavior, physical or verbal
3. Behavioral changes
    a. Unexplained missing of practices/classes
    b. Loss of commitment/dedication (e.g., broken promises)
    c. Lack or loss of participation in regular activities
4. Mood changes
    a. Shifts in mood, sometimes extreme (e.g. euphoric to hostile)
    b. Personality changes (e.g., gregarious to aloof)
5. Eating/Sleeping behavior
    a. Erratic sleep habits; extremes of too much or too little; frequent naps.
    b. Erratic eating habits - again, ranging from extremes, possible anorexia/bulimia.
6. Intellectual functioning
    a. Attentional difficulties
    b. Decreased concentration
    c. Confusion/Disorientation
7. Performance deterioration
    a. Falling grades
    b. Declining sport performance
8. Physical
    a. Alcohol can be smelled on breath
    b. Bloodshot eyes or frequent use of eyedrops
    c. Increased frequency of injury

Figure 1. Common indicators of drug use or abuse.

Referral to a potential outsider meet resistance. Colleges and universities sometimes manifest a "We take care of our own" approach to problems, which can create some barriers (see Chapter 1). It may be difficult to obtain outside help because these institutions fear potential embarrassment when the media confirms or announces a problem that it may already suspect. It is a variation on the adage: "Better to remain silent and be thought a fool than to speak out and remove all doubt." Thus, athletes may receive counseling by "party-line" therapists who may say what someone wants to hear rather than what needs to be said.

Student-athletes may be hesitant to consult an outsider as well. They may be accustomed to privileged or protected status and have reservations about talking with an outsider, especially about their drug use. If they feel that the referral is unnecessary, they themselves may sabotage the process.

The referring individual can expect a drug counselor to ask pointed questions concerning the student-athlete's drug use. This process typically begins with screening, during which the clinician interviews the referral for appropriateness for drug counseling. The next step involves the intake. At intake the athlete enters the system (i.e., hospital, community mental health center), and biographical data is collected. A formal assessment of the student-athlete's drug use is then conducted. The referring person is a potentially important source of additional information. As stated earlier, the student-athlete may minimize the extent of the drug use. A collateral interview with someone who knows the student well and who is willing to be honest is an integral part of the assessment process.

Once the suspicion of drug abuse has been confirmed, the next step is to determine the appropriate treatment. Once a student-athlete who is experiencing problems related to drug use has been identified, an important factor in obtaining the appropriate treatment is the response of the college, athletic department, coaches, and/or team-mates to the discovery of this problem. Many people take a moralistic or judgmental stance toward all people with drug-related problems. This righteous indignation seems to help others to feel superior to these athletes and impedes any real understanding of the problem. Despite the beliefs of many, athletes with drug-related problems do not like, enjoy, or want those problems. People do not choose to be "druggies" or alcoholics: drug abuse happens for a variety of psychological, biological, social, and environmental reasons. Anything less than a true understanding of the troubled student-athlete's problem is likely to meet a negative reaction, and so the opportunity for help may be lost.

Coaches, teammates, and college administrators would be wise to treat the student-athlete as a friend in trouble. When they approach this person as one who has (depending upon the severity of the problem) a potentially life threatening disease (such as cancer), the attitude of caring and compassion that is transmitted encourages the student-athlete to admit that problems exist and thus to seek help investing in the treatment process. Treating people who are in trouble with drugs allows a far greater potential for change than does making the drug issue a battle of wills.

This does not mean that the athlete should be treated with "kid-gloves." Although people working with the student-athlete should be understanding and compassionate, it should also be understood that changes are necessary and that continued drug use will not be condoned. Thus, the athlete should be informed of the consequences of continued use (suspension from the team, expulsion from the institution, loss of eligibility) although these consequences should not be communicated as a threat. It is better to explain to the student-athlete that the university, coaches, and teammates are concerned about him/her and would like to see improvement. However, if the student-athlete is unwilling to change, then coaches and teammates will not support the continued drug use and the stated sanctions will be necessary. This hard-line approach is fairly common among professionals working with drug abusers and addicts.

Interventions. In the 1960s, attempts were made to address the problem of drug abuse through educational means (Bry, 1978). Early programs of this kind were traditional lecture presentations, sometimes intended to scare young people out of or away from drug use. Such an approach was generally ineffective. Goodstat (1974) reviewed the effectiveness of 21 drug education programs. These studies were conducted mainly with junior and senior high school students. Goodstat reported a lack of evidence supporting beneficial effects of drug education. Very few of these programs showed any significant improvements in any change area other than increasing levels of knowledge.

Similar findings were obtained by Schaps, DiBartolo, Moskowitz,

Palley, and Churgin (1981), who reviewed the drug education literature spanning the years 1968-1977, which included evaluations of 127 programs. Their findings relative to the effectiveness of these programs were not encouraging. Overall, only minor effects on drug behavior and attitudes were observed, although the programs were consistently able to increase knowledge about drugs and their effects.

The author believes that the student-athlete alone has the right to decide whether or not to use drugs. Many of the problems that resulted from the early drug education efforts were the result of scare tactics, exaggerated accounts or blatant falsehoods about the effects of drug use (e.g., one-time use results in permanent brain damage). Consequently, many young people, including student-athletes, disregarded what they heard from adults because they knew that they were being lied to. Student-athletes deserve valid information concerning the effects of drugs on the body, both positive (e.g., relieve pain) and negative (e.g., health problems).

Such a credibility gap causes obvious problems when one attempts to provide student-athletes with accurate information. Therefore, it is not the author's intention to bring back prohibition and take a paternalistic stance regarding college student-athletes and drug use. As noted by Lipsyte (1985) earlier, athletes of all ages are given a bewildering array of drugs by a variety of others—often to help them hasten back into competition. Drug abuse is a complicated, often intensely personal issue. For example, it is apparent that drug abuse and drug addiction are a completely separate issues from simple drug use. The use of performance enhancing drugs by student-athletes is personally distressing. Such drugs alter fair competition and transform the genuine test of skill and training into a hunt for the best dealer. Decisions about drugs are going to be made by the student-athletes. Our focus needs to be on making sure that drug-related decisions are based on accurate information.

Certainly, these forms of drug use behavior are much more serious than simple use; at times, it may be necessary to become more active in helping the student-athlete either to discontinue drug abuse or discontinue drug use entirely. There are many forms of treatment available discussed later in this chapter.

Drug education for college student-athletes usually takes the form of a required one to two hour presentation, one time per year (Tricker & Cook, 1989). Often, this information is provided by a university substance abuse coordinator, athletic trainer, or a nationally known athlete who abused or was addicted to drugs. As stated earlier, these programs have been found to be essentially ineffective. Such presentations provide student-athletes token education at best. (They probably know as much or more about the topic than those giving the presentation.)

One of the purposes of these educational programs is the prevention of the onset of drug use (i.e., primary prevention). Unfortunately, this approach is largely inappropriate because many college student-athletes begin using drugs prior to entering college. At the college level, programming should focus on increasing their knowledge about drug abuse and their awareness of the various consequences, rather than on deluding ourselves into believing that primary prevention is the issue. Secondary or tertiary prevention efforts are more appropriate for this population. For example, attention should be given to teaching and developing skills (e.g., refusal or stress management skills) that help student-athletes decrease or discontinue established drug use behaviors.

During the 1980s, a variety of programs, based on several different models (e.g., cognitive, behavioral, social influence) were developed to reduce drug use onset among junior high and high school students (Bell & Battjes, 1985). These skills were found to be effective within these populations. One such approach, known as "lifeskills training" was developed by Botvin (1980). The main purpose of this approach was to facilitate the development of generic coping skills as well as of skills and knowledge more specifically related to resisting the social influences to smoke, drink, or use drugs. An essential feature of the lifeskills program was the teaching of several cognitive-behavioral skills that included cognitive strategies for enhancing self-esteem, techniques for resisting persuasive arguments to use drugs, techniques for coping with anxiety, verbal and nonverbal communication skills, and a variety of social skills. The incorporation of a program that addresses the development of these skills is essential for college student-athletes and represents another means by which to address the problem of drug abuse that is more effective than drug education (Botvin & Eng, 1980, 1982; Koll & Pearman, 1990).

Once an athlete is identified as a drug abuser or addict, there are several components to successful treatment that those who counsel student-athletes should be familiar with. The least restrictive of these approaches is outpatient individual or group counseling with a qualified professional. These sessions usually involve educating the student-athlete about the effects (e.g., physical, emotional, spiritual) of drug abuse/addiction and attempting to break through the denial of the seriousness of the consequences of continued use. This approach differs from traditional education as it is tailored to individual needs, based upon individual drug use history. Once these data are obtained, the professional uses the specific information to educate the student-athlete of the consequences of drug use relevant to her or him. Traditional education takes a broad approach to providing information. The superiority of this approach is that it deals specifically with the individual and can be adapted to individual needs.

Depending on the severity of the athlete's drug use, more intensive treatment may be necessary. Outpatient intensive programs usually consist of scheduled outpatient visits to a hospital 3 times a week, for sessions that may last up to 3 hours per session. These programs are designed for those individuals who need more intensive therapy than 1-2 hours a week (i.e., traditional therapy). These individuals probably possess a greater number of drug abuse/ addiction symptoms and stronger denial of any related problems.

Finally, residential hospitalization (voluntary or involuntary) is the most restrictive (in terms of the client's freedom to come and go at will) and the most intensive. This treatment usually require patients to be involved in therapeutic activities (i.e., individual, family, and group counseling/education; alcoholics anonymous meetings; recreational activities) for the majority of their waking hours. Thus, this approach is more intensive as it requires much more of the patient each day for about 30 days. Patients are typically involved in therapy and education (group and individual) for 12 to 14 hours per day. Therapeutic activities are usually provided by a diverse staff (nurses, physicians, counselors) whose primary goal is to help the athlete admit to being unable to control drug use. Depending upon the physical condition of the individual, medical observation may be required; thus some individuals require detoxification first.

Again, the appropriate treatment modality depends upon the severity of the student-athlete's drug use, among other factors (existing support for drug-free living, previous treatment, insight into the severity of the drug problem, etc.). Most treatment milieus include the use of 12-step support groups, such as Alcoholics Anonymous, Narcotics Anonymous, and Al-Anon.

Nace (1987) offered four reasons why 12-step programs work: 1) unconditional acceptance of the individual as he or she is, 2) overcoming denial of the seriousness of the problem, 3) group process, and 4) deflation of pathological narcissism. Most people who effectively work with this program are those who have reached bottom and believe that they have exhausted all other options for change. This may be difficult for some young student-athletes to accept, given their limited life experiences and their belief that physical superiority extends to their ability to handle drugs. Despite this, self-help groups can be invaluable to the college student-athlete. Such programs usually require no fees, and anonymity is a central tenet.

The effectiveness of these programs is difficult to assess. The literature does not indicate that one approach (i.e., outpatient, intensive outpatient, residential) is superior to another. What is likely is that the most important factor is matching the treatment to the individual. However, the use of support groups seems important. Hoffman, Harrison, and Belille (1983) indicate that alcoholics who regularly attend AA meetings may be more than twice as likely to be abstinent as the alcoholic who does not attend the meeting.

Another approach to combating the problem of drug abuse among college athlete was instituted by the National Collegiate Athletic Association (NCAA) in 1986, when it developed guidelines for institutional drug screening programs and sanctions for positive (i.e., substance present) urine analysis. Most colleges in the United States are attempting to comply with the NCAA proposals. The NCAA also compiled an extensive list of banned substances that are purported to affect athletic performance and therefore have led to unfair advantages when taken.

Initially, the NCAA recommended that testing occur only during NCAA championships (Wagner, 1987). At that time, voluntary testing was conducted for football players in the off-season and then only for steroids. Specific consequences were mandated by the NCAA for athletes who tested positive for banned substance use in postseason competition. The first positive test report resulted in the athlete's being ineligible for same-season post-season play for a minimum of 90 days beyond the test date. A second positive test (either during the suspension or after return to active status) resulted in the loss of postseason eligibility for all sports and continued for such postseason competition through the succeeding academic year.

The NCAA has recently updated these guidelines to require year round, short notice testing programs(for all student-athletes) for steroids and drugs associated with their use (Lederman, 1989a). Most institutions have developed their own guidelines concerning additional measures that would be taken following the student-athlete's involvement in counseling and subsequent offenses (e.g., suspension from the team, termination of scholarships). Drug testing is perhaps one of the most controversial and important issue of the 1990s in intercollegiate athletics. Although drug testing may be an effective tool to detect drug abuse, it is questionable as to whether is reduces the incidence of drug use and abuse (Benson, 1988). Drug testing works best as part of a comprehensive program, which would include education, skills training, assessment, and treatment.

Singularly, drug testing appears to be a narrow, inefficient approach to reducing the prevalence of drug use among college student-athletes. Society at large has many rules, regulations, and consequences for unacceptable behavior. Yet the establishment of such sanctions alone may not decrease the frequency of inappropriate behavior. (Behavior cannot be legislated.) Drug testing should be viewed as one part of a substance abuse prevention program rather than as the answer to combatting drug abuse. Additionally, the question of who should be tested, the legal issues involved in drug testing, and the intent of drug testing are all important issues that should be further addressed.

The NCAA has been challenged on the constitutionality of its proposed program. Student-athletes at Stanford University and the University of Washington in Seattle were among the first to challenge the legality of drug testing in college sports (Cowart, 1987; Monaghan, 1989). The Stanford lawsuit was filed by diver Simone LeVant, who stated that the tests degraded her, invaded her privacy, and constituted an illegal search. She was joined by the American Civil Liberties Union, which opposed drug testing in principle. In February, 1987 LeVant won a court order that prohibited the NCAA from requiring her to take the drug test. Two other athletes joined LeVant in her fight against Stanford's practices and forced a court order prohibiting the university from requiring its students to sign the consent forms for drug testing as a condition for participation in collegiate sports (Cowart, 1987). Several additional hearings were held after this decision. As it last stood, a California Superior Court ruled that the NCAA violated only the California, and not the U.S. Constitution. It was ordered that the NCAA change its procedures so that athletes were not required to urinate in the presence of a testing official. In addition, testing was discriminatory in that it was used only for men's football and basketball.

At the University of Washington, Elizabeth O'Halloran filed a suit against the University stating that the school's program, which included observation of urine sample collection was dehumanizing and unwarranted. Initially, a superior court ruled the university drug testing program unconstitutional for violating state and federal guarantees of individual privacy rights. The NCAA then entered into the picture and asked that the case be moved to a federal court, where in 1988 a judge ruled that the NCAA testing program was constitutional.

In another case, the University of Colorado's drug testing program was ruled unconstitutional by a district court judge. The Colorado testing program consisted of random urine test and rapid eye examination both designed to reveal drug use. The judge ruled that these measures amounted to intrusive unreasonable searches and that they violated the Colorado constitution and the fourth amendment of the U.S. Constitution (Lederman, 1989b). For the program to meet constitutional requirements, the institution should have tested athletes only when probable cause of drug use was suspected.

The urine screening process is intrusive at the least and potentially dehumanizing. As an observer, the author can speak of this from experience. Athletes are sometimes herded into a locker room or bathroom and given a small bottle in which to urinate. Athletes are searched to ensure that they did not bring "clean" urine samples with them. This process in itself is embarrassing. Next, the athlete is directly observed urinating into the container, to verify its authenticity. Imagine someone standing very close to you watching you urinate into a bottle so as to insure that "the product" is indeed yours. Clearly the drug testing process can be seen as a paternalistic, condescending process that can impart the feeling that student-athletes are not to be trusted and need to be watched over.

The issues of who should be tested, for what, and when are only parts of the overall drug testing dilemma. The bigger question involves the intent of the NCAA and the colleges and universities across the United States in the development of their drug-testing and treatment programs. Sperber (1990) believes that the NCAA is using drug testing not only to promote its public relations value but also to maintain considerable revenues that might be lost if these athletes were caught using drugs. It is arguable that athletic programs condone drug testing because it helps to protect their investment in their athletes. Athletes would appear then to be possessions of the institution rather than people, if Sperber's supposition is correct. This would be a sad statement indeed. In the end, the health and welfare of the student-athletes should come first. Therefore, we should focus on helping student-athletes avoid or discontinue drug abuse and related activities. This problem is primary, not secondary to the student-athlete's eligibility, ability to play on or at any given competitive events, or other scholarship-related issues. Once the university has made a commitment to the student-athlete, it assumes some of the responsibility for assuring that student-athletes receive the appropriate services for problems that occur during their attendance at the university. Hopefully, student-athletes will be viewed as people first, students and athletes second.

This may not always be the case. Much depends upon the university's perception of its student-athletes, the sport the athletes participate in, the skill level of the athletes and the university's perspective on drug abuse. Sometimes it appears that drug testing and treatment programs are developed as face saving devices, rather than as expressions of genuine concern for the welfare of student-athletes.

Many of us are aware of student-athletes who exhibit obvious symptoms of drug abuse or drug addiction. For a variety of reasons these problems often go untreated. Although the student-athlete is ultimately responsible for seeking out and complying with whatever services are necessary to alleviate such problems, there are times when universities could influence student-athletes to obtain appropriate treatment out of their concern for these individuals. Unfortunately, many people are aware of situations in which such action was not taken. We must then ask what is the purpose of drug testing and drug treatment, if not for the well-being of the college student-athlete?

Any drug testing/treatment program developed by a university is only as good as its intentions. Student-athletes, will often explain how rules and policies are bent or overlooked to suit the needs of the university (e.g., keep a star player active or eligible). Perhaps students are informed in advance when drug testing will be performed. Perhaps some student-athletes are given additional chances to "clean up their act" that other athletes may not receive. Perhaps such programs are used to weed out unwanted student-athletes. Like any other system, drug testing procedures are susceptible to abuse on different levels.

It is the author's opinion that the purpose of a well-defined drug education and prevention program should be to protect the welfare of student-athletes. Such programs should clearly explain the purposes of the program, procedures for testing, and consequences of positive test results. This information should be presented to prospective student-athletes during the recruiting process well before they enroll at the school of their choice. The student-athlete must choose to participate in a program only after having voluntarily provided informed consent, based upon a clear and fair agreement between the athlete and the university. This agreement should involve the provision of specific information in writing about the program's purposes, procedures and consequences, accompanied by an explanation of the program by a responsible and knowledgeable representative of the institution. Since an explanation of the program does not guarantee a person's understanding of its nature, it is also recommended that institutions assess each student-athlete's understanding of the program before they are asked to provide informed consent. This may be accomplished by administering a quiz or conducting an interview with each student-athlete.

Furthermore, it is essential that the results of drug testing remain confidential. Those who need to know such information should be clearly identified professionals (e.g., head physician, head athletic trainer) within the program and very limited in number. The private behavior of student-athletes who test positive must not be compromised so as not to become fodder for the morning sports page.

It is hoped that primary concern is for the personal welfare of the student-athlete as a person. The establishment of these programs seem to have been undertaken with the intent of providing college student-athletes with services that they may not otherwise have access to or seek out until their drug problems were overwhelming. College athletes are not superhuman: they are people who are susceptible to the same pitfalls and problems that most of us experience. Although they are often quite gifted, we must not lose sight of their human limitations. These young people are not objects, nor a draw at the gate. They are human just like the rest of us. Consequently, those who work with student-athletes need to be aware of the problems they experience, particularly drug abuse. Hopefully, the reader has become more aware of the serious nature of drug abuse in college student-athletes and has acquired a better understanding of indicators of drug abuse, as well as an acquired appreciation of the legal and political issues that surround drug testing and treatment programs within college sports.

REFERENCES

Anderson, W.A. & McKeag, D.B. (1985). *The substance use and abuse habits of college student-athletes.* East Lansing, MI: College of Human Medicine. Michigan State University.

Bell, C.S., & Battjes, R., (Eds.) (1985). *Prevention research: Deterring drug abuse among children and adolescents.* National Institute on Drug Abuse Research Monograph 63.(DHHS Pub. No. ADM 89-1334). Washington, D.C.: U.S Government Printing Office.

Bell, J., & Doege, T. (1987). Athletes' use and abuse of drugs.*The Physician and Sportsmedicine, 15*, 99-108.

Benson, D.C. (1988). A perspective on drug testing. *The Physician and Sportsmedicine, 16(2)*, 151.

Botvin, G., & Eng, A. (1980). A comprehensive school-based smoking prevention program. *The Journal of School Health,50*, 209-213.

Botvin,G.,& Eng. A. (1982).The efficacy of a multicomponent approach to the prevention of cigarette smoking. *Preventive Medicine, 11*, 199-211.

Bry, B.H. (1978). Research design in drug abuse prevention:

Review and recommendations. *The International Journal of the Addictions, 13*(7), 1157-1168.

Chaikin, T., & Telander, R. (1988). The nightmare of steroids. *Sports Illustrated, 69*(18), 82-102.

Cooter, G. (1980a). Amphetamine use, physical activity and sport. *Journal of Drug Issues, 3*, 323-330.

Cooter, G. (1980b). Amphetamines and sports performance. *Journal of Health, Physical Education and Recreation*, October, 63-64.

Cowart, V. (1987). Some predict increased steroid use in sports despite drug testing, crackdown on suppliers. *Journal of the American Medical Association, 257*, 3025-3026.

Dezelsky, T., Toohey, J., & Shaw, R. (1985). Non-medical drug use behavior at five United States universities: A nine-year study. *Bulletin on Narcotics, 37*, 49-53.

Duda, M. (1984). Drug testing challenges college and pro athletes. *The Physician and Sportsmedicine, 12*, 109-118

Duda, M. (1986). Do anabolic steroids pose an ethical dilemma for U.S. physicians? *The Physician and Sportsmedicine, 14* (11), 173-175.

Eichner, E. (1986). The caffeine controversy: Effects on endurance and cholesterol. *The Physician and Sports-medicine, 14*, 124-132.

Evans, R., Hansen, W., & Mittlemark, M. (1977). Increasing the validity of self-report of smoking behavior in children. *Journal of Applied Psychology, 62*, 521-523.

Goodstat, M.S. (1974). Myths and mythology in drug education: A critical review of the research evidence. In M. Goodstat,(Ed.) *Research on methods and programs of drug education*, Toronto, Canada.

Hoffman, N.G., Harrison, P.A., & Belille, C.A. (1983). Alcoholics Anonymous after treatment: Attendance and abstinence. *International Journal of Addictions, 18*, 311.

Koll, L., & Pearman, F. (1990). A life skills approach. *Student Assistance Journal*, May-June, 32-34, 51-52.

Lederman, D. (1989a, July 19). NCAA panel backs year-round,

mandatory drug testing. *The Chronicle of Higher Education,* July 19, p. A28.

Lederman, D. (1989b, September 6). Drug testing program at University of Colorado ruled unconstitutional. *The Chronicle of Higher Education,* p. A33-34.

Lipsyte, R. (1985). Baseball and Drugs. *The Nation,* p. 613.

Monahan, P. (1989, July 19). Runner drops legal charges to drug testing. *The Chronicle of Higher Education,* p. A28.

Murphy, A. (1988). Low tide at Alabama: Unsavory off-the-field incidents have tarnished the image of 'Bama football. *Sports Illustrated, 69* (6), 30-32.

Nace, E. (1987). *The treatment of alcoholism.* New York: Brunner-Mazel.

Neff, C., & Selcraig, B. (1986). One shock wave after another. *Sports Illustrated, 65* (20), 33-40.

Ryan, A. (1986). Drug abuse in sports: A physician's view. *Postgraduate Medicine, 80* , 213-217.

Schaps, E., DiBartolo, R., Moskowitz, J., Palley, C., & Churgin, S. (1981). A review of 127 drug abuse prevention program evaluations. *Journal of Drug Issues, 11(*1), 17-43.

Sperber, M. (1990). *College sports inc.: The athletic department vs. the university.* New York: Henry Holt.

Spitzer, R., & Williams, J. (1987). *Diagnostic and statistical manual of mental disorders.*(4th ed., rev.). Washington, D.C.: American Psychiatric Association.

Taylor, W. (1988). Prescribing for the competitive athlete. *Journal of Sports Medicine, 2,* 15-26.

Toohey, J. (1974). Trends in drug use behavior at ten Arizona high schools. *Arizona Journal of Health, Physical Education and Recreation, 18,* 6-8.

Toohey, J. (1978). Non-medical drug use among intercollegiate athletes at five American universities. *Bulletin on Narcotics, 30*(3), 61-65.

Toohey, J., & Corder, B. (1981). Intercollegiate sports participation and non-medical drug use. *Bulletin on Narcotics, 33*(3), 23-27.

Toohey, J., & Cox, B. (1971). Steroids and the athlete. *Journal of Health, Physical Education and Recreation, 14, 15-17.*

Tricker, R., & Cook, D. (1989). The current status of drug intervention and prevention in college athletic programs. *Journal of Alcohol and Drug Education, 34* (2), 38-45.

Ungerleider, J., & Andrysiak, T. (1984). Changes in the drug scene: Drug use trends and behavioral patterns. *Journal of Issues, 2,* 217-221.

Wadler, G.I., & Hainline, B. (1989) *Drugs and the athlete. Contemporary exercise and sports medicine series.* Philadelphia: F.A. Davis Company.

Wagner, J. (1987). Substance-abuse policies and guidelines in amateur and professional athletes. *American Journal of Hospital Pharmacy, 44,* 305-310.

CHAPTER 10

Identification and Treatment of the Athlete with an Eating Disorder

Richard Seime and Diana Damer

Eating disorders are common serious problems with which large numbers of male and female student-athletes struggle. The authors discuss the nature of eating disorders, factors that contribute to their onset, and maintenance as well as state of the art treatment approaches.

Health professionals and counselors who work with competitive athletes will be confronted with issues involving both appearance and weight control. This chapter will deal with those athletes who have developed clinical eating disorders, an important problem and one that often can go unrecognized among athletes. We describe how the athlete may be at particular risk, define eating disorders, and review the negative consequences of eating disorders. This is followed by a description of ways to identify athletes who are having trouble, a description of assessment and therapeutic resources for working with an athlete with an eating disorder, and suggestions for intervention.

COMPETITIVE ATHLETICS—A HIGH RISK SETTING

Maximum athletic performance in sports is intimately related to the physical condition of the athlete. Increasingly, coaches have begun to emphasize reduction of body fat as a way to develop maximum strength, endurance, and speed per pound of body weight (Smith, 1980). Young athletes in competitive sports receive strong pressure to reduce fat (Harris & Greco, 1990). High school girls will average 20-22% body fat, whereas girls involved in competitive sports such as gymnastics and distance running, are often asked to maintain body fat at less than 10% (Smith, 1980). Data supporting the advantage of lower body fat on performance can be conflicting. For example, one study found that collegiate gymnasts with lower body fat placed higher (Falls & Humphrey, 1978), yet another suggested that thinness was not an advantage in other sports (Dummer, Rosen, Heusner, Roberts & Counsilman, 1987). In spite of few studies addressing the optimum weight:height ratios or percent body fat for athletes, emphasis on leanness is a widely held value among coaches (Calabrese et al., 1983; Dummer et al., 1987; Rosen & Hough, 1988; Rosen, McKeag, Hough, & Curley, 1986).

The widely accepted notion that minimal levels of body fat are linked with maximal performance combines with societal dictates about thinness to create strong pressures on the young athlete (Dummer et al., 1987). The "pressure for thinness when augmented by high performance expectations is the ideal social medium for the expression of anorexia nervosa" (Garner & Garfinkel, 1980, p. 653). From a broader perspective, the competitive athletic environment with its emphasis on performance and the value placed on weight and appearance in achieving success is an ideal setting for student-athletes to develop patterns of hazardous weight loss practices and attitudes about weight and shape that prove to be detrimental to their physical and emotional well-being.

Smith (1980) noted that athletes are faced with fear of failure at two levels: 1) fear of making the team and 2) fear of failing in competition. Weight criteria set forth by the coach and the not so subtle pressure to be thin are usually accepted by the athlete without question. The athlete's efforts to achieve an athletic ideal are positively reinforced by coaches, parents, and teammates (Dummer et al., 1987; Smith, 1980). For vulnerable individuals, competitive athletics will be a factor in the development and maintenance of anorexia nervosa or bulimia nervosa.

Being achievement-oriented and perfectionistic have been cited repeatedly as individual risk factors for eating disorders (e.g., Bruch, 1973; Bruch, 1981; Garner, Olmsted, & Polivy, 1983; Root, Fallon, & Friedrich, 1986). Rodin, Siberstein, and Striegel-Moore (1985) contend that women's pursuit of thinness is a form of competition and achievement behavior. When other areas of life appear beyond control, weight may be viewed as the only factor that can be manipulated (Hood, Moore, & Garner, 1982). The drive for thinness provides feelings of control, a sense of identity, and a definable goal (Yates, Leehey, & Shisslak, 1983).

Competitive athletics attract and foster persons who are perfectionistic and high achieving (Borgen & Corbin, 1987; Druss & Silverman, 1979), and evidence suggests that elite performers are at the greatest risk to develop eating disorders (Hamilton, Brooks-Gunn, & Warren, 1985; Smith, 1980; Weight & Noakes, 1987). When warned about weighing too much, perfectionistic and hard-driving athletes are vulnerable to excessive weight loss and food aversion.

WHAT CONSTITUTES AN EATING DISORDER?

Preoccupation with weight and shape especially among women has been described as a "normative discontent" (Rodin et al., 1985) and, as described earlier, a preoccupation highly prevalent in athletes. It is when the preoccupation leads to persistent use of hazardous weight loss methods (i.e., self-induced vomiting, laxative abuse, diet pill abuse, unrelenting exercise and extreme dieting measures, or bingeing in combination with purging) that a diagnosis of an eating disorder is made. However, eating disorders clearly present along a continuum from preoccupation with body size to life-threatening medical emergencies. Likewise, eating disorders exist on a continuum from the presence of hazardous weight loss practices that constitute a set of bad habits to severe complicating psychopathology that accompanies the eating disorder.

Diagnostic Criteria. The two disorders of most interest to the professional working with competitive athletes are anorexia nervosa and bulimia nervosa. The diagnostic criteria for these disorders are described in the *Diagnostic and Statistical Manual of Mental Disorders, 3rd edition, Revised* (DSM-III-R) of the American Psychiatric Association (1987). Anorexia nervosa has been known for centuries, yet bulimia nervosa has existed as a separate diagnostic entity only for the last decade (Boskind-White & White, 1986). The defining feature of anorexia nervosa is obvious weight loss. The diagnostic criteria for anorexia nervosa include:

1. Refusal to maintain body weight over a minimal normalweight for age and height (e.g., weight loss leading to maintenance of body weight 15% below that expected).
2. Intense fear of gaining weight or becoming fat, even though underweight.
3. Disturbance in the way in which one's body weight, size, or shape is experienced, (e.g., "feeling fat" when emaciated, or believing one area of the body to be "too fat" even when underweight).
4. In females, absence of three consecutive periods. Bulimia nervosa has as its defining feature recurrent episodes of binge eating, but individuals with the disorder may be of below average to overweight. Periods of dieting and restrictive eating coupled with stress precipitate bingeing behavior. Typically, bingeing develops first followed later by the use of purging (i.e., self-induced vomiting, laxatives, etc.). The diagnostic criteria for bulimia nervosa are:

   1. Recurrent episodes of binge eating (rapid consumption of a large quantity of food in a discrete period of time).
   2. A feeling of lack of control over eating behavior during the eating binges.
   3. Regular self-induced vomiting, use of laxatives, strict dieting or fasting, or vigorous exercise in order to prevent weight gain.
   4. A minimum average of two binge eating episodes a week for at least three months.
   5. Persistent overconcern with body shape and weight.

Bulimia nervosa and anorexia nervosa are separate diagnostic categories, but there is much overlap. Approximately 40-50% of individuals with anorexia nervosa display bulimic behaviors (Hsu,

1990; Kennedy & Garfinkel, 1985). Research also indicates that about 50% of individuals who have bulimia nervosa have a history of anorexia nervosa (Hsu, 1990; Mitchell, Pyle, & Eckert, 1985). Hsu (1988) has pointed out that it is relatively rare for normal-weight bulimics to revert to a pattern of restrictive anorexia.

PREVALENCE OF EATING DISORDERS

The development of an eating disorder is multifactorial (see Yates, 1989 for an excellent review of these factors). However, eating disorders almost always emerge from a desire to be thin and a history of dieting (Agras & Kirkley, 1986, Hsu, 1988; Hsu, 1990; Striegel-Moore, Silberstein, & Rodin, 1986).

Anorexia Nervosa. The prevalence of anorexia is generally accepted to be about 0.31-1% among adolescent girls ages 15-19 (Hsu, 1990; Yates, 1989). The peak incidence for anorexia is during the adolescent years from 15-19 with the disorder rarely occurring before age 10 and the incidence dropping dramatically after age 29 (Lucas, Beard, O'Fallon, & Kurland, 1988). It should be noted that this is also the period when individuals become involved in competitive athletics.

Bulimia Nervosa. Because bulimia nervosa is new to the diagnostic nomenclature (i.e., 1980), early estimates of the prevalence of bulimia were inflated. Hart and Ollendick (1985) found a high prevalence of binge eating among university women (about 5 times higher than among working class women) but many fewer women who met diagnostic criteria for bulimia. Among college-age women the prevalence of bulimia nervosa is about 4% (Drewnowski, Yee, & Krahn, 1988; Pyle, Mitchell, Eckert, Halvorson, Neuman, & Goff, 1983; Katzman, Wolchik, & Braver, 1984) and among women in general about 1.9% (Cooper & Fairburn, 1983). Anorexia and bulimia are largely female disorders with a 10:1 ratio of women to men suffering from the disorders (Hsu, 1990).

Prevalence Among Athletes. Prevalence of eating disorders among athletes is difficult to pinpoint, and the data have been described as slippery (Thornton, 1990, p. 119). Certainly, athletes are viewed as a very high-risk population (Hsu, 1990; Thornton, 1990). There is evidence to suggest an increased risk for eating disorders among athletes, but an exact prevalence figure is impossible to calculate. However, the prevalence of hazardous weight loss practices among athletes is more firmly established and reported.

In one study of female collegiate athletes, 32% of the 182 athletes practiced at least one pathogenic weight-control behavior (i.e., vomiting, bingeing, laxatives, or diet/diuretic pills) (Rosen et al., 1986). In another study of girls and boys at a competitive swimming camp, 24.8% postmenarcheal adolescent girls used pathogenic weight-control behaviors whereas 3.6% of the boys did the same (Dummer et al., 1987). This is in contrast to a study of 1000 high school students showing 2.3% of girls vomiting, 2.1% using laxatives, and 8.15% using diet pills (no boys used vomiting or laxatives) (Rosen & Gross, 1987). In another study of 42 gymnasts ages 17-22, 62% were engaging in at least one form of pathogenic weight-control behavior, and all were dieting. This figure is higher than among female college students in general, where 4% were using laxatives or vomiting (Button & Whitehouse, 1981). Finally, in a study of 42 college wrestlers, 5% were using laxatives, 5% diuretics, and 11% vomiting to lose weight (Steen & McKinney, 1986).

It is safe to say that women athletes are at risk to use hazardous weight loss practices. However, these student-athletes may not have all the features of an eating disorder. What is of most concern are those athletes for whom weight loss is no longer a means of improving performance but an end in itself. In these athletes, hazardous weight loss practices, weight preoccupations, and distortions about self-worth and weight become ingrained and continue to affect their lives long after the competitive season is over.

Negative Consequences of an Eating Disorder. Within the scope of this chapter, it is not our intent to review in great detail the detrimental health consequences associated with these disorders. However, major organ systems are affected (i.e., renal, metabolic, gastrointestinal, cardiopulmonary, neurologic, and endocrine systems); serious complications can arise. Although anorexia nervosa involves weight loss and emaciation, there are few signs and symptoms that easily identify nonanorectic bulimics (Mitchell, 1984). Physical complications arise from the consequences of the hazardous weight loss practices in both anorexia and bulimia nervosa. The sustained loss of weight in anorexia nervosa causes severe physical problems. In both disorders, purging (e.g., self-induced vomiting, laxative use, use of emetic agents, fluid pills, excessive exercise, food restriction) causes disturbances in metabolic function. Readers can refer to several excellent reviews of the negative health consequences of hazardous weight loss practices (see, Mitchell, 1984; Mitchell, 1986a, 1986b; Mitchell, Pomeroy, & Huber, 1988).

Menstrual problems, including the absence of periods, are common in both disorders (Copeland & Herzog, 1987). However, it is common for menstrual dysfunction to occur in athletes without eating disorders as well (Shangold, Rebar, Wentz, & Schiff, 1990). Often there is little concern about the absence of periods shown by the athlete with an eating disorder because of the high prevalence of menstrual problems. (See Riggotti, Nussbaum, Herzog, & Neer, 1984, or Shangold et al., 1990, for a review of the consequences and management of menstrual dysfunctions.)

The emotional correlates of bulimia nervosa are most commonly depression and reduced self-esteem that result from the secretive pattern of bingeing and purging (Fairburn, Cooper, & Cooper, 1986; Mitchell et al., 1985). Anorectic individuals can also display depressive symptoms and these often are related to poor nutrition (see Hsu, 1990 and Kennedy & Garfinkel, 1985 for excellent reviews). As individuals become more ingrained in their eating disorder, their mood, self-esteem, and self-worth will largely be determined by a weight on a scale and whether or not certain foods have been eaten. For those with an eating disorder, the solution to all stresses becomes food and is weight related.

NEGATIVE CONSEQUENCES AS
A REASON FOR CHANGE

It is important to remember that most competitive athletes will not complain of physical symptoms. In spite of having an eating disorder and engaging in high-frequency hazardous weight loss practices, most individuals will minimize the effect of these behaviors on their physical health. Likewise, it is not uncommon for blood chemistry assays to be normal in the presence of a serious eating disorder. As a result, scare tactics that try to shock a person into a healthy pattern usually do not work because the physical consequences may not be as salient to the individual engaged in a hazardous pattern as they are to those who have some knowledge of possible negative consequences. Typically, family and friends of those with an eating disorder are more concerned than the individual about the immediate health risk of the problem.

Special Considerations in Evaluating and Treating Athletes. The athlete with an eating disorder will need to be referred to a professional for treatment. In our experience, a treatment team needs to include a mental health clinician, a physician (may be a team physician), and a dietitian aware of the demands of athletic competition. It is best that relationships between the clinician and the athletic staff be established proactively so that referrals can be handled effectively. It is most effective to have a specific eating disorder clinician as a contact person with the athletic staff. The athletic training staff has proven to be an efficient liaison between the eating disorder treatment team and the athletic department. The person in charge of the eating disorder program should establish positive rapport with coaches and athletic trainers. The athletes need to know that their problems will be addressed by concerned professionals who are aware of their status as athletes. Likewise, coaches need to be reassured that the treating professional has an understanding of the unique demands on the athlete. Professional fees for treatments should be directly arranged with the athletic department. In our university, treatment for student-athletes is funded by the athletic department. With these comments as a backdrop, the evaluation and treatment of the eating disordered athlete will be addressed.

ASSESSMENT

Although diagnostic criteria are fairly specific, identification of individuals with eating disorders is not always an easy task. This can be especially true among athletes. It is important to remember that for bulimic individuals there are no unequivocal signs that the disorder is present. Individuals can be engaging in a secretive pattern of bingeing and purging for many months and years without anyone else's knowing. Similarly, with the leanness expected among athletes, the rigid exercise regimens, and the denial of any distress, it is often difficult to identify those who are, or who are becoming anoretic.

The issue of what criteria to use in determining the absence or presence of an eating disorder is complicated with respect to the competitive athlete. It is difficult to determine when the athlete's behavior has crossed the boundary from normal to unhealthy (Chipman, Hagan, Edlin, Soll, & Carruth, 1983). McSherry (1984) listed dietary "faddism," restricted calorie intake, avoidance of carbohydrates, low body weight, increased physical activity, and amenorrhea or oligomenorrhea (light periods) as shared features. He also outlined several distinguishing characteristics. The athlete's exercise involves purposeful training, whereas exercise in the anorexic is often aimless and extreme. An athlete will demonstrate good muscular development, a level of body fat within normal limits, and increased exercise tolerance. In contrast, an anorexic will exhibit poorly developed muscles, a subnormal level of body fat, and decreased performance. Empirical support for reduced aerobic capacity among anorexics is provided by Einerson, Ward, and Hanson (1988).

Clinicians need to be aware of the potential for both underdiagnosing or overdiagnosing eating disorders in athletes due to the overlap of signs and symptoms. The following section will provide some further guidelines for identifying athletes who have eating disorders.

IDENTIFYING THE ATHLETE WITH AN EATING DISORDER

Typically, an athlete with an eating disorder comes to the attention of the trainer or coach through reports of other athletes. The individual may have been observed vomiting or not eating for lengthy periods of time. Similarly, a coach may note a deterioration in performance that seems unusual. Precipitous weight loss and physical symptoms such as lightheadedness or fainting during competition can also be a clue.

Initial Evaluation. Even if an athlete has admitted he or she might have a "problem," expect the individual to minimize difficulties. In general, bulimic symptoms (specifically, bingeing and self-induced vomiting) are disturbing for the individual. However, low body weight, highly restrictive eating, and weight loss are not seen as problematic. Typically, athletes will view themselves as being particularly special and unique. It is important to understand that these high- functioning individuals see their eating disorder behaviors as a means to a positive end, and even more than nonathletes with eating disorders, they do not typically view inadequate diet or excessive weight loss as problematic. Many will deny that any problem exists. In a few cases, the individual will be openly hostile and disparaging of the professional who is conducting the evaluation. This can usually be handled by acknowledging the anger, clarifying with the client your purpose for evaluating, determining the client's expectations of the evaluation, emphasizing that information obtained will be treated confidentially and that only with the knowledge of the athlete will information be disclosed to the athlete's coaches or trainers. It is best to proceed by conducting a thorough interview augmented with appropriate behavioral and psychological measures.

Evaluation should include a thorough review of presenting problems: events or actions that led to the evaluation, the chief complaints, a review of daily patterns of eating and purging practices, a review of physical symptoms, a review of psychological symptoms, and a review of history. Blood chemistry evaluation may be obtained from a consulting physician usually through a college or university health service (if no eating disorder clinic exists). High-frequency purging (use of large doses of laxatives, multiple daily episodes of vomiting, and severe dietary restriction) coupled with physical symptoms such as lightheadedness or paresthesias (numbness and tingling) are good indicators for blood chemistry evaluation. In our experience, routine blood chemistries on every patient regardless of pattern of weight loss or symptoms is not warranted.

Assessment of Weight. It is useful to weigh the client as part of the evaluation. This simple request can often elicit, more effectively than interview alone, the weight phobia and body-image distress that are cardinal features of those with an eating disorder. Two measures are particularly useful for assessment at the time of weighing: the Body Image Anxiety Scale and Weight Distress Scales. The Body Image Anxiety Scale (Thompson, 1990, Appendix C) measures anxiety and distress about appearance and weight. We use the Trait Body Image Anxiety Scale (TBIAS). The

TBIAS is an effective way to assess distress and it easily can be used to monitor changes in distress with treatment. The Weight Distress Scales were developed by the author (Seime) to assess distress about weight before and after weighing. Two questions are asked both before and after weighing: 1) How distressed do you feel about your weight right now? and 2) To what extent do you think you are overweight right now? Responses are marked on a 10 cm visual analog scale anchored at the extremes by the statements "not at all" to "extremely." Responses are transformed to a 1-10 value with high scores indicating distress.

Body weight can be assessed for normativeness by using the Body Mass Index (Bray, 1978). The Metropolitan Life Insurance Weight Tables (Metropolitan Life Insurance Company, 1983), widely used, are not very useful because the athlete is not an average person and rarely will these tables be of any usefulness for this group of clients.

Psychometric Assessment. The athlete, for whom a diagnosis is difficult as noted above, can be reliably assessed using several existing measures. Particularly useful are the Bulimia Test (Smith & Thelen, 1984), the Bulimia Investigatory Test (Henderson & Freeman, 1987), and the Body Shape Questionnaire (Cooper, Taylor, Cooper, & Fairburn, 1987), all of which have cutoff scores for ease of interpretation. The Eating Disorders Inventory (Garner & Olmsted, 1983) is widely used but we have not found it a practical tool for diagnosing eating disorders among athletes.

Several self-report questionnaires are available that are a thorough review of eating-related behaviors, attitudes and problems (such as, the Diagnostic Survey for Eating Disorders (Johnson, 1985) and the West Virginia Eating Behaviors Questionnaire. These can very efficiently obtain a wealth of important information that may be difficult to obtain during an interview. Finally, a brief measure of depression (Beck Depression Inventory [Beck & Steer, 1987]) is valuable for quick assessment of this important dimension. (The reader is referred for more comprehensive information about assessment to *Assessment of Eating Disorders* [Williamson, 1990] and *Body Image Disturbance* [Thompson, 1990]).

Self-Monitoring. Assessment of the athlete with an eating disorder needs to rely on more than retrospective self-report, and self-monitoring accomplishes this nicely. Self-monitoring of dietary intake, feelings, and self-talk is essential both in the initial evaluation and subsequent treatment. Self-monitoring forms have been developed that can assist clinicians in targeting appropriate issues (e.g., Fremouw, Wiener, & Seime, 1987). The dietary monitoring will be necessary for the dietitian evaluating nutrition. However, self-monitoring is also a way for the clinician to assist the client to see relationship between eating-related behaviors and thoughts, feelings, and stressors.

Utilization of Assessment Data. The clinician needs to be very clear with the student-athlete about how the assessment will be used. Athletes will be particularly sensitive that their competitive eligibility may be undermined as a result of the finding of an eating disorder. It is recommended that all communication with the athletic staff be done with the knowledge of the athlete. Unless the eating disorder is an immediate, serious health hazard, participation in athletic activity should not be terminated.

Assessing the Athletic Environment. Evaluation of the athlete must also include some assessment of the type of environment he or she is confronting with their sport and the particular coach. Coaches with rigid weight-related rules that include frequent weighing are a very detrimental force for combating an eating disorder. The clinician needs to be able to discuss these practices with the coach. We have found that an atmosphere of cooperation develops with frequent contact and meetings that take place even before any athletes are in treatment. This can help detoxify any fears that coaches may have that athletes will be advised to withdraw from competition if an eating disorder is found (c.f., Zucker et al., 1985). Receptivity is also enhanced when the athletic administrators (especially the director of women's athletics) understand and support the clinician's treatment approach.

TREATMENT

Individuals with eating disorders tend to be bright and verbal. This is even more the case with competitive student-athletes. They have achieved much and have reached the pinnacle of competition. The athlete lives in an environment that enhances the likelihood that an eating disorder will develop. However, the student-athlete also has many resources for dealing with the problem if it develops.

Generally, the athlete is a high-achieving, successful, and psychologically healthy individual. The clinician can build upon these strengths in therapy, yet it may be difficult to establish therapeutic rapport because the therapist may be viewed as very threatening. Before treatment can be successful, therapeutic rapport must be established. (See Hsu, 1990, for a discussion of therapist variables related to success with these clients.) The athlete must understand that the clinician has both expertise in evaluating and treating eating disorders and an understanding of athletes' special needs and problems.

Treatment Setting. Most athletes can be treated on an outpatient basis. If they are still competing, most are not so physically impaired as to need hospitalization. Generally, clients who have experienced severe weight loss (i.e., they weigh <70% of their normal weight) and have metabolic abnormalities associated with starvation or purging are candidates for inpatient care (Anderson, 1986). Treatment on an outpatient basis is done on an individual and group basis. The group treatment is especially helpful in breaking through denial and the illusion athletes may have that all of their attitudes and feelings are normal and related to the demands of athletic competition. Participation in a group with others who have bulimic and anorexic symptoms quickly dispels that myth.

Garner (1986), in an excellent chapter on cognitive therapy for anorexia, recommends a "two-track" approach to treatment. The therapist consciously deals with eating behavior and physical condition in the first track. On the second track, the clinician assesses and begins to modify self-concept deficiencies, emotional fears, perfectionism, and disturbed relationships with others. This is a useful orientation to the treatment of a competitive athlete.

We will present a treatment approach, but it is beyond the scope of this chapter to go into great detail about therapy methods with the eating disorder client. We recommend that clinicians familiarize themselves with chapters on treatment by Fairburn (1985) and Garner (1986). In addition, books on the subject by Agras (1987), Hsu (1990), Johnson and Connors (1987), and Weiss, Katzman, and Wochik (1985) may prove very helpful to clinicians as they strive to develop expertise.

AN APPROACH TO TREATMENT

The following outline is based on our experience and the recommendations of the authors noted above.

1. Education. The importance of providing information about nutrition, the ineffectiveness of bingeing and purging for weight control, and the hazards of medical complications needs to be underscored. Nutritional issues are of particular importance to the athlete. Individuals with eating disorders are notorious for having inaccurate information and beliefs about food and weight. Athletes generally seem to be uninformed about nutritional issues (e.g. Loosli, Genson, Fillien, & Bourdet, 1986). Hazardous weight loss methods especially the ineffectiveness of laxatives and vomiting for weight control, need to be discussed in a straightforward fashion, (see Bo-Linn, Santa Ana, Morawski, & Fordtran, 1983; Lacey & Gibson, 1985). Irrational fears about gaining excessive weight can be addressed at this point. The reference materials on medical consequences in the earlier section of the chapter will also prove useful. Finally, an excellent chapter by Garner, Rockert, Olmsted, Johnson, and Coscina (1985) should prove very useful to clinicians seeking material for educating those with eating disorders.

The education of the athlete with an eating disorder can also be enhanced by use of video tapes. Several tapes have proven to be very valuable for the purpose of education. The NCAA-produced video tape series: *Afraid to eat: Eating disorders and the student athlete, Out of balance: Nutrition and weight,* and *Eating disorders: What can you do?,* specifically deal with the challenges confronting the athlete (available from Karol Media, 350 N. Pennsylvania Avenue, Wilkes Barre, PA 18773-7600). The video *Bulimia: The binge-purge obsession* is excellent for education about bulimia nervosa (available from Carle Medical Communications, 110 W. Main Street, Urbana, IL 61801-2700). Finally, two videos about dieting and anorexia have proven valuable in use with athletes: *Fear of fat: Dieting and eating disorders* and *Portraits of Anorexia* (available from Churchill Films, 12210 Nebraska Avenue, Los Angeles, CA 90025).

It is also important to set some expectations about the course of treatment and what can be expected in terms of outcome. Many individuals will leave treatment after the initial evaluation: many expect a "magical" solution and become easily frustrated when symptoms intensify shortly after the initial consultation.

2. Self-Monitoring. The importance of self-monitoring throughout treatment needs to be underscored. This is a tool for breaking through the denial and retrospective distortion/minimization that so often is present (e.g., "How have you been doing? Fine, no problem!"). Accurate record keeping permits the clinician to address specific problem-solving with the client. It leads to increased awareness of the role of certain situational cues in bingeing, purging, or dietary restriction. Self-monitoring also highlights the role of emotions and cognitions in triggering unhealthy patterns of eating and purging. Importantly, the self-monitoring serves as a way of monitoring nutrition that can counteract the effects of dichotomous (all-or-none) thinking when a client does experience periods of relapse. The self-monitoring serves as a permanent record of both success and problems that can be translated into graphic representation of progress in self-control (see, healthy days graph, Fremouw et al, 1987). Most clients will react negatively to self-monitoring initially (especially if they perceive themselves as doing poorly). The therapist needs to take this task seriously and use the information for therapeutic work so it is not perceived as " busy work."

3. Directive approach to changing behavior patterns. Clients are directed to regularize their eating to include three meals each day, improve food choices, avoid foods associated with a binge, and avoid high risk situations (e.g., eating alone when under stress). Dietitian consultation and collaboration are essential at this juncture. Dietary restriction is the norm among those with eating disorders, and its role in triggering bingeing and purging needs to be stressed continuously.

Individuals are also requested to change certain ritualistic behaviors, especially frequent weighing. Excessive weighing behavior is very common. (For example, one of our athlete-patients carried a scale in her backpack so she could weigh herself between classes—until she became too weak to transport the scale.) Initially, we ask the client to weigh no more than twice, preferably only once each week.

For those who are binge-purgers, we ask that they not engage in purging even if they have binged. Once a bulimic pattern has developed, purging tends to maintain the pattern because it is the "out" from the bingeing episode. A simple instruction is simply to avoid bathrooms after eating and to repeat the statement "Purging is not an option." Generally, individuals will vow to change things "tomorrow" and fail to interrupt the pattern once it has started. We recommend that they engage in alternative behaviors (leaving the house, talking with friends, listening to music, doing relaxation exercises) to avoid purging after a binge. For those who restrict their diet, we recommend they eat a preplanned menu regardless of their perceived hunger, at least initially. Likewise, bulimic individuals can benefit from preplanned meals so that in the midst of distress and excessive hunger they do not have to face difficult choices.

Finally, it is important to remember that hazardous weight loss practices are highly valued. Bingeing, purging, and dietary restriction all have rewarding aspects to them. Specific behavior change suggestions will be resisted because they increase distress. This distress will need to be addressed. Use of in-session eating in the form of a minibinge (Agras, 1987) and exposure plus response prevention (Rosen & Leitenberg, 1985) have proven effective in directly accessing the irrational fears of those with ingrained patterns of bingeing and purging.

4. Addressing Beliefs and Emotions. Beliefs about weight, looks and their relationship to "success" are important in the maintenance of eating disorders. Athletes are particularly vulnerable to believing that their success is directly the result of weight and food restriction. Body image issues need to be addressed, especially the misbelief that an ideal body will make everything in life wonderful. The hallmark of those with an eating disorder is an extreme reaction to weight change in the forms of depression and elation. Both extremes need to be addressed therapeutically. Readers should refer to chapters by Freedman (1990) and Rosen (1990), as well as the book by Thompson (1990) for detailed guidance in treating body image issues. Similarly, a audio tape program, *Body-image therapy: A program of self-directed change* by Cash, is available (Guilford Publications, 72 Spring Street, Dept 1V, New York, NY 10021).

Those with eating disorders use bingeing and purging and

restriction both to feel in control and to avoid emotions. The role of emotional feelings and highly perfectionistic attitudes needs to be addressed. Self-monitoring data are a rich resource for identifying feeling and mood states as well as dysfunctional identifying cognitions and self-statements. By exploring these emotions and cognitions, the clinician will be able to assist the client in identifying situations that trigger certain feelings. The binge and purge pattern usually is triggered by certain events, and the individual with an eating disorder uses eating related behaviors to cope inappropriately with a range of emotions. Within the therapeutic setting, the individual begins to experience feelings that have been numbed by the eating disorder. Group therapy sessions are a very good setting for eliciting feelings and reactions. In addition, many individuals with eating disorders are unassertive, yet they have high expectations of others. The role of interpersonal style and patterns also needs to be addressed by the clinician.

5. Maintenance and Relapse Prevention. Those who are in treatment for an eating disorder may be faded to fewer individual sessions with successful treatment. We have found that continuation in group therapy or support groups can serve as a nice bridge from intensive individual sessions. In the latter stages of therapeutic intervention issues of body image, the effect of feelings and thoughts on behavior, and self-esteem issues continue to be addressed. As stated earlier, the individual with an eating disorder usually has trouble viewing restrictive dieting as a problem—this needs to be a continual focus during maintenance sessions.

It is difficult for clients to experience lapses and these need to be addressed before becoming relapses. The client needs to be prepared to problem-solve when problematic behaviors reemerge. Most clients and the general public are quite unaware of the success achieved by those who have overcome their eating disorders through treatment. It is important to convey that although eating disorders have chronic features, individuals can get well. However, those who have had an eating disorder certainly have a vulnerability to resume the use of hazardous weight loss practices to cope with stress in the future. Clinicians should develop some familiarity with outcome studies in the eating disorder research literature so that realistic attitudes about outcome can be fostered (See Hsu, 1990, for an excellent review of the current state of knowledge.)

Relapse and the Athlete. In our experience, athletes with eating disorders and those who have features of a clinical disorder are at particular risk when not training. The rigorous training regimens serve to structure the athlete's life, and exercise itself may serve to suppress appetite. On vacation breaks or during periods of enforced inactivity due to injury, the vulnerable athlete who has an eating disorder will usually experience a resurgence of dietary restriction or bulimic behavior. Special efforts during this high-risk time should include increased frequency of visits even if the athlete has been tapering frequency of sessions and the situation has been stable.

Athletes should also be aware of the risks following participation in highly competitive sports. There is some evidence that bulimic symptoms are more likely to develop after an athlete is no longer competing (Katz, 1986).

CONCLUDING REMARKS

This chapter has provided an overview of eating disorders and the student-athlete. The recognition of the risk factors facing the athlete may lead to earlier detection and successful intervention. Women athletes are at particular risk to develop a longstanding disorder that will affect their lives long after their athletic eligibility is exhausted.

Clinicians with expertise in eating disorders need to become more involved in consulting athletic departments, coaches, and trainers. Research on coaching practices and healthy weight management in athletics needs to be conducted. Much work remains to be done in early identification of those at greatest risk. Hopefully, those reading this chapter can take leadership in developing more specific methods for treating the athlete and shaping the athletic environment to minimize the development of eating disorders.

REFERENCES

Agras, W. S. (1987). *Eating disorders: Management of obesity, bulimia, and anorexia nervosa.* New York: Pergamon Press.

Agras, W. S., & Kirkley, B. G. (1986). Bulimia: Theories of etiology. In K. D. Brownell & J. P. Foreyt (Eds.), *Handbook of eating disorders: Physiology, psychology, and treatment of obesity, anorexia and bulimia* (pp. 367-378). New York: Basic Books.

American Psychiatric Association. (1987). *Diagnostic and statistical manual of mental disorders* (3rd Edition, Revised). Washington, D. C.: Author.

Andersen, A. E. (1986). Inpatient and outpatient treatment of anorexia nervosa. In K. D. Brownell & J. P. Foreyt (Eds.), *Handbook of eating disorders: Physiology, Psychology, and treatment of obesity anorexia and bulimia* (pp. 333-350). New York: Basic Books.

Beck, A. T., & Steer, R. A. (1987). *Beck Depression Inventory manual.* New York: The Psychological Corporation.

Bo-Linn, G. W., Santa Ana, C. A., Morawski, S. G., & Fordtran, J. S. (1983). Purging and calorie absorption in bulimic patients and normal women. *Annals of Internal Medicine, 99,* 14-17.

Borgen, J. S., & Corbin, C. B. (1987). Eating disorders among female athletes. *The Physician and Sportsmedicine, 15(2),* 89-95.

Boskind-White, M., & White, W. C. (1986). Bulimarexia: A historical-sociocultural perspective. In K. D. Brownell & J. P. Foreyt (Eds.), *Handbook of eating disorders: Physiology, Psychology, and treatment of obesity anorexia and bulimia* (pp. 353-366). New York: Basic Books.

Bray, G. (1978). Definitions, measurement, and classification of obesity. *International Journal of Obesity, 2,* 1-14.

Bruch, H. (1973). *Eating disorders: Obesity, anorexia nervosa, and the person within.* New York: Basic Books.

Bruch, H. (1981). Developmental considerations of anorexia nervosa and obesity. *Canadian Journal of Psychiatry, 26,* 212-217.

Button, E. J., & Whitehouse, A. (1981). Subclinical anorexia nervosa. *Psychological Medicine, 11,* 509-516.

Calabrese, L. H., Kirkendall, D. T., Floyd, M., Rapoport, S., Williams, G. W., Weiker, G. G., & Bergfeld, J. A. (1983). Menstrual abnormalities, nutritional patterns, and body composition in female classical ballet dancers. *The Physician and Sportsmedicine, 11(2),* 86-98.

Chipman, J. J., Hagan, R. D., Edlin, J. C., Soll, M. H., & Carruth, B. R. (1983). Excessive weight loss in the athletic adolescent. *Journal of Adolescent Health Care, 3,* 247-252.

Cooper, P. J., & Fairburn, C. G. (1983). Binge-eating and self-induced vomiting in the community. *British Journal of Psychiatry, 142*, 139-144.

Cooper, P. J., Taylor, M. J., Cooper, Z., & Fairburn, C. G. (1987). The development and validation of the Body Shape Questionnaire. *International Journal of Eating Disorders, 6*, 485-494.

Copeland, P. M., & Herzog, D. B. (1987). Menstrual abnormalities in bulimia. In J. I. Hudson & H. G. Pope (Eds.), *The psychobiology of bulimia* (pp. 29-54). Washington, D.C.: American Psychiatric Press.

Drewnowski, A., Yee, D. K., & Krahn, D. D. (1988). Bulimia in college women. *American Journal of Psychiatry, 145*, 753-755.

Druss, R. G. & Silverman, J. A. (1979). Body image and perfectionism of ballerinas: Comparison and contrast with anorexia nervosa. *General Hospital Psychiatry, 1*, 115-121.

Dummer, G. M., Rosen, L. W., Heusner, W. W., Roberts, P. J., & Counsilman, J. E. (1987). Pathogenic weight-control behaviors of young competitive swimmers. *The Physician and Sportsmedicine, 15*(5), 75-86.

Einerson, J., Ward, A., & Hanson, P. (1988). Exercise responses in females with anorexia nervosa. *International Journal of Eating Disorders, 7*, 253-260.

Fairburn, C. G. (1985). Cognitive-behavioral treatment for bulimia. In D. M. Garner & P. E. Garfinkel (Eds.), *Handbook of psychotherapy for anorexia nervosa and bulimia* (pp. 160-192). New York: Guilford Press.

Fairburn, C. G., Cooper, Z., & Cooper, P. J. (1986). The clinical features and maintenance of bulimia nervosa. In K. D. Brownell & J. P. Foreyt (Eds.), *Handbook of eating disorders: Physiology, psychology, and treatment of obesity anorexia and bulimia* (pp. 389-404). New York: Basic Books.

Falls, H. B., & Humphrey, L. D. (1978). Body type and composition differences between placers and nonplacers in an AIAW gymnastics meet. *Research Quarterly, 49*(1), 43.

Freedman, R. (1990). Cognitive-behavioral perspectives on body-image change. In T. F. Cash & T. Pruzinsky (Eds.), *Body images: Development, deviance and change* (pp. 272-295). New York:

Guilford Press.

Fremouw, W. J., Wiener, A. L., & Seime, R. J. (1987). Self-monitoring for bulimia. *Innovations in Clinical Practice, 6,* 325-332.

Garner, D. M. (1986). Cognitive therapy for anorexia nervosa. In K. D. Brownell & J. P. Foreyt (Eds.), *Handbook of eating disorders: Physiology, Psychology, and treatment of obesity anorexia and bulimia* (pp. 301-327). New York: Basic Books.

Garner, D. M., & Garfinkel, P. E. (1980). Socio-cultual factors in the development of anorexia nervosa. *Psychological Medicine, 10,* 647-656.

Garner, D. M., Olmsted, M. P., & Polivy, J. (1983). Development and validation of a multidimensional eating disorder inventory for anorexia nervosa and bulimia. *International Journal of Eating Disorders, 2,* 15-34.

Garner, D. M., Rockert, W., Olmsted, M. P., Johnson, C., & Coscina, D. V. (1985). Psychoeducational principles in the treatment of bulimia and anorexia nervosa. In D. M. Garner & P. E. Garfinkel (Eds.), *Handbook of psychotherapy for anorexia nervosa and bulimia* (pp. 513-572). New York: Guilford Press.

Hamilton, L. H., Brooks-Gunn, J., & Warren, M. P. (1985). Socio-cultural influences on eating disorders in professional female ballet dancers. *International Journal of Eating Disorders, 4,* 465-477.

Harris, M. B., & Greco, D. (1990). Weight control and weight concern in competitive female gymnasts. *Journal of Sport & Exercise Psychology, 12,* 427-433.

Hart, K. J., & Ollendick, T. H. (1985). Prevalence of bulimia in working and university women. *American Journal of Psychiatry, 142,* 851-854.

Henderson, M., & Freeman, C. P. L. (1987). A self-rating scale for bulimia: The "Bite." *British Journal of Psychiatry, 150,* 18-24.

Hood, J., Moore, T., & Garner, D. (1982). Locus of control as a measure of ineffectiveness in anorexia nervosa. *Journal of Consulting and Clinical Psychology, 50,* 3-13.

Hsu, L. K. G. (1988). The outcome of anorexia nervosa: A reappraisal. *Psychological Medicine, 18,* 807-812.

Hsu, L. K. G. (1990). *Eating disorders*. New York: Guilford Press.

Johnson, C. (1985). Initial consultation for patients with bulimia and anorexia nervosa. In D. M. Garner & P. E. Garfinkel (Eds.), *Handbook of psychotherapy for anorexia nervosa and bulimia* (pp. 19-51). New York: Guilford Press.

Johnson, C., & Connors, M. E. (1987). *The etiology and treatment of bulimia nervosa: A biopsychosocial perspective*. New York: Basic Books.

Katz, J. L. (1986). Long-distance running, anorexia nervosa, and bulimia: A report of two cases. *Comprehensive Psychiatry, 27*, 74-78.

Katzman, M., Wolchik, S., & Braver, T. (1984). The prevalence of frequent binge eating and bulimia in a non-clinical college sample. *International Journal of Eating Disorders, 3*, 53-62.

Kennedy, S., & Garfinkel, P. E. (1985). Anorexia nervosa. In R. E. Hales & A. J. Frances (Eds.), *American Psychiatric Association: Annual Review* (Vol. 4, pp 438-463). Washington, D.C.: American Psychiatric Association.

Lacey, J. H., & Gibson, E. (1985). Controlling weight by purgation and vomiting: A comparative study of bulimics. *Journal of Psychiatric Research, 19*, 337-341.

Loosli, A. R., Genson, J., Fillien, D. M., & Bourdet, K. (1986). Nutrition habits and knowledge in competitive female gymnasts. *The Physician and Sportsmedicine, 14*(8), 118-130.

Lucas, A. R., Beard, C. M., O'Fallon, W. M., & Kurland, L. T. (1988). Anorexia nervosa in Rochester, Minnesota: A 45-year study. *Mayo Clinic Proceedings, 63*, 433-442.

McSherry, J. A. (1984). The diagnostic challenge of anorexia nervosa. *American Family Physician, 29*, 141-144.

Metropolitan Life Insurance Company (1983). *Statistical bulletin, 64*, 2-9.

Mitchell, J. E. (1984). Medical complications of anorexia nervosa and bulimia. *Psychiatric Medicine, 1*, 229-255.

Mitchell, J. E. (1986a). Anorexia nervosa: Medical and physiological aspects. In K. D. Brownell & J. P. Foreyt (Eds.), *Handbook of eating disorders: Physiology, psychology, and treatment of obesity anorexia and bulimia* (pp. 247-265). New York: Basic Books.

Mitchell, J. E. (1986b). Bulimia: Medical and physiological aspects. In K. D. Brownell & J. P. Foreyt (Eds.), *Handbook of eating disorders: Physiology, psychology, and treatment of obesity anorexia and bulimia* (pp. 379-388). New York: Basic Books.

Mitchell, J. E., Pomeroy, C., & Huber, M. (1988). A clinician's guide to the eating disorders medicine cabinet. *International Journal of Eating Disorders, 7*, 211-223.

Mitchell, J. E., Pyle, R. L., & Eckert, E. D. (1985). Bulimia.In R. E. Hales & A. J. Frances (Eds.), *American Psychiatric Association: Annual Review* (Vol. 4, pp 464-480). Washington, D.C.: American Psychiatric Association.

Pyle, R. L., Mitchell, J. E., Eckert, E. D., Halvorson, P. A., Neuman, P. A., & Goff, G. M. (1983). The incidence of bulimia in freshman college students. *International Journal of Eating Disorders, 2*, 75-85.

Rigotti, N. A., Nussbaum, S. R., Herzog, D. B., & Neer, R. M. (1984). Osteoporosis in women with anorexia nervosa. *New England Journal of Medicine, 311*, 1601-1606.

Rodin, J., Silberstein, L. R., & Striegel-Moore, R. H. (1985). Women and weight: A normative discontent. In T. B. Sonderegger (Ed.), *Nebraska symposium on motivation: Vol. 32, Psychology and Gender* (pp. 267-307). Lincoln: University of Nebraska Press.

Root, M. P., Fallon, P., & Friedrich, W. N. (1986). *Bulimia: A systems approach to treatment.* New York: Norton.

Rosen, J. C. (1990). Body-image disturbance in eating disorders. In T. F. Cash & T. Pruzinsky (Eds.), *Body images: Development, deviance and change* (pp. 190-214). New York: Guilford Press.

Rosen, J. C., & Gross, J. (1987). Prevalence of weight reducing and weight gaining in adolescent girls and boys. *Health Psychology, 6*, 131-147.

Rosen, L. W., & Hough, D. O. (1988). Pathogenic weight-control behaviors of female college gymnasts.*The Physician and Sportsmedicine, 16* (9), 141-144.

Rosen, J. C., & Leitenberg, H. (1985). Exposure plus response prevention treatment of bulimia. In D. M. Garner & P. E. Garfinkel (Eds.), *Handbook of psychotherapy for anorexia nervosa and bulimia* (pp. 193-209). New York: Guilford Press.

Rosen, L. W., McKeag, D. B., Hough, D. O., & Curley, V. (1986). Pathogenic weight-control behavior in female athletes. *The Physician and Sportsmedicine, 14* (1), 79-86.

Shangold, M., Rebar, R. W., Wentz, A. C., & Schiff, I. (1990). Evaluation and management of menstrual dysfunction in athletes. *Journal of the American Medical Association, 262,* 1665-1669.

Smith, M. C., & Thelen, M. H. (1984). Development and validation of a test for bulimia. *Journal of Consulting and Clinical Psychology, 52,* 863-872.

Smith, N. J. (1980). Excessive weight loss and food aversion in athletes simulating anorexia nervosa. *Pediatrics, 66,* 139-142.

Steen, S. N., & McKinney, S. (1986). Nutrition assessment of college wrestlers. *The Physician and Sportsmedicine, 14* (11), 100-116.

Striegel-Moore, R. H., Silberstein, L. R., & Rodin, J. (1986). Toward an understanding of risk factors for bulimia. *American Psychologist, 41,* 246-263.

Thompson, J. K. (1990). *Body image disturbance: Assessment and treatment.* New York: Pergamon Press.

Thornton, J. S. (1990). Feast or famine: Eating disorders in athletes. *The Physician and Sportsmedicine, 18(4),* 116-122.

Weight, L. M., & Noakes, T. D. (1987). Is running an analogue to anorexia? A survey of the incidence of eating disorders in female distance runners. *Medicine and Science in Sports and Exercise, 19(3),* 213-217.

Weiss, L., Katzman, M., & Wolchik, S. (1985). *Treating bulimia: A psychoeducational approach.* New York: Pergamon Press.

Williamson, D. A. (1990). *Assessment of eating disorders: Obesity, anorexia, and bulimia nervosa.* New York: Pergamon Press.

Yates, A. (1989). Current perspectives on the eating disorders: I. History, psychological, and biological aspects. *Journal of the Academy of Child and Adolescent Psychiatry, 28,* 813-828.

Yates, A., Leehey, K., & Shisslak, C. M. (1983). Running—an analogue of anorexia? *New England Journal of Medicine, 308,* 251-255.

Zucker, P., Avner, P., Bayder, S., Brotman, A., Moore, K., & Zimmerman, J. (1985). Eating disorders in young athletes. *The Physician and Sportsmedicine, 13(11),* 89-106.

CHAPTER 11

Counseling Injured and Disabled Student-Athletes: A Guide for Understanding and Intervention

Roy Tunick, Edward Etzel, and John Leard

Thousands of college student-athletes are injured during practice and competition every year. This chapter provides information about the psychological aspects of injury and suggestions for those who work with people who have suffered an athletic injury.

Recently, the incidence of athletic injuries and related disabilities experienced by college student-athletes has been increasing. This increase has occurred despite the fact that the quality of athletic equipment, facilities and physical conditioning techniques continue to improve. A recent survey of some 4,000 National Collegiate Athletic Association (NCAA) Division I student-athletes revealed that approximately 50% had experienced an athletic-related injury (American Institutes for Research, 1988). Furthermore, it is apparent that the injury rates of those involved in intercollegiate athletics are greater than the injury rates of those who participate in other collegiate extracurricular activities (American Institutes for Research, 1988; MacIntosh, Skrien, & Shepard, 1971). Worse, for the student-athletes, a considerable number of respondents in the first study (i.e., approximately 25% of the football and basketball players and 12% of participants in other sports) said that they felt "extremely intense" or "intense" pressure to ignore their physical problems.

These data stand in contrast to the widespread perception that athletes in general and injured athletes in particular are "super healthy" and that injury, especially related psychological considerations, should perhaps not be major concern (May & Sieb, 1987). Many authors of sports medicine, counseling, and sport psychology studies maintain that this assumption is far from the truth (Danish, 1984; Ermler & Thomas, 1990; McDonald & Hardy, 1990; Nideffer, 1983; Rotella & Heyman, 1986; Samples, 1987). Short or long-term loss of functioning associated with an injury can have a considerable, often unrecognized impact on student-athletes, whose "livelihood" and well-being depend to a great extent upon their physical health and skills. For those who work with student-athletes (e.g., counselors, trainers, coaches), knowledge about injury and its far-reaching effects is something of great value and utility.

Today, several hundred thousand young people participate in intercollegiate athletics in universities, colleges, junior, and community colleges. Within the 900 universities that belong to the NCAA alone, some 270,000 young people participate in intercollegiate athletics. This figure translates to approximately 300 student-athletes per campus on the average. If roughly 50% of student-athletes are injured at some time during their time on campus, those who provide services to student-athletes face the considerable problem of attending to the needs of hundreds of people with a disability.

Injured student-athletes have many needs as they embark upon the road to recovery. Attention usually focuses on the necessary medical assistance provided by trainers and physicians. Unfortunately, the psychological needs of the injured are typically unattended.

Although informal supportive counseling is provided by some sports medicine staff members, few are trained to provide psychological first aid to the injured. The presence of a professional psychologist, counselor, or psychiatrist on the sports medicine staff is apparently rare. Nevertheless, there are many ways that such professionals can help injured student-athletes psychologically cope with their losses. Without psychological rehabilitation, many student-athletes may be unprepared to return to training and competition, feel afraid about doing so, remain vulnerable to reinjury, and demonstrate puzzling performance decrements (Rotella & Heyman, 1986).

The three purposes of this chapter are: 1) to review some definitions and theoretical notions regarding the nature and consequences of injury/disability, examining some psychosocial and somatopsychological aspects of injury/disability; 2) to share and discuss various intervention strategies for helping those who work with injured and disabled student-athletes; and 3) provide a brief case example of a helping professional's work with a student-athlete who suffered a career-ending physical problem. Hopefully, by addressing this often neglected topic, the following information will assist those who work with injured student-athletes to better help the afflicted cope with their losses.

INJURY, DISABILITY, AND SOMATOPSYCHOLOGY

Before proceeding much further, it seems appropriate to attempt to define two important terms: injury and disability. No generally agreed-upon definitions seem to exist for both terms. Perhaps the most useful one is the definition of a "reportable injury" used by the National Collegiate Athletic Association's "Injury Surveillance System." An injury is considered to be a loss of physical functioning that 1) "occurred as a result of participation in an organized intercollegiate practice or game", 2) "required medical attention by a team athletic trainer or physician", and 3) "resulted in restriction of the student-athlete's participation for one or more days beyond the day of the injury" ("Injury Rates", 1990). As used in this chapter, injury implies that the affected person will probably return to athletic participation. Examples of an injury viewed in this way are nonsurgical sprains or strains.

A term used in conjunction with injury is disability. Here,

disability will generally refer to a medically defined state or condition that imposes longer term or permanent limitations or handicap upon an individual's independent functioning. Disability then is seen as a consequence of a student-athlete's incurring an injury. Moreover, disability implies that the injured individual is unable to or limited in his or her ability to perform the various expected roles and tasks (Whitten, 1975). Injury to a paired organ (e.g., eye or kidney) is an example of a disabling athletic condition.

Student-athletes who are disabled by injury are often limited in their ability to continue to participate in their usual routine of attending classes, training and competing with their team, caring for their day-to-day personal responsibilities, and carrying on with their everyday personal lives. Injury and disability disrupt the balance in their already stressful life-styles.

Injury and disability not only disrupt a student-athlete's daily patterns of functioning but can also have great psychosocial impact on those who are struggling to adjust to their changed physical condition, which is typically unexpected and unwanted. Barker, Wright, Myerson, and Gonick (in Wright, 1960) refer to "variations in physique that affect the psychological situation of a person by influencing the effectiveness of this body as a tool for actions or by serving as a stimulus to himself or others" as "somatopsychological" (p.2). Somatopsychology is a generally accepted theory that presumes somatic disturbances have an effect on one's psychological functioning. Garner (1977) identifies a number of somatopsychic concepts relevant to injured or disabled persons. A few are presented below.

First, a person's total personality prior to the development of the disturbed structural and physiological functioning crucially affects the response to injury. All life experiences are important factors that influence how one is affected by the change. Some of these factors may include one's developmental history, family, cultural and social experiences, motivation, level of aspiration, tolerance for stress and frustration, and self-concept. Each individual will interpret their changed physical condition based on his or her personality. A student-athlete's prior level of psychological functioning will affect his or her unique reaction to a disabling condition (Samples, 1987). The preinjury mental health condition of a person is often called one's "pre-morbid" personality.

As an aside, the investigation of personality variables as predictors of injury proneness has been a popular avenue of research (Burckes, 1981; Rosenblum, 1979; Sanderson, 1977). Some investigators (Holmes & Rahe, 1967; Jackson et al, 1978; Valliant, 1981) have observed a relationship between injury and certain psychological factors (e.g., life stress, soft mindedness, dependency). Some of this research suggests a causal relationship between injury and personality characteristics, instead of assuming a somatopsychological relationship (i.e., the effect of bodily function or malfunction on psychological functioning) (Wright, 1960). In contrast, other researchers (Abadie, 1976; Brown, 1971; Gover & Koppenhaver, 1965) have found no significant connection between athletic injury and personality.

Summarizing the literature on psychological variables relating to the incidence of athletic injury, Bergandi (1985) concluded that the causes of athletic injury are complex. He determined that many individual variables such as size, strength, level of conditioning, personality characteristics, combined with the demands of a particular sport, influence the incidence of athletic injury. Overall, the research in this area does not point to any highly reliable personality predictors of injury (Rotella & Heyman, 1986).

The personal meaning of the disturbance can have far-reaching implications for injury rehabilitation. In general, the greater the severity of the physiological damage and loss of functioning, the greater the somatopsychic influences. Furthermore, it is known that we all value certain parts of our body more than others. Therefore, a broken thumb on a quarterback's throwing hand may have some special symbolic significance that may lead to disability disproportionate to the functional loss. It is important to realize that an individual's experience of physical loss can surpass the objective impact of damage and often affect self-concept. Furthermore, the same medically defined condition can produce a different set of psychological problems for different owners (i.e., the impact may be quite different for those who play different sports or positions). Sensitivity to the different response patterns of each student-athlete to injury is an important concept to keep in mind.

Second, Garner (1977) has pointed out that anxiety typically accompanies any injury or illness in which physical integrity is threatened. The person who is disabled is confronted with many threats to personality and life that often create anxiety. Uncertainties about the nature, consequences, and duration of the impairment are thought to contribute to this anxiety.

STAGES OF ADJUSTMENT: A SEQUENCE OF EMOTIONAL RESPONSES

Emotional reactions to disability are commonly described in terms of stages or phases of adjustment, or in terms of theories of mourning or grieving as they relate to loss. Engel (1961), Kerr (1969), Kubler-Ross (1969), Schlossberg (1981), Schneider (1984), Shontz (1965), and Tunick and Tunick (1980), have characterized common psychological reactions that a disability or loss of functioning can impose on an individual's adjustment to loss. Although some propose that only two stages of adjustment exist (McDonald & Hardy, 1990; Shontz, 1975), the process of reacting to loss is most often divided into five phases: 1) shock, 2) realization, 3) mourning, 4) acknowledgement, and 5) coping/reformulation. Each phase is associated with certain emotional and behavioral responses that change as an individual progresses through it. It is important to keep in mind that each person reacts to his or her condition in a unique manner. Therefore, reactions may vary, resulting in some phases and behaviors not appearing at all, appearing in combination with others, or being repeated or recycled. Nevertheless, Athelstan (1981) cautions helpers to be sensitive to these phases and their associated behaviors so that we can be alert to the impact a person's psychological responses can have on an individual's progress and rehabilitation.

Shock. This phase is usually observed soon after the injury. Most often, shock occurs during the first few hours or days of the disability. The injured individual usually experiences muted reactions to the condition, reacting minimally with little apparent understanding that something is wrong with his or her body. The person may deny the condition or be so unaware of it that he or she does not demonstrate any noticeable anxiety. In this state, the individual is still viewing him or herself as before the injury, rejecting all incongruence between body and function. The sudden onset, unexpectedness, and seriousness of the athletic injury may intensify the shock reaction.

During this phase, student-athletes will often reject the assistance of a counselor, trainer, or physician because they view such help as unnecessary. If the defense of denial is being used by the injured person (as it frequently is), helpers should be prepared to feel quite frustrated. Indeed, as Nideffer (1983) tells us, it is very hard to develop a working relationship with a person who is avoidant or even laughs at you. In such situations, the counselor may have little to offer but friendly support. Counseling interventions during this phase may have little observable impact on the student-athlete who is now a patient. The counselor should be primarily concerned with establishing rapport with the injured person to build a foundation for possible future interventions. However, the student-athlete may be receptive to assistance during this phase due to the relative absence of intense emotionality usually confronted in some latter phases. Again, each injured person's response will be unique.

Realization. In this phase the disabled individual begins to realize that something is wrong. This realization is usually accompanied by anxiety and in some cases even panic, anger, and depression. It is important to appreciate that in the person's mind (and very often in reality) the disability has created a seemingly insurmountable barrier to leading a "normal life," as the individual begins to recognize that independent functioning and athletic participation are threatened. The student-athlete progressing through this phase, may express anger toward others for not being able to be cured quickly. At times, the injured person may make statements such as "As soon as I'm well", and "When I get out of here ...I am going to...." Implicit in these messages is striving toward goals that were embraced prior to their acquired condition, goals that presuppose a normal body. The astute clinician should be sensitive to the possibility of this anger turning inward, resulting in the person's experiencing a variety of depressive symptoms.

During this phase, the disabled student-athlete may be fearful. Helpers need to acknowledge and accept such fear and demonstrate that they will be there for the person when times are tough. Well-intended statements such as "Don't worry, things are bound to get better soon" should be avoided. Instead, recognizing the seriousness of the problem and the injured person's intense reaction to the condition, statements like "I realize that this is a scary time for you because you don't know what to expect, but I will help you work with difficulties as they come up... I cannot promise you miracles, but I can promise you help when you want it" will probably be more helpful. Helpers should be accepting of the student-athlete and attempt to normalize the person's experience when it is appropriate.

Mourning. This phase is characterized by intense distress. Overwhelmed, the disabled individual may feel hopeless and helpless. The finality of what has been lost has fully entered the person's consciousness. The student-athlete (especially the seriously injured) is often convinced that everything has been lost and that he or she can no longer achieve life-long ambitions. The disability has spread or metastasized, to all functions and aspirations. Depression and suicidal ideation are not unusual. The disabled person's ability to tap available sources of support to cope dissipates. The student-athlete may avoid contact with others, become uncommunicative, and even resist treatment as the physical and psychological battle against the disability appears to have been lost. During this phase, it is important for helpers to avoid being critical. Statements such as "Stop feeling sorry for yourself" or "Tough it out" are counter-productive: they make the individual more introspective and demonstrate to the injured person that indeed no one understands the situation. Instead, those trying to help the afflicted person need to listen carefully, provide support and encouragement, disseminate small doses of information, and attempt to arrange the environment so that it is responsive to the person's needs. The purpose of such efforts is gradually to change the figure-ground relationship between what the person can no longer do and what they still retain.

Acknowledgment. In this phase the injured student-athlete begins to come to grips with the disability by gradually appreciating the nature of the loss and its associated limitations. Depression and anxiety often continue to be experienced. The depressed person, particularly someone who has incurred a severe injury and/or endured prolonged hospitalization, may still experience a loss of control, choices, independence, and perceived loss of identity (Grief & Matarazzo, 1982).

It is often mistakenly assumed that depression during the phase of acknowledgment is a necessary prerequisite for adjustment; that is, if depression does not occur the person will never adequately or completely adjust to the condition. Although depression during the acknowledgment phase occurs often, it is not experienced by everyone.

Another common feature of this phase is that people with disabilities often may rely too much on others for help accomplishing tasks they can perform themselves. Here too the counselor must listen carefully to the client, encourage activities that will likely be self-reinforcing, recognize and call attention to personal resources and progress, as well as allow for as many choices as possible (Greif and Matarazzo, 1982). Encouraging the injured student-athlete to assume personal responsibility and giving the individual the opportunity to do so are important strategies in this phase of recovery. Furthermore, increasing social contact (i.e., the frequency and variety of visitations from others) may help the injured person work through this stage.

Coping and Reformulation. This phase normally occurs after some degree of resolution of the disability has occurred. Schneider (1984) stated that the resolution liberates energy once tied to the past. Now this energy is available to broaden personal awareness in ways perhaps never before acknowledged. Having learned to cope with any residual limitations that may remain, the person reasserts him or herself emotionally. Having worked through the disability the person is ready to get on with life.

In this phase, the disability remains mostly in "ground" (i.e., in the background of awareness) as the injured person does not continually attend to the limitations (if any) imposed by the condition. However, at times, the disability may reemerge into "figure" (i.e., becomes the focus of awareness). This regression may be prompted, for example, when the student-athlete sees someone injured, encounters a similarly injured person in the training room, or is personally reinjured. When this happens, the student-athlete must face the loss and any related limitations once again. When this occurs the student-athlete may re-experience emotional distress upon being reminded of the past. Reluctance to train or compete (which may involve considerable anxiety even to a phobic degree) as well as performance decrements on the part of those who continue to train and perform is sometimes observed. Fears about reinjury typically underlie such responses. Although they may be irrational to coaches and trainers, such fears are real for the student-athlete and should not be discounted by others. Regardless of the rationality of the fears, helpers must work to appreciate what the student-athlete is experiencing and work with that person to help overcome this problem. Hopefully, at this stage, the person has the experience and resources to make the duration of these responses brief. It is important for the counselor to educate the client and normalize these regressions so that they can be seen as what they are; that is, they do not reflect poorly on the person's ability to cope or self-worth. It is also critical for the counselor to avoid using language like "You need to accept your disability." Thoreson and Kerr (1978) also caution us to stop using terms like "acceptance" when working with persons who are disabled because the communication has intrinsically derogating aspects.

Given the opportunity, counselors can help educate coaches, teammates, and trainers about the language to use around injured student-athletes. Statements commonly voiced by coaches and teammates like "Tough it out" or "Suck it up" as well as questions about the person's "giving 100%" are clearly not useful. Rotella and Heyman (1986) point out that sport leaders (coaches in particular) need to know that it is essential to make the injured people feel cared for and important, not as if they are worth less than they were when they were fully functioning. During this critical period, such influential people can foster or destroy trust and confidence by their treatment of the injured. They must not ignore or discourage injured or disabled student-athletes.

SOCIAL IMPACT OF INJURY ON THE STUDENT-ATHLETE

Together with the emotional consequences experienced by the disabled or injured student-athlete, loss of functioning can have a profound social impact on the person's ability to cope with his or her condition. The student-athlete may experience a loss of social status, value loss, isolation and altered or strained interpersonal relations, as well as academic performance problems.

Social Status. Once injured, student-athletes tend to lose social status. (They are not part of the same world they once belonged to.) Because they no longer appear to serve as a contributing members of the team, they often are not seen in the same light as before their injury. Removed from the day-to-day activities of the team, the injured may no longer receive the same amount of attention from coaches and teammates, and may be ignored altogether. The "on-the-shelf" or "down" athlete is no longer a part of the team or its social activities, unless (rare) efforts are made to keep the individual engaged in team activities. This transition is often rapid and demoralizing.

Injured student-athletes also stand to lose special status among the student body and the public. Out of the limelight, they can no longer discuss personal athletic exploits, respond to admiring interrogatives, or share other customary interpersonal interactions. The injured student-athlete's comparative value to fans and the media is quickly reduced as the focus of attention shifts to the new faces and numbers of replacements.

Isolation. Not only do student-athletes lose perceived value and status, but they may now also have to brave considerable social isolation associated with their new, unwanted status. An injury can drastically change the usual interaction patterns with others because the student-athlete cannot train, compete, and may not be allowed to travel with the team. Isolation can be exacerbated by teammates' and coaches' avoidance of contact with the injured student-athlete. It may create a situation in which the student-athlete feels "invisible," unable to make sense of the apparent rejection by others who previously valued him or her (Ermler & Thomas, 1990). This avoidance comes from three fronts. Others may avoid the injured person from a sense of awkwardness; that is, coaches or teammates may feel uncomfortable or not know how to interact with the injured person. The second is a function of "out of sight, out of mind;" since the injured student-athlete is not part of the team's routine activities, he or she is not thought about. Third, the injured athlete may serve as a threat to other athletes and coaches, in that the injury confronts them with their own vulnerability or uncomfortable memories of past losses. Therefore, they intentionally or unintentionally avoid the injured student-athlete, making him or her feel alienated.

Academic and Developmental Concerns. Injury may not only affect the individual's physical, emotional, and social functioning, but it can also have a major impact on the student's academic status and person from a developmental standpoint. The injured student-athlete must often confront new or ignored academic problems and changing priorities. Previously caring and understanding instructors may now appear to be aloof, demanding and unsympathetic. At one time, instructors may have afforded the student-athlete additional time to complete required tasks or administered examinations at different times due to unique training or travel demands, but now may not understand the need for accommodation. Familiar training, conditioning, and studying routines have been replaced with different schedule demands of physical rehabilitation, doctor visits, and personal care. These and other changes in routine may create additional problems with fatigue, motivation, and concentration, resulting in poor academic performance.

Disabled student-athletes (particularly those who must cope with a lasting, serious impairment) may be forced to face developmental concerns never before considered or face such concerns earlier than planned. Confusion about one's self, personal values, life goals, relationships with others and dealing with ambiguity may be experienced. Suddenly, life appears telescoped, decision making appears more crucial, career choices more difficult, as concern about other areas of life beyond sport becomes much more important. If physical prowess and athletics have been emphasized over intellectual pursuits, injury will probably have some profound implications. Those who have foreclosed their identities (Chartrand & Lent, 1987), having banked on the wish to become professional athletes, can find the loss of functioning personally devastating. Career and academic goals based on physical assets now must be drastically altered. The problem of "Who am I now that I cannot play" often has more impact on this type of student-athlete than on one who valued and developed both physical and intellectual assets. Therefore, it is important for those who work with student-athletes to actively encourage them to be realistic in setting long-term goals, so as to avoid the discouragement of not having their dreams come true.

IMPLICATIONS FOR HELPERS

It is easy to see that injury can have numerous, often profound effects on a student-athlete's psychosocial and academic functioning and future goals. Implications for those in contact with the injured student-athlete, including sports medicine staff, coaches, counselors and sport psychologists will follow.

Sports Medicine Staff. Sports medicine professionals (e.g., team physicians and trainers) are in a unique position, in that they interact with the student-athlete almost exclusively in the early phases of injury. From the start, they need to provide concrete information to the injured person regarding the severity of injury, potential and assumed limitations of the injury, and the likelihood of a full recovery, as well as information on treatment plans. Sports medicine staff must be aware that these issues may need to be addressed repeatedly, due to the disabled athlete's inability to appreciate the implications of the injury at various stages of adjustment to his or her condition.

Furthermore, sports medicine staff need to avoid or disown two common misconceptions: 1) student-athletes are somehow well-equipped to cope with their newly acquired condition, and 2) they are somehow more likely than nonathletes to recover fully from a severe injury because of their exceptional pre-morbid physical condition. The second misconception, in particular, can potentially encourage mistreatment of the athlete, in that one could easily dismiss unusual behavior associated with the grieving process as being "not like him or her." The injured student-athlete's need for psychological as well as medical help must not be overlooked.

Another implication for sports medicine professionals is to recommend that treatment be provided within an athlete's customary environment whenever possible. When this is done, the disabled person has the opportunity to continue to interact with peers in a familiar setting, thus reducing the sense of isolation from others. Ermler and Thomas (1990) recommend providing variability and choices of treatments whenever possible, which can foster a sense of involvement within the athlete and thereby reduce the sense of isolation. In addition, they suggest that trainers avoid treating injured athletes in separate areas, continue to conduct strength training for unafflicted body parts, and utilize alternative training equipment in order to enhance the athlete's involvement. Setting specific, realistic short-term rehabilitation goals is also seen as helpful because they can increase the injured athlete's sense of personal involvement and satisfaction with the process of recovery (DePalma & DePalma, 1989).

Athletic trainers probably have more opportunities to interact with injured student-athletes than do any other professionals. They can use this time not only to physically treat the athlete but also to be alert to changes in the athlete's emotional equilibrium. The trainer is in an excellent position to monitor the injured person's mental status and make timely referrals to on-campus mental health professionals to promote the athlete's psychological well-being.

Sports medicine staff should be careful when communicating with injured student-athletes. They need to avoid communicating negative, judgmental attitudes regarding the athlete's condition by not using statements that convey disability or inferiority. For example, phrases such as "Move your bad knee," "Lift your broken hand", or "Push off with your good foot" serve to communicate a negative message to the athlete regarding his or her condition. Alternatively, language such as "Move your left knee" that does not convey judgment about the athlete's condition should be used. Another more nonverbal approach involves the trainer placing a hand on the athlete's body part and asking the person to move that particular part of the body during an exercise.

As suggested above, trainers can also assist the injured person by providing concrete information concerning the athlete's prescription of treatment, expected rate of recovery, changes in range of motion, and any somatosensory experiences that may occur during treatment. Such information can help reduce the anxiety the injured student-athlete experiences. Sports medicine staff should also be realistic in communicating about what to expect from a forthcoming treatment intervention. They should avoid phrases such as "This shouldn't hurt much," when in fact pressure and some pain is the usual reaction and expected response.

Coaches. As teachers, disciplinarians, and parental figures, coaches have a great deal of direct and indirect influence on the disabled student-athlete. When a student-athlete is injured, the coach is in a position to facilitate or hinder the adjustment process of the athlete to the disabling condition. Understandably, the coach must be concerned about and responsible for more than one athlete. However, the injured person needs to know that he or she is still part of the team or "family" even though loss has changed the person's ability to function as before. The coach needs to act as a facilitator for the athlete and demonstrate that the coaching staff is concerned about the student as a person and not just as a performer.

Many simple actions on the part of the coach can go a long way toward communicating concern. Simply going onto the field or court with trainers when a person is injured is an important initial gesture that many coaches unfortunately eschew. Other ways in which to assist student-athletes in their adjustment process are to involve the injured person as a resource for other athletes and to have injured athletes attend practices and competitions on the bench or sidelines with other teammates. The coach is also in the position to encourage the athlete to continue physical rehabilitation and counseling. The longer or more frequently the coach and/or his staff avoid contact and neglect the injured athlete via avoidance, the greater the likelihood the athlete will feel used, isolated, and rejected.

For the most part, the coach (or an assistant coach) has the means with which to make periodic contact with injured student-athletes to review their physical and emotional status. A helping professional could help model this process and promote the importance of contact by coaches after injury and during recovery. Indeed, spending time regularly to visit the injured in the training room can be a powerful, supportive endeavor. At the very least, the coach should instruct his assistants to make periodic contact with the student in order to assess the athlete's progress and express the staff's interest. Often the injured athlete, like other people who become disabled, has many well-wishers during the early phases of their condition, but as the condition and the recovery period continue, fewer and fewer people make such needed contact. This often results in a pronounced feeling of isolation and exploitation for the student-athlete. The coach can also assist injured athletes in their adjustment by encouraging noninjured athletes to maintain contact with their injured peers. Such contact by teammates not only helps the injured athlete but can also assist teammates confront their own vulnerability.

The Sport Psychologist. The sport psychologist is often the person called to assist the athlete either after a crisis has occurred or when the physician and or trainer cannot understand why the athlete does not seem to respond to treatment. The sport psychologist is often the person of last resort. However, as noted earlier, the sport psychologist should be involved with the injured athlete as early as possible in the athlete's injury and recovery process. This allows the professional to be in a position of support and guidance for the injured athlete throughout the rehabilitation process.

The sport psychologist needs to encourage student-athletes to express themselves both affectively and cognitively concerning their condition. The meaning and implications that loss may have for them should be explored. The injured person may need to consider aspects of life outside of athletics including work, relationships, and avocational interests that can have an impact on the adjustment process. Although previous decision making may have been avoided or ignored, the injured student-athlete's life has been abruptly disturbed. He or she is now in the position of having to confront many life decisions in what may seem to the athlete an accelerated pace. The sport psychologist is well suited to assist the injured athlete in reframing the crisis of loss as an opportunity for challenge and growth. By helping the disabled individual cope and readjust, the sport psychologist can help move the disability from "figure" to "ground," thus allowing the injured athlete to view him-or herself in a more realistic, healthy light.

From time to time, a resistant or uncooperative athlete who does not want to become involved in physical treatment or counseling may be referred to the sport psychologist. Unfortunately, these people are often dismissed as unmotivated and untreatable, thus absolving others of responsibility in their treatment. The resistant person's problem often lies within the framework of interpersonal and environmental influences. Some of these determinants may involve conflicting pressures from coaches, peers, trainers, physicians, and parents. Other factors may consist of obstacles such as time requirements for physical rehabilitation and a demanding course of study. Cognitive limitations can contribute to resistance brought about by stress affecting the student-athlete's ability to concentrate, comprehend, or execute appropriate expected behaviors resulting in actions and moods that appear to be uncooperative or resistant. Then too, the student-athlete may be resistant because he or she does not understand the purpose and meaningfulness of recommended treatments, and therefore does not become involved in or complete them.

In order to work effectively with such a person, various strategies need to be employed. First a positive relationship between the athlete and the sport psychologist must be developed providing the student-athlete with realistic support, encouragement, and reinforcement. Second, it is important that the athlete understand the rationale for suggested treatment approaches. Such information needs to be dispensed in small bits and often reviewed. Third, the athlete should have clear guidelines as to what must be done and what can realistically be expected from treatment. Fourth, a well-organized daily, weekly, and monthly schedule needs to be developed so that the athlete can have a reasonable routine to follow and look forward to, thus providing environmental structure and security for the athlete. Lastly, the sports psychologist needs to help appropriately normalize the athlete's emotional response to the condition communicating to the athlete that what he or she is experiencing is consistent with what others have also weathered. In any case, such people present a challenge to those who want to help the injured person. The clinically trained sport psychologist can serve as a most useful resource to everyone concerned.

THE IMPACT OF INJURY AND DISABILITY: A CASE EXAMPLE.

The following case is an example describing the impact that an athletic injury can have on various aspects of a student-athlete's life. It also provides an illustration of the course that counseling can often take when an injury is experienced, as well as how counseling can be helpful to the victim of a disability.

C. was a twenty-year old upperclass student at the time of our first meeting. He was referred to the Counseling and Psychological Services Center by an astute athletic trainer late in the fall semester. C. had been receiving treatment from the sports medicine staff for a chronic physical condition, exacerbated by play that had been causing pain for several months. His ability to participate in practice and competition had gradually been decreasing as pain increased, despite conscientious, time-consuming rehabilitation efforts on his part. C.'s trainer had noticed his increasing frustration with the rehabilitation process. The trainer spent considerable time providing informal counseling to C., all the while encouraging him to come by for a consultation. It took C. several weeks before he decided (with great reluctance) to make an appointment for counseling, which he made only after a team physician warned him that continued participation would cause more, probably permanent, physical damage.

C. was quite distraught during the initial phase of our work together. He reported feeling depressed, anxious, and confused in the face of his situation. C. also revealed that he had occasional suicidal thoughts. Struggling to make sense of something that he had never expected would happen to him, he tearfully wrestled with a set of undesirable options ranging from risky surgery that would possibly allow him to play again to the untimely end of his ten year athletic career. Furthermore, C. was uncertain about whether he would receive a medical waiver that would allow him to still receive financial aid, without which he might have to leave the university to finish college at home at a school his parents would be better able to afford. C. was afraid to approach his coach, who was similarly frustrated with C.'s situation, wanting him to return to play if at all possible. C. wondered if he could really trust his coach and count on him for support if C. had to leave the team. While we were working on these issues, it became progressively more difficult for C. to attend practices in an observer status and even to be around his teammates, his closest friends on campus for three years, who he did not want to let down if he left.

Over the course of the next several weeks, we developed a good therapeutic relationship. C. was willing and able to express his feelings about his disability, while we explored his options together. It became obvious that he had to retire prematurely, despite his great reluctance to do so. He spoke regularly with his understanding parents and teammates. Eventually C. met with his coach, and along with the sports medicine staff, they supported his leaving and arranged for a medical waiver.

Although this was a great relief to C., he experienced considerable grief as a consequence of his loss, the adjustment to which became the focus of our work. Up to that point, C's identity had been to a great extent that of a player in his chosen sport. It was very difficult for him to sort out who he was if he was not a student-athlete. What would others think of him? How did he see himself? What would he do with his new-found free time now that he did not have to train and compete? In what directions would he redirect his energies during the time that remained before graduation, and what would he do after college?

Over the course of the sessions that remained, we were involved in grief work, decision making, and career counseling. We were eventually able to reframe the situation as "a blessing in disguise," that is, an opportunity to grow as a person in ways that he might not have considered if he had continued to be involved in athletics. He struggled with the boredom and occasional depression associated with his newly found free time. C. struggled with the notion of transferring, which he eventually decided against. He struggled with the question of what to do with his life at this point, choosing to work even harder at his studies in which he had been very successful to date. Results of a vocational interest inventory and related counseling pointed to a inclination to pursue graduate school and a professional career. Although he would always regret his loss, in the end, C. emerged from his trying experience as a healthy, reoriented young person.

On follow-up nearly a year later, C. reported that he was doing fine. He had adjusted well to his life outside of athletics and was not interested in playing any more. C. was surprised how much university life had to offer him outside of the life style he had once lived. He had decided to accept a challenging job after graduation and was considering returning to graduate school after a few years in the world of work.

Summary. In this chapter the authors have attempted to address the psychosocial consequences associated with the acquisition of an injury and disabling condition. Specific terms were defined. Various stages of adjustment and sequelae of emotional reactions to a disabling condition were identified in concert with various helping strategies for those who work with student-athletes. Additional recommendations were made for those most often interacting with the injured student-athlete including the physician, trainers, coaches, and sports psychologist. Finally, a case study was presented in order to illustrate some of the psycho-social factors associated with an injured student athlete.

REFERENCES

Abadie, D.A. (1976). Comparison of the personalities of non-injured and injured athletes in intercollegiate competition. *Dissertation Abstracts, 15*(2), 82.

American Institutes for Research (1988). *Summary results from the 1987-88 national study of intercollegiate athletics.* (Report No.1). Palo Alto, CA: Center for the Study of Athletics.

Athelstan, G.T. (1981). Psychosocial adjustment to chronic disease and disability. In W. C. Stover & M. R. Clower (Eds.) *Handbook of severe disability* (pp. 13-18). Washington, D.C.: U.S. Government Printing Office.

Bergandi, T.A. (1985). Psychological variables relating to the incidence of athletic injury. *International Journal of Sport Psychology, 16* (2), 141-149.

Brown, R.B. (1971). Personality characteristics related to injuries in football. *The Research Quarterly, 42(2)*, 133-138.

Burckes, M.E. (1981). The injury prone athlete. *Scholastic Coach, 6* (3), 47-48.

Chartrand, J., & Lent, R. (1987). Sports counseling: Enhancing the development of the student-athlete. *Journal of Counseling & Development, 66*, 167.

Danish, S. J. (1984). Psychological aspects in the care and treatment of athletic injuries. In P.E. Vinger & E.F. Hoerner (Eds.), *Sports Injuries: The unthwarted epidemic* (2nd ed.). Boston: John Wright.

DePalma, M.T., & DePalma, B. (1989). The use of instruction and the behavioral approach to facilitate injury rehabilitation. *Athletic Training, 24*, 217-219.

Engel, G. (1961). Is grief a disease?: A challenge for medical research. *Psychosomatic Medicine, 23*, 18-27.

Ermler, K.L., & Thomas, C.E. (1990). Intervention for the alienating effects of injury. *Athletic Training*, 25, 269-271.

Garner, H.H. (1977). Somatopsychic concepts. In R.P. Marinelli, & A.E. Dell Orto (Eds.), *The psychological and social impact of physical disability* (pp. 2-16). New York: Springer.

Gover, J.W., & Koppenhaver, R. (1965). Attempts to predict athletic injuries. *Medical Times, 93* (4), 421-422.

Greif, E., & Matarazzo, R.G. (1982). *Behavioral approaches to rehabilitation*. New York: Springer.

Holmes, T.H., & Rahe, R.H. (1967). The social readjustment rating scale. *Journal of Psychosomatic Research, 11*, 213-218.

Injury rates below average in four of six NCAA sports. (1990, May 9). *The NCAA News*, p.3.

Jackson, D.W., Jarret, H., Bailey, D., Kausek, J., Swanson, J., & Powell, J.W. (1978). Injury prediction in the young athlete: A preliminary report. *American Journal of Sports Medicine, 6* (1), 6-14.

Kerr, N. (1969). Understanding the process of adjustment to disability. *Journal of Rehabilitation, 27*(6), 16-18.

Kubler-Ross, E. (1969). *On death and dying*. New York: McMillan.

MacIntosh, D. L., Skrien, T., & Shepard, R. J. (1971). Athletic injuries at the University of Toronto. *Medicine and Science in Sports, 3* (4), 195-199.

May, J.R., & Sieb, G.E. (1987). Athletic injuries: Psychosocial factors in the onset, sequelae, rehabilitation, and prevention. In J.R. May & M.J. Asken (Eds.) *Sport psychology: The psychological health of the athlete.* (pp.157-185). New York: PMA.

McDonald, S., & Hardy, C. (1990). Affective responses patterns of the injured athlete: An exploratory analysis. *The Sport Psychologist, 4*, 261-274.

Nideffer, R. (1983). The injured athlete: Psychological factors in treatment. *Orthopedic Clinics of North America. 14*, 373-385.

Rosenblum, S. (1979). Psychologic factors in competitive failures in athletes. *American Journal of Sports Medicine, 7* , 198-200.

Rotella, R., & Heyman, S. (1986). Stress, injury and the psychological rehabilitation of athletes. In J.M. Williams (Ed.), *Applied sport psychology: Personal growth to peak performance* (pp. 343-362). Palo Alto, CA: Mayfield.

Samples, P. (1987). Mind over muscle: Returning the injured athlete to play. *The Physician and Sportsmedicine, 15*(10), 172-180.

Sanderson, F.H. (1977). The psychology of the injury prone athlete. *British Journal of Sports Medicine, 11*(1), 56-57.

Schlossberg, N.K. (1981). A model for analyzing human adaptation to transition. *Counseling Psychologist, 9*, 2-18.

Schneider, J. (1984). *Stress, loss, & grief.* Baltimore: University Park Press.

Shontz, F.C. (1965). Reaction to crisis. *Volta Review, 67*, 364-370.

Shontz, F.C. (1975). *The psychological aspects of physical illness and disability.* New York: MacMillan.

Thoreson, R.W., & Kerr, B.A. (1978). The stigmatizing aspects of severe disability: Strategies for change. *Journal of Applied Rehabilitation Counseling, 9*(2), 21-26.

Tunick, R.H., & Tunick, R. (1982). Content narratives for "The disability experience" for the Institute of Information Studies adapted to multimedia computer programs for the Control Data Corp.

Valliant, P.M. (1981). Personality and injury in competitive runners.

Perceptual and Motor Skills, 53, 251-253.

Whitten, E.B. (Ed.). (1975). *Pathology, impairment, functional limitation and disability: Implications for practice, research program and policy development and service delivery.* Washington, D.C.: National Rehabilitation Association.

Wright, B. (1960). *Physical disability: A psychological approach.* New York: Harper & Row.

CHAPTER 12

The Athletic Trainer-Helping Professional Partnership: An Essential Element for Enhanced Support Programming for Student-Athletes

Rod Compton and A.P. Ferrante

Through cooperative efforts, athletic trainers and helping professionals can better assist the student-athlete to cope with injury and other psychosocial problems.

Athletic trainers have long enjoyed a special relationship with student-athletes, coaches, and athletic department personnel. However, for psychologists or counselors whose intent is to help provide support services for student-athletes, gaining a similar degree of acceptance for themselves and their services can be an uphill battle. For even the most competent and well-intentioned helping professional, the world of intercollegiate athletics can be a complex system at best difficult to become assimilated into and at worst closed to most outsiders. Athletic trainers are generally valued and trusted insiders who provide understandable and necessary health care services to those within the domain of athletics. On the other hand, helping professionals are often seen as offering assistance (e.g., personal-social or career counseling) that does not readily appear to tie into the paramount missions of helping student-athletes train for successful competition.

Assuming that knowledgeable and competent helping professionals are responsible for providing comprehensive services to student-athletes, their success will seemingly depend upon two things: 1) the degree of accessibility to student-athletes, and 2) the degree of acceptance and positive regard that the helping professional is afforded by student-athletes, coaches, and staff. We believe that a close working relationship between athletic trainers and helping professionals represents a necessary and beneficial linkage that can ultimately serve to extend the degree of care available to the student-athlete. Such a cooperative relationship can facilitate accessibility and acceptance of helping professionals into the intercollegiate athletic world. Developing a colleagial relationship can also increase the probability of shaping an effective referral network through which student-athletes may be helped to cope with their stressful lives. Furthermore, the likelihood of athletic trainers and student-athletic trainers becoming consumers of services (e.g., becoming involved with in-service training or seeking help for personal concerns) is yet another way in which the nurturing of this partnership may benefit many people.

Recent literature in the fields of athletic training and sport psychology has focused on such topics as the need for athletic trainers to have basic psychological knowledge and counseling skills in order to understand the psychosocial factors that precipitate injury and influence rehabilitation (Ermler & Thomas, 1990;

Furney & Patton, 1985; Kane, 1982, 1984; LaMott et al, 1989; Rotella & Heyman, 1986; Smith, Scott, O'Fallon, & Young 1990; Smith, Scott, & Wiese, 1990; Weise, Weiss, & Yukelson, 1991; Yukelson, 1986). The knowledgeable helping professional, working in cooperation with athletic trainers and student trainers, would appear to be the most appropriate professional resource to provide related educational and direct service functions. This approach is apparently being employed on a growing number of university campuses (e.g., Ohio State, Florida State). It was successfully used in another realm by the United States Olympic Committee (USOC) during the 1988 Olympic Games in Seoul, Korea, where a pair of clinical sport psychologists were selected to work with USOC sports medicine staff members (Ferrante, 1989; Murphy & Ferrante, 1990). The decision to utilized the expertise of these helping professionals on behalf of our country's elite athletes lends credence to the notion that athletes are people first and that what occurs "above the neck" is relevant to their performance and well-being.

Further support for the use of the helping professionals within intercollegiate athletics can be found in the literature pertaining to college student health and development. Accordingly, the past decade has reflected increased interest in the plight of student-athletes (Chartrand & Lent, 1987; Ferrante, 1986; Ferrante, 1989; Lanning, 1982; Pinkerton, Hinz, & Barrow, 1987; Sowa & Gressard, 1983). Most authors appear to agree that student-athletes constitute an at risk population who could benefit from specialized support services geared toward factors associated with personal development (see Chapter 1). Formal efforts intended to reach out to this diverse and often needy group have recently begun. Indeed, comprehensive developmental support service programs for student-athletes have been started at schools such as The University of California at Los Angeles, The University of Delaware, The University of Notre Dame, The Ohio State University, Pennsylvania State University, Washington State University, and West Virginia University.

Much of the success of these programs appears in large part due to the establishment of cooperative working relationships developed between helping professionals hired to work with student-athletes and athletic trainers (E. Etzel, personal communication, December 7, 1990; M. Anderson, personal communication, February 14, 1991). Athletic trainers are seen as knowledgeable colleagues who serve both as sources and consumers of professional consultation as well as essential front line referral sources.

The two purposes of this chapter are: 1) to review the factors that appear to contribute to the unique relationship that exists between athletic trainers and student-athletes and 2) to provide insight into how a good working relationship between athletic trainers and helping professionals can be developed to enhance the overall effectiveness of their efforts to assist student-athletes.

THE ATHLETIC TRAINER AND THE STUDENT-ATHLETE

As noted earlier, the athletic trainer has traditionally enjoyed a unique relationship with student-athletes. It is normally a trusting, close relationship that requires honesty and free communication. Interactions range from obtaining an athlete's medical history to discussing nonathletic personal concerns. The trainer sees student-athletes in the extremes of human experience and emotion—from the "thrill of victory and the agony of defeat" to the physical and mental struggles of practice and competition, after having incurred an injury, through the process of rehabilitation and return to activity. The athletic trainer is there throughout the hot and cold, sunny and rainy practices and games. He or she is often a privileged participant in most of the struggles the student-athlete experiences.

Accordingly, the trainer has numerous, often daily opportunities to observe and interact with student-athletes. Perhaps, other than teammates and coaches, student-athletes interact more with trainers than anyone else. Over time, they learn that trainers are some of the most dependable and accessible people within the athletic family to turn to in times of distress. Trainers are there for the student-athlete at times of greatest physical and emotional vulnerability, such as after having incurred an injury, after surgery, and/or during the shared long hours of rehabilitation.

In such situations, student-athletes often cannot disguise their pain and emotions. They reveal themselves and depend upon the trainer for support and comfort. During these difficult times, trainers and student-athletes often form close personal relationships. Therefore, the existence of trust in their relationships is critical, because an injury situation is not one in which to deny pain, to be macho, or to exaggerate complaints. To properly evaluate and treat an injury, the athletic trainer must be able to obtain accurate information from the injured person.

If the athlete knows that the trainer is concerned and always there to help, a good relationship will probably develop. A relationship between student-athlete and trainer will be enhanced when the former realizes that the latter has the student-athlete's best interest as a top priority. Furthermore, it is expected that the trainer treat all student-athletes equally, whether they are scholarship players or walk-ons—on the first team or the scout team. Unlike the coach, the trainer is not responsible for determining the starting lineup or the traveling team roster. Consequently, from the student-athlete's viewpoint, the trainer may be a less threatening person, a person in whom the student-athlete can have faith.

Athletic trainers recognize their professional and ethical limitations in caring for athletes. They cannot be all things to all people. That is to say, while they are responsible for the initial care of athletes, they recognize that they are neither equipped or prepared to deal with all of the various personal concerns that student-athletes may possibly present. It is our experience that most trainers actually seek out and welcome any and all resources that can help them to care for their student-athletes.

Furney and Patton (1985) tell us that "Athletic trainers seem to realize that the pain or problems which student-athletes present to them may not always be in the body" (p.297). Clearly, there seems to be increased awareness among athletic trainers that student-athletes are subject to stresses that affect not only their athletic performance, but also their everyday activities. The athletic trainer is in a unique and privileged position to observe and assist with other difficulties (e.g., personal-social problems) if he or she knows what to look for and when referral to a helping professional is appropriate. With some training and experience in these areas, the athletic trainer can recognize a broad range of possible concerns worthy of referring a student-athlete to someone else and go about doing so in a timely and sensitive professional manner. In this way, the athletic trainer can greatly improve the overall scope and quality of care available to student-athletes.

HELPING STUDENT-ATHLETES BY
DEVELOPING THE TRAINER-HELPING
PROFESSIONAL RELATIONSHIP

Helping professionals possess unique skills and training that can complement the base of existing services offered to student-athletes. Because the advent of human service professionals (e.g., counselors and psychologists) working in intercollegiate athletics is a relatively new phenomenon, the helping professional must be prepared to encounter some degree of hesitancy on the part of others to engage his or her services. This is not a personal issue, but rather something to be expected. Instead, this hesitancy probably reflects a lack of information and understanding regarding both the developmental needs of student-athletes and the ways in which the services provided by helping professionals can meet those needs. In addition, several other barriers to the use of helping services by student-athletes are known (see Chapter 1).

The saying "actions speak louder than words" holds particular relevance here. Therefore, we provide below a number of suggestions that involve both the athletic trainer and helping professional which we believe can enhance program acceptance by student-athletes, coaches, and staff. Furthermore, these aspects of involvement can serve as a springboard for the use of available services.

To begin with, it is important to recall that a major factor associated with the bond shared by student-athletes, trainers, and coaches is the recognition that regardless of the time, day, or weather conditions, the athletic trainer is always around to help. Although we are not suggesting that the helping professional try to become an omnipresent entity, we believe that the helping professional must regularly seek opportunities to interact with student-athletes and staff in athletic settings.

Just like the athletic trainer, the helping professional must be willing to leave the counseling office and work beyond the traditional 5 o'clock quitting time and five day week. Indeed, athletic activities usually occur during odd hours of the day and on nearly every day of the week. The helping professional cannot afford to sit in the office and await a call for help. In fact, some of the most valuable opportunities for professional interaction and programming occur in the training room, ready rooms, and on the practice and playing fields.

Association with the athletic trainer provides the helping professional with an invaluable means of contact with virtually all teams, student-athletes, and coaches. This also allows the helping professional to be identified as a resource for all teams and coaching staffs. With this visibility, student-athletes and staff learn that the helping professional is an interested, available resource.

The helping professional needs to assess carefully his or her willingness and ability to commit to this type of nontraditional involvement. It is important that the helping professional be seen regularly. In fact, it is our perception that infrequent visits to athletic facilities can have a potentially deleterious effect on efforts to provide services. Experience has taught us that infrequent visits sometimes lead student-athletes and staff (even if they are familiar with you) to assume incorrectly that there must be some serious problem or crisis or the helping professional would not be present.

Other types of involvement can assist the helping professional to provide services. If possible, traveling with each team to at least one away competition per season can be invaluable for relationship building and programming. The presence of the helping professional on trips helps to communicate that the individual is regarded as a valuable member of the support team, one whose skills are relevant and can be useful.

Involvement in athletic department social events represents another informal way by which the helping professional can indirectly gain acceptance and support for programs. Attending such events, allows the helping professional to interact with student-athletes and staff in ways that enable them to learn more about the helping professional and program in a nonthreatening manner.

The athletic trainer can play a central role in the assimilation of the helping professional into the athletic setting. The acceptance and use of the helping professional's services by athletic trainers can serve as a model for student-athletes, coaches, and staff who may be reluctant to contact, consult or refer potential clients. The trainer's use of the helping professional's services acts as an informal endorsement of the counselor or psychologist and his or her organization, thus encouraging others to use available assistance.

Conversely, the involvement of the helping professional can directly and indirectly have a significant positive impact on the scope and quality of athletic training staff care of student-athletes. As noted previously, recent contributions to the athletic training and applied sport psychology literature indicate several areas of need and potential benefit to trainers efforts to better serve student-athletes. Kane (1982, 1984) suggested that trainers' can benefit from refining basic learning and communication skills. Learning about the stressful life styles and developmental needs of student-athletes represents another fertile area where athletic trainers, student-trainers, and other selected athletic department staff could benefit from in-service training and consultation provided by a knowledgeable helping professional. Drug and alcohol education and counseling represent yet other areas in which the trained helping professional can help trainers assist student-athletes through programming and consultation. Helping professionals are encouraged to seek opportunities to make presentations introducing and explaining the nature and accessing of their services in team and small group meetings with athletic trainers, student-athletes and coaches. This can be done in a timely and cost-effective manner at the beginning of the school year. Finally, helping professionals who have been trained in research methods can assist athletic trainers in the conduct of various forms of research (e.g., evaluations of services and psychological correlates of injury). Such information can be very beneficial to staff and student-athletes in both the short and long run.

SUMMARY

The helping professional attempting to enter the world of intercollegiate athletics often feels like a stranger in a strange land. Due to their valued role related to the care of student-athletes, athletic trainers can function not only as an allies who are knowledgeable guides and colleagues, but also as crucial referral sources and consumers of consultation services. In these ways, the athletic trainer can provide invaluable assistance to the helping professional in the quest to gain access to student-athletes and staff. To assist student-athletes and staff, the helping professional must be willing to invest considerable time and energy in unconventional ways. The rewards for these efforts are manifested in the forms of increased awareness of the nature and value of available helping services as well as by the use of those services by student-athletes and staff. The relationship between athletic trainers and helping professionals represents a resource by which student-athletes can benefit greatly. Regular effort should be undertaken to nurture its development.

REFERENCES

Chartrand, J. & Lent, R. (1987). Sports counseling: Enhancing the development of the student-athlete. *Journal of Counseling and Development, 66*, 164-167.

Ermler, K., & Thomas, C. (1990). Interventions for the alienating effect of injury. *Athletic Training, 25, 269-271*

Ferrante, A. (1986, February). *Outreach programming for the student-athletes: The problem, the need.* . Paper presented at the annual meeting of the Southeastern College Counseling Center Association, Asheville, NC.

Ferrante, A. (1989). Sport psychology at the XXXIVth Olympiad: Prologue to the future? *North Carolina Medical Journal, 50*(9), 474-478.

Furney, S., & Patton, B. (1985). An examination of health counseling practices of athletic trainers. *Athletic Training, 21*, 294-297.

Kane, B. (1982). Trainer in a counseling role. *Athletic Training 17*, 167-168.

Kane, B. (1984). Trainer counselor to avoid three face-saving maneuvers. *Athletic Training, 19*, 171-174.

LaMott, E. Petlichkoff, L., VanWassenhove, J., Stein, K., Wade, G., & Lewis, K. (1989, September). *Psychological rehabilitation of the injured athlete: An educational approach to injury.* Paper presented at the annual meeting of the Association for the Advancement of Applied Sport Psychology, Seattle, WA.

Lanning, W. (1982). The privileged few: Special counseling needs of athletes. *Journal of Sport Psychology, 4*, 19-23.

Murphy. S., & Ferrante, A. (1990). Provision of sport psychology service to the U.S. Team at the Summer Olympic Games. *The Sport Psychologist, 3*, 374-385.

Pinkerton, R., Hinz, L., & Barrow, J. (1987). The college student-athlete: Psychological considerations and interventions. *Journal of American College Health, 37*, 218-226.

Rotella, R. & Heyman, S. (1986). Stress, injury, and the psychological rehabilitation of athletes. In J. Williams (Ed.), *Applied sport psychology: Personal growth to peak performance* (pp. 343-364). Palo Alto, CA: Mayfield.

Smith, A., Scott, S., O'Fallon, W. & Young. M. (1990). The emotional responses of athletes to injury. *Mayo Clinic Proceedings, 65*, 38-50.

Smith, A., Scott, S., & Wiese, D. (1990) The psychological effects of sports injuries: Coping. *Sportsmedicine*, 352-369.

Sowa, C., & Gressard, C. (1983). Athletic participation: Its relationship to student development. *Journal of College Personnel, 24*, 236-239.

Weiss, M., Smith, R., Smoll, F. & Hardy, C. (1987). *Psychosocial factors in injury occurrence*. Paper presented at the annual meeting of the North American Society for the Psychology of Sport and Physical Activity, Vancouver.

Wiese, D., Weiss, M. & Yukelson, D. (1991). Sport psychology in the training room: A survey of athletic trainers. *The Sport Psychologist, 5*, 15-24.

Yukelson, D. (1986). Psychology of sport and the injured athlete. In D.B. Bernhart (Ed.), *Clinics in physical therapy* (pp.175-195). New York: Churchill Livingstone.

CHAPTER 13

Improving the Residence Hall Experience of Student-Athletes, Resident Advisors, and the University

Rebecca Parker and Le'Roy Reese

Residence hall life is an important part of the overall experience of college students. Residence hall professionals can help student-athletes adjust to college life and enhance the holistic development of student-athletes in a number of ways.

The student who participates in intercollegiate athletics faces a variety of challenges and responsibilities. Several of these challenges evolve from the experience of living in a residence hall community composed of a diverse group of individuals with whom the student-athlete shares no prior knowledge or relationship. This new home environment is governed by a set of living guidelines that may or may not be as explicit or enforced in ways similar to those experienced at home. Student-athletes enter a community whose values and norms may differ from their own. The ability to accommodate these differences can be an important determinant of a student-athlete's successful adjustment to college. This is a time in the development of the young adult when autonomy is cherished and actively sought (Chickering, 1976; L'Abate, Ganahl & Hansen, 1986). The combination of guidelines to govern behavior in a manner that respects other athletes, nonathletes, people of different religions, races, and cultures, sexual orientations, and a variety of authority figures, with a life-style that allows and encourages increased freedom to make choices, can result in confusion for the student-athlete.

Various programs and interventions exist in the residence halls to assist student-athletes with these challenges and growth transitions. Of concern to the residence hall professional is how best to assist the student-athletes in taking advantage of those services and programs that would be most beneficial to them. Unfortunately, the hectic schedule of student-athletes often inhibits participation in many available programs. The typical day for a student-athlete is a rather inflexible one comprising classes, practices, meals, study time, and meetings. Frequently, the services offered by residence hall professionals take place at an inconvenient time for student-athletes.

This chapter explores issues that affect the student-athlete's experience in the residence hall. Our remaining discussion will examine barriers to the wellness and holistic development of the student-athlete. We will also highlight problems for residence hall professionals, athletic departments, and student-athletes. The information and suggestions are based on the current literature, our experience as student affairs professionals, conversations with athletic administrators and coaches, and the shared experiences of student-athletes.

In addition to the challenge of living in a different community, other variables affect the residence hall experiences of student-athletes. The variables under consideration for this discussion are:

1) gender, 2) size of institution, 3) type of sport, 4) biases and discrimination, and 5) the manner in which institutional resources are coordinated to best serve student-athletes.

GENDER

Gender, it seems, plays a significant role in the experience of the student-athlete both within the university and, more germane to our discussion, in the residence halls. Typically, female student-athletes do not receive high profile status, and consequently do not seem to receive much attention. Unfortunately, this leads some to believe that the needs of female student-athletes are not as important as the needs of their male counterparts. It is not uncommon for the starter on the football team to receive more attention than the All-American female on the basketball team. Accordingly, much of the available literature deals almost exclusively with male student-athletes. Much of the literature and many of our conversations have focused on high-profile athletes and revenue-generating sports (e.g., football and men's basketball). This type of sexism, which tends to diminish the needs and experiences of female student-athletes, exists not only in athletic departments but also within the ranks of student affairs professionals. Conversations with both athletic administrators and student affairs professionals indicate that more attention is directed to the needs of male student-athletes than to those of female student-athletes. What little time is spent discussing the experiences of the student-athlete in residence halls typically centers around football and men's basketball. Rarely do we engage in conversations or programming efforts that acknowledge women's athletics in any significant manner. The authors would suggest that female student-athletes face challenges similar to those of male student-athletes. Issues relates to schedules, classes, traveling, and roommates as well as to available support services are just as real for the female student-athlete.

Male student-athletes also experience sexism. They are expected to be tough, durable, and able to handle any difficulties. How often do we think of the male student-athlete as a sensitive, caring individual who has the same psychological and social needs as all young people? When one author reflects back on his personal experience as a student-athlete, it seemed that the only other people who experienced the emotional expressions of the male athlete were teammates and significant others. Frequently, when residence hall staff think of male student-athletes expressing emotion, it is a destructive expression. Athletic departments, residence hall staffs, and members of the university community often inadvertently encourage this bravado by failing to recognize and assist in the development of a full range of expressed emotions. In general, it seems that male students have difficulty requesting emotional assistance from others. This is due in part to how we socialize males in Western society. This situation may be exacerbated for male student-athletes. If they are not seeking support from professionals on campus, how are they responding to their developmental needs and the demands of a very stressful life-style?

Another gender-related issue that is that of superstar status. Conversations with athletic counselors have yielded stories about high-performing and highly visible student-athletes who are frequently harassed in their residence halls by both fans and media. Indeed it is difficult to find time alone when one is the Big Ten Player of the Week. One star quarterback at a large institution reported having to take the phone off the hook so he and his roommate could sleep and study in their room.

A challenge for residence hall staff is to normalize the living experience for student-athletes in response to increased media attention. Successful student-athletes also tend to receive increased amounts of support and attention from the residence hall staff. The residence hall professional must decide whether or not this attention serves to assist the student-athlete or to differentiate him from others. Equally important is the intentional outreach to student-athletes of both genders and in all sports.

INSTITUTION SIZE

The size of the institution, and more specifically, the size of the residence hall affects the student-athlete's attempts to become acclimated to a new environment. For student-athletes from small towns or cities, getting acclimated to the large residence halls at many institutions can prove traumatic. Conversely, student-athletes coming from a large metropolitan area to a smaller institution may encounter a social and political milieu that is different from the one to which they are accustomed. Conversations with student-athletes who have experienced both scenarios sometimes produce comments such as "I can handle school and my athletic demands, but I don't feel especially comfortable in my dormitory."

It is not uncommon for larger universities to have residence halls specifically intended for student-athletes. Despite the fact that the National Collegiate Athletic Association rules state that "an institution may not provide an on-campus or off-campus housing benefit for student-athletes that is not available on the same basis to the general student body" (Sperber, 1990, p. 256), very few Division I institutions appear to allow for the full integration of student-athletes in the general student populace throughout the residence halls. These special halls, which frequently offer a more lavish environment than that found in typical residence halls, usually cater to football and men's basketball teams. The use of these facilities segregates athletes. The result for the student-athlete is a quite limited experience. In addition, these types of facilities can indirectly encourage student-athletes to view themselves as privileged and special, further allowing critics to use these facilities as evidence of the closed nature of intercollegiate athletics.

TYPE OF SPORT

The type of sport in which a student-athlete participates seems to influence the student-athlete's experience in the residence hall. The differences associated with participation in revenue-producing and non-revenue-producing sports can have a significant impact on the student-athlete's experiences. Pressures often arise for the individual who has All-American aspirations or who may be performing poorly in a sport that typically generates moneys for the athletic department and the university. Unfortunately, some athletic departments privilege the principles of capitalism over those of education (Gee, 1990). Evidence of such pressures on student-athletes can manifest itself in the residence hall. Examples of this may be observable irritability, difficulty getting along with others, and an inability to concentrate on studies. These behaviors may be the indirect product of the athletic director's chewing the coach's ear about not filling the stadium because of a losing record. The message that the student-athlete may then hear is "You're not working hard enough, we have to do better, we have to win."

Socioeconomic status (SES) also has important ties to the type of sport in which student-athletes participate. For example, young people who participate in sports such as swimming and golf are typically more upper-middle class. These student-athletes may have more resources that more positively influence their overall experience in the residence halls and school than do other student-athletes. It is not uncommon for these student-athletes to have siblings and parents who have attended college. Sometimes the experiences of these family members shape expectations for a successful collegiate experience. It is much more common for student-athletes in such sports as basketball, football, and track to be from lower-middle class and working-class backgrounds. These student-athletes typically have fewer resources entering the university, and they may encounter more difficulty acclimating to the residence hall and the university. Sometimes these young people are the first generation in their family to attend college. Being the first in your nuclear family to attend college has two implications: 1) although the family can be emotionally supportive, they typically do not have any personal experience with some of the demands and challenges facing the young person, and 2) such student-athletes may find themselves in a position where they do not know who to ask for assistance.

BIASES AND DISCRIMINATION

Much of our discussion thus far has focused on intervening variables that affect the experience of the student-athlete in the residence hall. While much of what has been described is discriminatory and would do little to enhance the experience of the student-athlete in the residence hall, student-athletes experience more overt types of discrimination. Frequently, this type of discrimination is a function of gender, race, sexual orientation, and perceptions about intelligence.

Minority students often have difficulty making the transition to residence hall living, particularly in predominantly white institutions (Fleming, 1984). It is common to encounter a minority student-athlete who has experienced some discriminatory behavior in either their residence hall or the classroom. Unfortunately, residence hall and athletic departments' supervisors still need to train staff to identify accurately and respond appropriately to incidents of racism. Perhaps what is more unfortunate in the residence halls occurs when students take their concerns about minority student-athletes to staff, and subsequent opportunities to educate are not embraced. When we do not take advantage of opportunities to educate, we have lost another chance to advance understanding about a group whose experiences we say we want to improve. According to Sperber (1990), the disproportionate numbers of African-Americans participating in some sports exacerbates the need for direct interventions that address issues such as home to residence hall transitions. If America's institutions of higher education are serious about the retention and graduation of minority student-athletes, appropriate resources should be put in place to attend to these important issues.

Perceptions of intelligence may also cause biased treatment of student-athletes. People express surprise when student-athletes achieve in the classroom. For example, it was recently reported at Ball State University that the cumulative grade point averages of their student-athletes were higher than those of the general student body (D. Dixon, personal communication, April 30, 1990). Although findings such as these are becoming common, some members of the academic community frequently greet them with mixed of skepticism and enthusiasm. We need to ask ourselves why we find it so incredible that student-athletes are capable of excelling both in school and on the athletic field. The perception of the student-athlete as intellectually inferior surely has important implications for the student-athletes and their residence halls peers. The greatest potential harm for the student-athlete is the unspoken message that this stereotype sends: "You're not smart enough to make it in the classroom, so you better excel on the athletic field if you expect to have any type of future." No wonder a disproportionate number of student-athletes come to college with unreasonable expectations for careers as professional or Olympic-level athletes (Sperber, 1990). How we educate the university community about student-athletes as well as how we provide academic support is something that needs to be considered by the academy and professionals concerned with the quality of residential life.

The topic of sexual orientation is one that is generally not discussed when considering the student-athlete. For example, it is easier to imagine the lesbian basketball player than the gay football player. This is a result of the tendency in our society to define what have traditionally been thought of as masculine and feminine characteristics in limited and biased ways. Classic studies by Kinsey, Pomeroy, and Martin (1948, 1953) provide evidence indicating that ten percent of any population of people are exclusively gay. Subsequent studies have provided a good measure of validity for their original findings. Given the results of these studies, it seems appropriate that some consideration be given to meeting the needs of student-athletes dealing with these issues. At stake is a basic identity issue that has important implications for how a young person will live his or her life. Young people in general dealing with gay issues frequently encounter homophobic attitudes and a lack of support. These experiences may be exacerbated for the student-athlete because of assumptions and expectations about sexual orientation.

A growing trend among residence hall staffs has been to provide educational programming on gay, lesbian, and bisexual issues. Unfortunately, these programs frequently fail to examine the diversity that exists within the gay community. That in fact that there are poor people, rich people, minority members, and student-athletes who are gay is needs attention. The gay student-athlete who contemplates "coming out" frequently has no support system in either the residence hall or athletic department. At one institution, the athletic counselor who most closely works with student-athletes living in the residence halls could recall only a handful of situations in which student-athletes approached him about resources for gay persons. He also shared that it was more common for female student-athletes to "come out" than it was for males. Reports like this about may send confusing messages to young student-athletes about these important identity issues.

The aforementioned variables interact with the residence hall environment to create a unique set of barriers to a holistic developmental experience for the student-athlete. Simultaneously, the opportunities to design and implement creative strategies are limited by our inability to make full use of our resources.

BARRIERS TO THE HOLISTIC EXPERIENCE OF STUDENT-ATHLETES LIVING IN UNIVERSITY RESIDENCE HALLS

In talking about barriers to the holistic experience of athletes living in residence halls, it is imperative that we understand the complexity and multifaceted sources of these barriers. Barriers do not merely exist; they typically have a history, often one that some people may want to hold on to, whether or not such an attachment is productive. Athletic department staff often blame residence hall staff and the intrinsic structures of the residence hall department. Residence hall staff often fault the expectations of the athletic department staff. Student-athletes are sometimes caught in the middle, not knowing where to turn or who to blame. The reality is that all three groups contribute to the failure of residence halls to live up to their potential as developmental environments for student-athletes.

Professional residence hall staff members are trained in student personnel work, counseling and guidance, educational administration, and other related areas. They seldom have much experience with or exposure to athletics. They are therefore unable to respond to some of the pressures faced by student-athletes that involve more than typical young adult development issues. According to Pearson and Petitpas (1990), "as a person's identity and activity increasingly center on athletics, the likelihood increases of encountering developmental issues and events that are unique, or are substantially different from those persons not engaged in careers centered on performance that demands high levels of physical excellence" (p.7). For example, student-athletes are exposed to the competitive pressure that includes the desire to win at all costs (Lope, 1990). As a result, they must endure the stress of frequent travel and demanding training schedules (Pearson & Petitpas, 1990). Whether or not they intended to, they are forced to surrender a large part of the privacy that other students enjoy (Meilman & Fleming, 1990). Further, the student-athlete who is managing an athletic role, is also attempting to balance academic and social roles. It should not be surprising that this is no simple task, when one fairly acknowledges that student-athletes have substantially less free time than do other students.

Even career issues acquire a unique perspective for the student-athlete. Most college students are studying in academic programs in preparation for a related career. The student-athlete may be similarly engaged. Perhaps too often, however, the student-athlete also has unrealistic expectations for a professional career related to his or her athletic skills. "In reality, no more than 1% of high school athletes make it in college sports; only 1 in 10,000 go on to the pros" ("Poll", 1990, p.4). Therefore, while most students including student-athletes are planning careers, student-athletes also need to be planning for athletic retirement (Pearson & Petitpas, 1990).

Residence hall professionals can learn about the variety of pressures faced by the student-athlete. In fact, increased knowledge about those stressors is critical if professionals are to help facilitate the overall development of the student-athlete. Unfortunately, the individual attitudes of athletic department staff, residence hall staff, and student-athletes often create barriers to collaborative, successful approaches to holistic experiences for student-athletes.

Athletic department staff are sometimes suspicious of residence hall staff. Interaction between these groups, as a result, occurs in a manner that often inhibits information sharing which might otherwise prove useful in their work with student-athletes. Athletic department staff are sensitive to the fact that staff members outside the athletic department sometimes treat student-athletes unfairly.

Unfortunately, residence hall staff are sometimes biased against student-athletes (particularly male athletes involved in revenue-generating sports). The student-athlete's involvement in violations of residence hall and university policies is sometimes assumed, and the level of their involvement in incidents is sometimes judged greater than the evidence would warrant. Some of these staff believe student-athletes are pampered people who are permitted to get away with anything. Consequently, these staff members believe they must personally introduce an element of accountability. To complicate matters, some student-athletes, having been over-indulged or over-protected for their athletic ability, develop an attitude of entitlement. As a result, they are less likely to develop the skills needed to function in other roles (Petitpas & Champagne, 1988). This mindset is exacerbated by the fact that student-athletes have been rewarded for rugged individualism and sometimes find it difficult to seek or request assistance from available resources (Pearson & Petitpas, 1990).

The student-athlete's inability to request assistance or use available resources in the residence halls may have a significant, long-lasting developmental impact. Although the athletic system promotes conformity that sometimes leads to the adoption of its community values and life-styles (Schaefer, 1971), this same promotion of conformity often inhibits the student-athlete's opportunities to question values and norms. The result may be a lack of various life experiences useful in personal problem solving and career planning (Blann, 1985; Sowa & Gressard, 1983).

The structure of living facilities can also be a barrier to the holistic development of student-athletes. Some believe it is more supportive to house all student-athletes together. It is thought that because they know one another, have similar schedules, and possess common motivations, they are in a position to provide each other with understanding, support, and assistance. Mitchell (1974) would refer to this as a "dense social system." According to Remer, Tongate, and Watson (1978), however, such systems may likely result in the restricting rather than broadening of perspectives and alternatives for action. Further, it has been noted that student-athletes living in special facilities tend to be more isolated and destructive (Sperber, 1990). Even when athletes live in facilities with nonathletes, the student-athlete's schedules make it sometimes difficult, if not impossible, for them to take advantage of available workshops and programs (Jordan & Denson, 1990).

It would appear, based on the information available and on the authors' experiences, that the barriers outlined above fall into one or more of the following four categories: 1) professional and paraprofessional staff training and communication skills for working with student-athletes, 2) facilities and environment planning, 3) access to programs and other resources, and 4) the quality of community life.

The next section of this chapter will be devoted to strategies for neutralizing, if not eliminating, barriers in these four categories, in an effort to improve the experience of student-athletes.

STRATEGIES FOR THE HOLISTIC DEVELOPMENT OF STUDENT-ATHLETES LIVING IN THE UNIVERSITY RESIDENCE HALLS

In actuality, there are many resources and much support available to student-athletes. Both athletic department and residence hall professionals, charged with the holistic development of these students, are committed to performing their roles with the highest professional ideals. Unfortunately, however, these professionals tend to act separately and may strive to accomplish different goals. Athletic department staff have knowledge and expertise about the unique challenges faced by student-athletes in the college environment, so they set about to design and implement programs and procedures to address those needs. Residence hall staff have knowledge and expertise about the developmental challenges faced by young adults in the college environment. So they both set about to design and implement programs and procedures to address those needs. It is time that these two groups of professionals collaborate to design and implement specific programs and procedures for student-athletes who are faced with the challenges of young adult development in the college environment. The benefit of this collaboration is at least threefold:

1. Student athletes are encouraged and able to take advantage of the opportunities that respond to their current needs as well as provide skill building for their future careers and adult interactions.
2. Athletic department staff are able to take advantage of the expertise of residence hall staff, relative to young adult development in general, and
3. Residence hall staff are able to take advantage of the expertise of athletic department staff, relative to the unique issues for young adults who are also facing the challenges of being student-athletes.

Using a team approach, these professionals can initiate strategies to overcome the barriers previously noted and can contribute to the holistic experience of student-athletes in the residence halls. Specifically, strategies can be implemented that focus on: 1) training staff in both residence halls and athletic departments about the unique challenges facing student-athletes and the resources available in both departments to help meet those challenges, 2) intentionally using residence hall facilities to enhance the quality of life for student-athletes, 3) improving the access of student-athletes to programs and facilities in the residence halls, and 4) developing an overall community environment that provides the interaction of challenge and support for students and student-athletes. Enhanced professional and paraprofessional staff training and communication can overcome some of the barriers to a holistic experience for student-athletes in the residence halls.

Every year countless hours are devoted to the training and preparation of residence hall staff hired to provide services and assistance to college students. Many residence hall programs offer courses for resident advisors that are designed to provide information and skills that enhance their ability to serve in helping roles with students. In addition, it is common to find both intensive pre-service training programs and year-round in-service training programs for staff at all levels of the residence hall department. Ideally, this training should assist the staff in working with the student population in general, as well as with the diverse populations represented in the residence hall community. Though it is clear that student-athletes represent a legitimate special population in the residence halls, it is common for information and discussion about their issues and role in the community to be omitted from these training sessions. This must change if we are to better assist student-athletes.

To enhance the success of such training programs, we propose that they be co-facilitated by athletic department and residence hall staff. Further we would also recommend that such training sessions be conducted for staff in both departments. Athletic department staff must work with residence hall staff to provide more accurate information, greater insight, and a shared understanding of purpose that will result in enhanced skills for staff working in the living environment. This training would include information about the unique experiences, challenges, and needs of student-athletes. It might also serve to increase staff awareness of the variety of circumstances, perceptions, and realities that affect the lives of student-athletes. In addition to helping staff understand the severe limitations on the student-athlete's time, training sessions could be designed to explore the diverse reactions to student-athletes that come from staff and other students. It is also helpful for staff members to know that student-athletes in the college environment may experience less support for being student-athletes than they did in high school. Often they are expected to be able to handle anything, and at any time. When they can not, it is expected that they are treated exactly like everyone else. To do otherwise is to feed the sentiment that student-athletes are pampered people rescued inappropriately and unfairly by the athletic department staff. Staff members need to understand that as a result of these experiences and circumstances, student-athletes are a special population. Staff training provides an opportunity for them to become more familiar with existing support services and with available helping professionals. Information concerning methods of making appropriate and timely referrals can also be presented and discussed.

The specific use of facilities, as well as general environmental planning, is another strategy that can be used to address some of the barriers to a holistic experience for student-athletes in residence halls. It is possible to take advantage of the support that can be found when people of similar interests and activities live together, without jeopardizing the development of critical life skills. We do not recommend separate facilities for student-athletes. Such arrangements, from our perspective, only make it harder for student-athletes to have a normal developmental experience away from home. Student-athletes, like anybody else, deserve to have time away from the stresses of constant competition and evaluation. We would, however, recommend taking advantage of roommate assignment patterns designed to promote both developmental challenge and support. This could be accomplished by having student-athletes live together as roommates in facilities that also house nonathletes in proximity. Community activities should be planned to balance a focus on general developmental issues with other issues specific to diverse populations. This also provides an environment both residence hall and athletic department staffs can use to focus efficiently on issues for students who are members of more than one population. For example, programs could be developed to focus on the issues faced by honors students, student-athletes, and honor students who are also athletes. Conversations with professionals in the field indicate that issues would vary for all three groups.

Improving the student-athlete's access to programs and other resources is a third category of strategies that can be used to enhance the holistic experience of residential living. The success of a residential community can be measured in part by the quality of its planned programming efforts. Professional staff in the residence halls should use an increased amount of primary prevention, which is an approach to assisting individuals by preventing problems before they occur (Pearson & Petitpas, 1990). The current literature and research inform us of some of the potential risks for student-athletes. These risks should be identified early, and programs should be developed to address potential difficulties.

For example, programs should be developed to assist student-athletes in gaining a sense of identity that is not totally dependent on athletic ability. The gap between their levels of athletic ability and levels of athletic career aspiration needs to be reduced. We need to help student-athletes develop the ability to adapt to change that is sometimes made difficult by personal challenges, convince them to develop supportive helping relationships, and then respond to issues when resources are limited or unavailable (Pearson & Petitpas, 1990). Further, knowing that student-athletes are often unaware of their vulnerability, residence hall and athletic department staff must educate the student-athletes, coaches, and family members about these potential risks (Pearson, 1986).

In residence halls, this type of education could occur in a variety of ways. Orientation sessions for incoming student-athletes and their parents could be offered. Training sessions designed to highlight the unique challenges of student-athletes and the resources available to respond to them, could be offered for residence hall and athletic department staffs prior to the opening of the residence halls. Workshops and community programs could be designed and implemented throughout the year for students and student-athletes living in the residence hall community. Both the student-athlete and the other student residents could benefit from such proactive programming.

An integrated example would be the development of a wellness program designed to operate with the collaboration of both residence hall and athletic department staffs to address general developmental needs as well as the unique needs of student-athletes. Wellness information, screening, counseling, and programming could be offered by both staffs in the residence halls and as a part of athletic training and study tables.

While we must try to be as proactive as possible in the programs we plan for our residential communities, it is often necessary for our programming strategies to evolve as a reaction to situations or circumstances. For example, it is acknowledged that substance abuse is a major problem among the college student population. It is a problem for residence hall students and a highly publicized problem for student-athletes. Professional staff from both residence halls and athletic departments could jointly develop and sponsor substance abuse programs that respond to this problem, in general, and for student-athletes, in particular. It has been noted that athletic teams represent self-contained support groups that may be especially helpful in such programming efforts (Meilman & Fleming, 1990)

Proactive or reactive planning does not matter if programs are offered in residence halls at times when student-athletes cannot attend. At the most popular times (early evening) for residence hall programs, this population is often engaged in practices or required study activities. Residence hall staff must work with athletic department staff to provide programs and other services to student athletes at nontraditional times. One way to accomplish this would be to provide guest speakers and developmental activities during a portion of the athlete's training or study table. Care must be taken, however, to balance the need for the information such programs would provide with the student-athlete's need for concentrated and uninterrupted study time. In addition, residence hall staff could work with athletic department staff to target specific locations and times when more concentrated programs could be made available to student-athletes.

Although effective programs and services are critical components of a successful residential community, they are not the sole indication of an environment conducive to the holistic development of its members. Facilitating and enhancing the overall quality of life in the residential community is a more comprehensive approach to the level of environmental management of most benefit to students and student-athletes.

The Carnegie Foundation for the Advancement of Teaching (1990) concluded that college campuses would benefit from a larger vision that should provide a new framework within which a community of learning might be built (Boyer, 1990). The 1990 special report outlines the following six principles around which campus life should be built:

1. The community should be purposeful. Specifically, students should work together with faculty and staff to strengthen teaching and learning.
2. The community should be just. All members of the community must be afforded dignity and equality of opportunity.
3. The community should be open. Honest communication should be encouraged. Freedom of expression should be protected. And messages of integrity must be clearly articulated.
4. The community should be disciplined. People must understand the obligations they have to others in the community.
5. The community should be caring. The well-being of each community member should be supported, and service to others should be encouraged.
6. The community should be celebrative. Traditions should exist to remember the past. Simultaneously, community members must be able to look to and plan for the future.

We propose that incorporating these principles into the community experience of students and student-athletes would improve their residence hall experience. If we strategically combine information about the experience of student-athletes on the college campus and the skills of residence hall staff to support and guide young adult development with the ability of athletic department staff to recognize, understand, and translate the unique challenges to student-athletes, we can reduce the Carnegie principles from the macro-level of human development on the college campus to the micro-level of quality of life for student-athletes in residence halls.

If we want to enhance the sense of purpose for student-athletes living in the residence halls, we can design and facilitate programs and experiences that encourage student-athletes to work closely with faculty members, coaches, and resident advisors around academic and intellectual issues. Specific attention could be given to study skills, time management, and stress management strategies that address the unique needs and experiences of the student-athlete, while helping maintain priorities and perspectives appropriate for the collegiate environment. Using both the residence hall lounge and the athletic study table as learning sites helps to reinforce the overall goals of both the academy and the student-athlete.

If the residence hall community is to be an environment of justice, all of its members must be treated with dignity and respect at all times. Student-athletes should be able to expect to enjoy the living environment, engage in positive interactions with other students and staff, and take full advantage of the other available resources. Student-athletes should be afforded the opportunity to interact with others in the community without the handicap of biased perceptions and isolating assumptions. Further, regardless of their race, gender, or type of sport, student-athletes are entitled to live in communities where prejudice of all forms is challenged by the residence hall community and staff. Athletic department staff are responsible for providing that challenge on behalf of student-athletes on the playing field, in the locker room, and at the study table. Residence hall staff have the same responsibility in the living environment. Activities and programs can be designed that develop a sense of personal well-being and interpersonal respect. Intentional conversations, educational discipline, workshop training, and leadership experiences are all examples of the intervention that can be provided here.

Achieving an open community is a special challenge. We say we want honest communication and freedom of expression. Simultaneously, however, we expect civility on our campuses, on our playing fields, and in our residence halls. We must work with students and student-athletes so that we might better understand their feelings and concerns, and assist them in better communicating those concerns to the appropriate persons and in the appropriate arenas. Residence hall programs could be designed to allow healthy and facilitated discussions about issues that are central to the lives of student-athletes. Such discussions could occur in various settings, ranging from the one-on-one conversation with a resident advisor to the guest speaker sponsored by the residence hall council. This approach allows students, student-athletes, and staff to express concerns, opinions, and ideas in an environment that affirms their right to do so. At the same time, however, it seeks to maintain civility by having staff members present and responsible for sharing messages of integrity that represent the university.

For example, students and student-athletes may choose to engage in a debate over the perceptions of women's intercollegiate athletics. The fact is that women's programs do not receive the support, enthusiasm, or publicity of men's revenue sports. Students and student-athletes should be encouraged to share their opinions and experiences in this area. Staff members must be able to help them understand, however, that there is a failure to think of females as student-athletes dealing with the same issues that males deal with. Further, this would be an appropriate time to provide educational messages about the costs and dilemmas associated with sexism, both for men and women. We have allowed open expression in the community. We have also articulated a clear message of integrity intended to govern the community in a manner that empowers one of its identified populations.

In a disciplined community such as a residence hall, policies and procedures exist to maintain an environment that serves the good of the whole. Residence hall staff should be available to assist student-athletes in learning, understanding, and maintaining the obligations they have to other community members. Athletic department staff should reinforce the merits of a disciplined community. It is most effective, however, when the residence hall staff and the athletic department staff work together to create teachable moments that foster an environment that recognizes the special needs and issues of all its participants, while reinforcing the mission of the university.

For example, upon being demoted from first string, a student-athlete may return to the residence hall and engage in disruptive or destructive behaviors. Then, the residence hall and athletic department staffs could respond with educational discipline. The goal is to choose the most effective means of resolving problems and of maintaining conduct that is congruent with the academic purposes of the institution. Additionally, responses to behavioral problems should be aimed at maximizing student understanding of the constraints of group living (Dunn, 1990). This is most effectively achieved when staff and students understand the intensity of emotion that may be involved for the student-athlete, refrain from a desire to punish the student-athlete, and communicate to the student-athlete the expectation that he or she take responsibility for behavior while continuing to be a valued member of the community.

The ability to adopt and facilitate such attitudes and approaches depends, in part, on the amount of information, insight, and collaboration that exists among the residence hall staff, athletic department staff, student-athletes, and other students.

If a community is to be caring, the well-being of each community member should be supported. Simultaneously, service to others should be encouraged. This creates an infinite amount of opportunities for students and student-athletes. Honors students living in residence halls could serve as tutors at athletic study tables. This is even easier to facilitate when those honors students are also student-athletes. Student-athletes in residence halls could serve as trainers for students interested in the physical dimensions of wellness. These and other service projects could be jointly established and monitored by athletic department and residence halls staff.

In celebrative communities, traditions exist to remember the past. At the same time, community members must have an eye on the future. This necessitates representative student leadership in the community, and is predicated on the assumption of representative participation in the community. All students must be involved, including the student-athlete with the busy schedule. Undoubtedly, this means changing residence hall governance to make it more inclusive. Residence hall staff may be in the best position to initiate the challenge. Athletic department staff may be in the best position to encourage student-athlete participation.

Residence halls are environments that exist within a community of scholars. Student-athletes are scholars who often live in residence halls. Athletics and residence hall professionals are the environmental catalysts who encourage and manage the utilization of resources in a manner that contributes to the holistic development of student-athletes. It is a huge task, and it will not be accomplished easily. It is a task that requires information, communication, caring, collaboration, and vision. That is what we are trained to do. That is what student-athletes deserve.

REFERENCES

Blann, F.W. (1985). Intercollegiate athletic competition and students' educational and career plans. *Journal of College Student Personnel, 26*, 115-121.

Boyer, E. (1990, February). *Campus life: In search of community.* Paper presented at the National Association of Student Personnel Administrators, New Orleans.

Carnegie Foundation for the Advancement of Teaching (1990). *A Special Report. Campus life: In search of community.* New Jersey: Princeton University, Princeton University Press.

Chickering, A.W. (1976). *Education and identity,* San Francisco: Jossey-Bass.

Dunn, M. (1990). *We become just through the practice of just actions: A judicial systems manual.* Columbus, Ohio: Office of Residence Life, The Ohio State University.

Fleming, J. (1984). *Blacks in college,* San Francisco: Jossey-Bass.

Gee, E. G. (1990, November). Greed and avarice: The crisis in collegiate athletics. *USA Today,* pp. 25-26.

Jordan, J.M. & Denson, E.L. (1990). Student services for athletes: A model for enhancing the student-athlete experience. *Journal of Counseling and Development, 69,* 95-97.

Kinsey, A., Pomeroy, W., & Martin, C. (1948). *Sexual behavior in the human male.* Philadelphia: W.B. Saunders.

Kinsey, A., Pomeroy, W., & Martin, C. (1953). *Sexual behavior in the human female.* Philadelphia: W.B. Saunders.

L'Abate, L, Ganahl, G, & Hansen, J.C. (1986). *Methods of family therapy.* Englewood Cliffs, NJ: Prentice-Hall.

Lope, M. (1990). Steroids in athletics: One university's experience. *Journal of College Student Development, 31,* 523-530.

Meilman, P.W. & Fleming, R.L. (1990). A substance abuse prevention program for student-athletes. *Journal of College Student Development, 31,* 477-479.

Mitchell, J. C. (1974). Social networks. *Annual Review of Anthropology, 3,* 279-300.

Pearson, R. E. (1986). Health promotion/primary prevention: Primary prevention-oriented groups. In R. J. Conye (Ed.) *The group worker's handbook: Varieties of group experience* (pp. 277-292). Springfield, IL: Charles C. Thomas.

Pearson, R. E. & Petitpas, A. J. (1990). Transitions of athletes: Developmental and preventive perspectives. *Journal of Counsel-*

ing and Development, 69, 7-10.

Petitpas, A. J. & Champagne, D.E. (1988). Developmental programming for intercollegiate athletes. *Journal of Student Development 29* (5), 454-460.

Poll: Student-athletes' expectations unrealistic (1990, November 15). *The Cleveland Plain Dealer* (Sports section), p. 4.

Remer, R., Tongate, R.A. & Watson, J. (1978). Counseling the overprivileged minority. *The Personnel and Guidance Journal, 56,* 616-629.

Schaefer, W. (1971). *Sport socialization and the school.* Paper presented at the Third International Symposium on the Sociology of Sport, Waterloo, Ontario, Canada.

Sowa, C.J. & Gressard, C.F. (1983). Athletic participation: Its relationship to student development. *Journal of College Student Personnel, 26,* 236-239.

Sperber, M. (1990). *College sports inc.: The athletic department versus the university.* New York: Henry Holt.

Subject Index